Donated
To The Library by

**Eleanor McCahill Denny
Book Fund**

PRESERVATION IN LIBRARIES

PRESERVATION IN LIBRARIES: PRINCIPLES, STRATEGIES AND PRACTICES FOR LIBRARIANS

Ross Harvey

Topics in Library and Information Studies

BOWKER
SAUR

London • Melbourne • Munich • New York

In association with the Centre for Information Studies,
Charles Sturt University, Wagga Wagga, New South Wales

British Library Cataloguing in Publication Data
Harvey, Douglas Ross
    Preservation in Libraries. - Principles,
    Strategies and Practices for Librarians.
    - (Topics in Library & Information
    Studies Series)
    I. Title II. Series
025.8

ISBN 0-86291-632-1

Library of Congress Cataloging-in-Publication Data
Harvey, Ross.
    Preservation in libraries : principles, strategies, and practices
for librarians / Ross Harvey.
        p. cm.
    Includes bibliographical references and index.
    ISBN 0-86291-632-1
    1. Library materials—Conservation and restoration.
    2. Books—Conservation and restoration.. I. Title.
Z701.H36 1992
025.8'4--dc20   92-17493
                                                            CIP

Published by Bowker-Saur
60 Grosvenor Street, London W1X 9DA
Tel: +44(0)71 493 5841 Fax: +44(0)71 580 4089
Bowker-Saur is a division of REED REFERENCE PUBLISHING
ISBN 0-86291-632-1
Cover design by John Cole
Printed on acid-free paper
Printed and bound in Great Britain by Antony Rowe Ltd, Wiltshire

TOPICS IN LIBRARY AND INFORMATION STUDIES

A series under the General Editorship of:

G.E. Gorman,   School of Information Studies, Charles Sturt
University, Wagga Wagga, New South Wales,
Australia

R.R. Powell,   School of Library and Informational Science,
University of Missouri-Columbia, Columbia,
Missouri, USA

Contents

Chapter 6. Disaster Preparedness   119

Chapter 7. Preserving the Artefact: Book Maintenance and Repair Procedures, and Binding   137

Chapter 8.   Preserving the Intellectual Content: Reformatting

List of Tables

Acknowledgements

I am grateful to the many colleagues and students who have enabled me to formulate my views on preservation. I wish to thank in particular Emeritus Professor Jean P. Whyte for encouragement, Ann Miller for alerting me to important sources, Sandra Cassano for her ideas on 'backsliding' in the library profession, and Rebecca Smale and Sheena Cuthbert for their assistance with identifying and locating relevant literature. Special thanks are due to Jeavons Baillie for his technical advice on conservation, and above all to Rachel Salmond for her assistance in ways too numerous to mention. Thanks are also due to the staff of the Graduate Department of Librarianship, Archives and Records at Monash University for their support: the assistance of Margaret Incoll in particular is gratefully acknowledged. I owe thanks also to the Faculty of Professional Studies, Monash University, for providing financial assistance and leave to enable this book to be written. However, although thanks are due to these individuals and organizations, the final responsibility for any errors or omissions lies with the author.

I also wish to thank those publishers who gave their permission to reprint material published here. I hereby acknowledge the permissions given by:

American Library Association (50 East Huron Street, Chicago, Ill., USA) for:
> *Preservation Microfilming: A Guide for Librarians and Archivists*, edited by Nancy E. Gwinn (Chicago, Ill.: ALA, 1987), p. 39.

The British Library (National Preservation Office, British Library, London, UK) for:
> 'Bacon' and 'Celery' bookmarks; posters 'Books Need a Velvet Glove', 'Life Can Be Rough' and 'Books Are Like Lovers'.

CAVAL Ltd (123 Dover Street, Richmond, Vic., Australia) for:
> *Disaster in Libraries: Prevention and Control,* edited by Max W. Borchardt (Camberwell, Vic.: CAVAL, 1988), p. 26.

Foreword by the General Editors

> Preservation has become one of the less predictable fashions in librarianship in the last decade of the twentieth century. Until comparatively recently, what was usually called 'conservation' was thought of as one of those esoteric matters which exercised the minds of archivists and rare book librarians, and was as remote as those specialists themselves from the concerns of other members of the profession. Suddenly, or so it seemed, conservation came out of the closet of the rare book rooms. It emerged under a new name – *preservation* – and with a new purpose. It was no longer merely a means of preserving the past for hypothetical readers in the indefinite future, but an essential part of the growing art of collection management.... (John Feather)

This 'indefinite future' is now, in the 1990s, only too patently definite – and has been since 1966, when international librarianship was first shocked and then mesmerized by the disastrous Florence flood and resulting damage to the priceless collections of the Biblioteca Nazionale. This event presented dramatic images that changed forever our perception of those strange people called conservators, who worked in splendid isolation, tucked away in forgotten sections of libraries. Conservators were generally viewed as the 'mad scientists' of our profession, people with strange fetishes about how materials should be handled and esoteric knowledge of chemistry, physics and technology. They were not true librarians but interlopers in a profession peopled by arts graduates; proof of this was found not only in the language they spoke but also in the esoteric papers they published in serials with such odd titles as *Journal of the Society of the Chemical Industry* and *Bureau of Standards Journal of Research*.

After Florence and the extensive media coverage of what conservators could do, all of this was set to change. Suddenly conservation chemists and technologists were heroes. In a sense 1966 can be viewed as a kind of *aggiornamento* for conservation, the beginning of a move to the broader perception known as preservation, in which conservators are recognized as key players. The next step was a more general conscientization of the profession at large, which occurred through a number of institutional and professional body initiatives. Throughout the 1970s and 1980s the United States and Britain were the focal points of these initiatives, particularly through such bodies as the Library of Congress, the American Library Association, the Association of Research Libraries, the Research Libraries

Group, the British Library and The Library Association. In addition a number of international organizations, primarily Unesco, IFLA and FID, contributed to a greater awareness of conservation and preservation at regional and international levels. Conservation and preservation offices and sections, task forces, standard-setting deliberations and conferences were the order of the day, with the inevitable increase in the number of publications on this topic.[1] Toward the end of this period even library science educators began to reflect in print on the nature, function and content of preservation education – a sure sign that changing perceptions were firmly part of the professional scene.[2]

Following the two steps of *aggiornamento* and general conscientization, we have now moved into a third stage, integration, in which preservation becomes recognized as an essential component in collection management. As Margaret Byrnes sees it, 'awareness of the integral and necessary relationship between collection management and development and preservation programs has been increasing in recent years. At long last, collection managers and preservation specialists have begun to work together more closely and to identify areas of common concern.'[3] This has begun to have an identifiable impact on larger academic and research libraries, with preservation coming formally within the professional responsibility of collection managers and funds for conservation activities allocated from the collection-building budget. Also, both nationally and internationally there have been moves to include preservation as an issue in the resource-sharing debate and to consider cooperative preservation programs.

One basic reason for this, of course, has been financial, as 'rising prices and falling budgets have forced librarians to reconsider the rate of redundancy and replacement of stock, while the continuous growth of the publishing industry places ever increasing demands on those same diminishing budgets.'[4] What this means in monetary terms in just one country and without reference to the cost of stock replacement has been estimated by Byrnes: 'to preserve only three million of the estimated 75 million brittle books in US research libraries will cost approximately $200 million over the next 10 to 15 years.'[5] Clearly the problem is of such a magnitude, and the prognosis so poor, that efforts must be redoubled to find practical, effective and realistic means of integrating preservation into all sectors of library practice, from the highest levels of national and international policy-making to the most specific areas of clerical activity.

From an educator's perspective part of this continuing conscientization and integration involves increased attention to preservation in library science, archives and records management curricula; this in turn requires the provision of superior teaching materials. Furthermore, such materials must be suited to the continuing educational needs of practitioners who find themselves faced with the task of improving their professional knowledge and skills. At the end of the 1980s there were no appropriate preservation texts in Australia or New Zealand, and it was for this reason that the Centre for Information Studies at Charles Sturt University approached Dr Ross Harvey, Senior Lecturer in the

Graduate Department of Librarianship, Archives and Records at Monash University, with a request that he prepare such a work. The result, *Preservation in Australian and New Zealand Libraries*, enjoyed significant antipodean and even international success, so much so that the first edition went out-of-print in less than two years.[6]

Elsewhere in the anglophone world there have been a number of publications over the years that seek to provide basic tuition in preservation. Recently, for example, John Feather has drawn on his considerable experience as a teacher of preservation at Loughborough University in preparing *Preservation and the Management of Library Collections*. However, neither Feather's introductory guide to preservation nor any other currently available title seeks to provide for an international audience what Dr Harvey has given his antipodean readers – a detailed and substantial 'framework for further reflection on the problems of preservation and for research into their solutions.' We believe that Ross Harvey offers a valuable perspective on the management of preservation activities and procedures in libraries and that his views will be of interest to students and practitioners in many countries.

Dr Harvey's scholarly and judicious approach is reflected not only in the care with which he presents sometimes contentious policy issues but also in the clarity with which he describes specific preservation procedures. The ten chapters of *Preservation in Libraries: Principles, Strategies and Practices for Librarians* offer, in our view, a detailed guide to all aspects of preservation, from deterioration of materials and methods of preservation to cooperative strategies and preservation programs. We are pleased, therefore, to include this volume and the accompanying collection of readings, *Preservation in Libraries: A Reader*, in Topics in Library and Information Studies.

Notes

1   Among the more notable publications of the 1980s from the United States one can cite the following: Library of Congress. Preservation Office, *A National Preservation Program. Proceedings of a Planning Conference* (Washington, DC: Library of Congress, 1980); J. Merrill-Oldham and M. Smith (eds.), *The Library Preservation Program. Models, Priorities, Possibilities* (Chicago, Ill.: American Library Association, 1985). Comparable British publications include: F.W. Ratcliffe, *Preservation Policies and Conservation in British Libraries: Report of the Cambridge University Library Conservation Project*. Library and Information Research Reports, 25 (London: British Library, 1984); R.E. Palmer (ed.), *Preserving the Word. Library Association Conference Proceedings, Harrogate, 1986* (London: The Library Association, 1987). And internationally the most notable collection was *Preservation of Library Materials. Conference Held at the National Library of Austria, Vienna, 7-19 April 1986, Sponsored by the Conference of Directors of National Libraries in Cooperation*

        with IFLA and Unesco. 2 vols. IFLA Publications, 40-41 (Munich: K.G. Saur, 1987).

2   Two of the more useful papers by educators are J.R. Turner, 'Teaching Conservation,' *Education for Information* 6 (1988): 145-151; and J. Feather and A. Lusher, 'Education for Conservation in British Library Schools: Current Practices and Future Prospects,' *Journal of Librarianship* 21 (1989): 129-138.

3   M. Byrnes, 'Preservation and Collection Management: Some Common Concerns,' In *The Collection Building Reader,* ed. by Betty-Carol Sellen and Arthur Curley (New York: Neal-Schuman Publishers, 1992), p. 57.

4   J. Feather, *Preservation and the Management of Library Collections* (London: Library Association Publishing, 1991) , p. 7.

5   Byrnes, *op. cit.*, p. 61. This estimate appears to be based on that provided by the Council on Library Resources. Committee on Preservation and Access, *Brittle Books: Report of the Committee on Preservation and Access* (Washington, D.C.: Council on Library Resources, 1986).

6   Ross Harvey, *Preservation in Australian and New Zealand Libraries: Principles, Strategies and Practices for Librarians.* Topics in Australasian Library and Information Studies, 3 (Wagga Wagga, NSW: Centre for Information Studies, 1990). A second edition of this work will be available at the end of 1992. Information on this and other titles is available from the Centre for Information Studies, Locked Bag 660, Wagga Wagga, NSW 2678, Australia.

Dr G.E. Gorman
Charles Sturt University – Riverina

Dr Ronald R. Powell
University of Missouri – Columbia

Introduction

The physical deterioration of library materials, especially of paper-based materials, is now recognized as one of the major professional issues of librarianship. The deterioration is on a massive scale, affecting such an immense volume of material in libraries throughout the world that to suggest it will become *the* major professional concern of the coming decades is no exaggeration. It results from factors such as the quality of the environment in which library collections are stored, the handling these collections receive, the increasing use of library resources as a consequence of improved education and recent awareness of our cultural heritage, and – equally important – the processes of decay inherent in the materials themselves.

Preservation of library materials has until recent years suffered from a bad press. It was long felt to be the concern only of rare books librarians or manuscript librarians in large academic and research libraries. No possible relevance was perceived by most librarians in public or special libraries, or indeed by librarians working in any type of library outside the very largest institutions. Over the last decade there has been a gradual recognition that the issues recognized and addressed (albeit by solutions which are still in the early stages of development) in a handful of research libraries have a much wider significance. The real issue is now stated more generally than merely in terms of unique, very expensive and otherwise demonstrably valuable items in a library's collection. Preservation is currently described in terms applicable to all libraries and all library materials: it is now about 'making our libraries useful' and is concerned with 'preserving materials for as long as they are wanted'.[1]

This book is written for practising librarians and information workers and for students of librarianship. It aims to provide for the thinking librarian and student a framework for further reflection on the problems of preservation and for research into their solutions. It is not primarily intended for archivists and records managers, although there will be much of interest to them in it. Nor is it a 'how-to-do-it' manual. It will not provide much assistance for those who want to learn how to carry out technical conservation procedures, and it does not purport to describe the technical procedures which are properly the province of trained conservators and trained conservation technicians. The examples it uses are mainly, but not exclusively, relevant to paper-based materials, for these are still by far the most strongly represented formats in our library collections. I have hypothesized as the reader a 'typical' librarian, one who is likely to have a modicum of secondary-school-level science background, who is probably concerned with general conservation issues such as those relating to the environment and to old buildings, and who has a more specific professional interest in, and possibly a need to know more about, all aspects of the preservation of library materials.

This book is, then, for those librarians who take an interest in this major professional issue and who want to acquire further knowledge about it. Such knowledge is essential for making informed decisions about the place of preservation in library procedures, for understanding which standard routines do not needlessly damage library materials and may therefore be retained, and which procedures are not acceptable and must be altered. Furthermore, such knowledge is required for deciding when a problem is beyond the resources of the library and its staff, and when technical advice from professional conservators should be sought.

In an ideal world such a book as this would not need to be written. In such a world all libraries would have the services of specialist conservators readily accessible to them, either on their staff in the case of medium-sized and larger institutions, or available through a consortium for smaller organizations. The reality does not even begin to approach this ideal. There is a shortage of conservators available and willing to work in libraries. Librarians at all levels cannot rely on the ready availability of advice from and services of conservators and must be willing themselves to put principles such as those expounded in this book into everyday practice. More importantly – and more lamentably – few library managers have recognized the problems of preserving library materials and even fewer have diverted resources to their resolution. This book may start to redress the balance. It will, it is hoped, be read by librarians and students of librarianship who will in future years become library managers in a position to put preservation principles into practice. If it is also read by some who are already library managers, and if it alters their attitudes to this issue, that will be an added bonus.

This book is based on four premises:

1   that preservation is a management responsibility, at the highest level;
2   that all collections need a preservation plan;
3   that the preservation plan must be adequately funded as part of the ongoing budget;
4   that preservation must be the concern of all library staff at every level and a part of all library routines: it is not just a technical specialist matter which takes place in a separate laboratory.[2]

In Chapter 1 an overview of preservation of library materials is given. Here the general nature of the problem is described and an indication is given of some of the methods to address it. Chapter 2 examines the physical nature of library materials, describes the inherent characteristics which cause deterioration, and looks at the major causes of deterioration – temperature, relative humidity, light, atmospheric pollutants, moulds and fungi, insects and rodents, abuse and mismanagement by curators and users of collections.

The third chapter is concerned with ascertaining the extent and nature of the preservation problem in collections by carrying out conservation surveys.

Chapter 4 covers methods of controlling the storage environment of the collection and addresses factors to consider when designing new buildings or renovating existing accommodation. In Chapter 5 handling of library materials and the education of librarians, staff working in libraries and users is described. Disaster response planning is addressed in Chapter 6.

Chapters 7, 8 and 9 comprise descriptions and evaluations of the many procedures available to managers to conserve library collections. Chapter 7 describes treatments which in the main can readily be implemented in-house, that is, simple procedures which can be carried out by non-specialist staff and without special equipment. It also notes the importance of binding as a preservation measure. Chapter 8 examines substitution media or reformatting, where procedures using equipment such as the photocopier, the microfilm camera, and the computer and optical disc transfer the content of the original item to another medium. Chapter 9 looks at strategies for preservation which require the development and application of technology to bulk treatment of materials, and also at cooperative preservation programs.

The final chapter specifically addresses that which has been implicit throughout the preceding chapters. In it the integration of preservation into all aspects of library management is described, and such matters as designing and implementing a preservation plan, adjusting existing procedures and introducing new procedures are addressed.

This book is clearly a personal one, reflecting my concept of what all librarians should know about preservation. I am diffident about adding yet another item to the already large number of writings about library preservation. If this one is different, it is because it is written by a librarian, not by a conservator. To the best of my knowledge this is different from most of the current general texts. I make no apology for this: the best, if not the only, way of addressing the preservation problem is for librarians to take charge of their preservation destiny and incorporate existing solutions, and any new solutions, into the everyday routines and administrative processes in their libraries.

Notes

1   John Feather, 'Preservation and Conservation: A Professional Issue for the 1990s', *New Zealand Libraries* 46, 2/3 (1989): 23.

2   A similar list is given in Mary Lynn Ritzenthaler, *Archives and Manuscripts: Conservation; A Manual on Physical Care and Management* (Chicago, Ill.: Society of American Archivists, 1983), p. 7.

Chapter 1

Overview: The Problem, Causes and Solutions

For most of us, preservation is about making our libraries useful:
preserving materials for as long as they are wanted. In that sense,
preservation is indeed a central issue in modern librarianship, and one
which will continue to be of concern to the end of this century and
beyond.(John Feather)[1]

PRESERVATION IS POINTLESS WITHOUT A PURPOSE – USE.
(Ina Bertrand)[2]

Definitions of Conservation and Preservation

The terms 'preservation' and 'conservation', and to a lesser extent the term
'restoration', have been used interchangeably in library literature until the last
few years. Present usage allocates to 'preservation' the more general, all-
encompassing meaning, while 'conservation' and 'restoration' are defined
more specifically. Care must be taken when reading the literature, as
publications before the early 1980s may not use these terms in the same sense
as the current terminology does. Take, for example, the terms used by the
National Conservation Advisory Council (United States) in 1983. Here
'conservation' is the all-encompassing term; it includes *examination*
(assessment of the item), *preservation* ('action taken to
retard...deterioration...by control of their environment and/or treatment of
their structure') and *restoration* ('action taken to return a deteriorated...artifact
as nearly as is feasible to its original form...with minimal further sacrifice of
aesthetic and historic integrity').[3]

Currently 'conservation' is the more specific term and is particularly
used in relation to specific objects, whereas 'preservation' is a broader
concept covering conservation as well as actions relating to protection,
maintenance and restoration of library collections. The eminent British
conservator, Christopher Clarkson, emphasizes this broader aspect when he
states that *preservation* 'encompasses every facet of library life': it is, he says,
'preventive medicine...the concern of everyone who walks into, or works in,

a library.' For Clarkson *conservation* is 'the specialized process of making safe, or to a certain degree usable, fragile period objects' and *restoration* 'expresses rather extensive rebuilding and replacement by modern materials within a period object, catering for a future of more robust use.' He neatly distinguishes the three terms by relating them to the extent of operations applied to an item: '*restoration* implies major alterations, *conservation* minimal and *preservation* none.'[4] Another British writer, Diana Grimwood-Jones, points out a further useful distinction between preservation and conservation: the former term applies to 'various strategies for preserving the intellectual content', whereas the latter 'is primarily concerned with ensuring that the original artefact is maintained and secure.'[5] This distinction and its implications are examined in more detail later in this chapter.

The definitions used in this book are taken from the IFLA (International Federation of Library Associations and Institutions) *Principles for the Preservation and Conservation of Library Materials.*

Preservation Includes all the managerial and financial considerations including storage and accommodation provisions, staffing levels, policies, techniques and methods involved in preserving library and archive materials and the information contained in them.

Conservation Denotes those specific policies and practices involved in protecting library and archive materials from deterioration, damage and decay, including the methods and techniques devised by technical staff.

Restoration Denotes those techniques and judgements used by technical staff engaged in the making good of library and archive materials damaged by time, use and other factors.[6]

Reasons for Preservation

The concept of preservation is firmly rooted in the idea that mankind learns from the past and that evidence of the past therefore has considerable significance to the human race and is worth saving. Libraries and archives are two of several kinds of institutions which have a primary role to play in collecting and preserving the records of the past. 'Past' as used here is a relative term, ranging from the very distant, whose records might be represented by fragments of text carved on stones, to the very recent, yesterday's newspaper or a computer-stored map of North America transmitted last week from a satellite to Washington. The implication of this definition is that *all* libraries are, or should be, involved in preservation. The recent concern with preservation is, of course, not solely the preoccupation of libraries and archives. It is to a large extent another aspect of the more general international concern with conservation of the environment. This augurs well for setting a more positive and more supportive scene for increased concern (translated into increased resources) about the preservation of library and archival materials.

Many writers have expressed the idea that we have a duty to preserve what went before us. One such view is that expressed by John Agresto, who in 1986 headed the National Endowment for the Humanities, one of the major funding agencies of preservation programs in the United States (it gave, for example, $22.6 million for preservation in the 1991 fiscal year).[7] Agresto considers that 'we have a human obligation *not to forget*' (italics in original). Preservation of library and archival materials is essential politically, for the well-being of democracies which, argues Agresto, 'depends on knowledge and the diffusion of knowledge' and on 'knowledge shared'. It is also essential to scholars and educators, who must rely on the availability of primary source materials as the basis for good teaching. For all teachers and scholars and all citizens, then, there is a duty to preserve. Agresto also makes the point that preserving the past 'is useful and practical to us, the living'.[8] One needs only to consider a present without Walt Whitman, Andrew Wyeth or Henry Moore (on the aesthetic level) or without information about the location of unsuccessful mining exploration carried out in Indonesia last year (on the economic level) to recognize the truth in this statement.

Libraries, archives and information agencies, then, have as a major responsibility, perhaps as *the* major responsibility, the preservation of the recorded word. The recorded word is still largely on paper, written and printed, and so preservation has until now been largely the province of 'traditional' librarians, those who deal with collections which are heavily paper-based; but to an ever-increasing extent media other than paper are assuming importance, magnetic media which store computer data being the most significant. If librarians as custodians of these records – both printed and in other forms – fail in their preservation duties, then it is not too fanciful to suggest that what is at stake is nothing less than 'the perpetuation of society as we are accustomed to conceive or idealize it'.[9]

What if we fail in this responsibility? Surprisingly, few writers on library preservation have addressed this question. Pamela Darling is one who has. She foresees that in twenty-five years libraries would no longer have space shortages, as the natural deterioration of retrospective collections would have advanced so far that most items would be useless and would have been discarded, 'the paper crumbled, photographic images vanished, magnetic tape charges jumbled.' (Paper fragments, thinks Darling, would perhaps be sold for use as filter material in air pollution masks.) Destruction of many collections would have occurred because of fires started by 'spontaneous combustion of densely packed paper' and exacerbated by crowded and unmaintained storage areas. Theft, she contends, would become a major problem as paper-based material from the nineteenth and twentieth centuries diminishes in availability and quantity and becomes scarcer.[10] Although this is probably an alarmist view which deliberately overstates for effect, it illustrates some of the potential results.

Professional Responsibilities of Librarians and Archivists

Archivists have a clearly and unequivocally stated preservation mission. For them, 'a concern for conservation is central to the true responsibilities of the archivist. To ignore the matter is to be professionally negligent. There can be no compromise on this point, and not even a shortage of resources can excuse a lack of concern for conservation.'[11] This view, usually neatly encapsulated in the phrase 'the physical defence of archives', was formulated by the British archivist Sir Hilary Jenkinson, whose words are worth quoting in detail.

> The duties of the Archivist...are primary and secondary. In the first place he has to take all possible precautions for the safeguarding of his Archives and for their custody.... *Subject to the discharge of these duties* he has in the second place to provide to the best of his ability for the needs of historians and other research workers. But *the position of primary and secondary must not be reversed.* (italics in original)[12]

This attitude is based on the logic of cause and effect: if materials are allowed to deteriorate, then it will become increasingly difficult, and finally impossible, to use them to access the information they contain.

While archivists are secure in their understanding of their preservation responsibilities, the library profession is not. In the past librarians did have a preservation mission, clearly stated; for example, the tasks of the librarian were identified by John Durie in 1650 as to build collections, care for them, and be 'dispensers to applie them for use, or to see them well used, or at least not abused.'[13] During the intervening centuries the relationship between access to materials in libraries and preservation of such materials has become unbalanced, so that the logic of cause and effect noted in the preceding paragraph in relation to archivists is no longer perceived as a truism by the library profession and does not form a significant part of the librarian's professional ethos. Librarians had devoted most of their energies towards providing access to the materials in their care and towards encouraging use and improving the mechanisms for use, without having proper regard to the physical deterioration caused by increased use.

The balance is fortunately changing, as evidenced by this and many similar publications in the last decade. Current library literature is now more likely than not to include the term 'preservation' in the same sentence with descriptions of other library management functions. One example is from the influential 1986 report, *Brittle Books*: 'Responsibility for preservation is inseparable from the work of building and maintaining research collections.'[14] This could be extended to read: 'Responsibility for preservation is inseparable from the work of building, maintaining and using all library collections.' Another statement, from the 1989-1990 annual report of the Commission on Preservation and Access, needs no qualification: 'The preservation function – the stewardship of the accumulated knowledge base – represents the central obligation of librarianship.'[15] Perhaps by the end of the 1990s such statements will be acceptable to all librarians; at present, however, there is still much convincing to be done. What must be stressed to librarians is the importance of access to the collections in their care. Preservation is pointless unless it enhances access; and usability of the collections is the ultimate aim of preservation.

The Extent of the Preservation Problem

The preservation problem is immense. This was forcibly brought to the attention of the library world in 1959 with the publication of William J. Barrow's key study, *Deterioration of Book Stock: Causes and Remedies; Two Studies on the Permanence of Book Paper.* Barrow, using evidence gained from the testing of 500 non-fiction books printed in the United States between 1900 and 1949, asserted that most books printed in the first half of the twentieth century would be unusable in the next century.[16]

Later studies of collections in the United States, while moderating Barrow's conclusions, have still emphasized the size of the problem. In 1973, for example, the Library of Congress estimated that 6 million items (34 per cent of its total of 17 million) were either completely unusable or irreparably damaged.[17] Major studies were carried out at the University of California Libraries, Stanford University and Yale University. In the Yale survey, the results of which were published in 1985, about 29 per cent of the large number of books sampled had very brittle paper, about 37 per cent had brittle paper, and about 83 per cent had acidic paper (with a pH level below 5.4). Thirteen per cent were in need of immediate treatment.[18] (More information on these surveys is given in Chapter 3.) Other recent studies, for example those at the Syracuse University Libraries and the University of Illinois at Urbana-Champaign, have confirmed the size of the problem.[19] In 1986 an estimate of the number of volumes affected in research libraries in the United States was made. Of 305 million volumes, 75 million (about 25 per cent) were then at risk. (This figure will have increased in the intervening six years.) Over the next twenty years, it was estimated, the contents of 3.3 million volumes 'of lasting importance' must be converted to another medium such as microfilm if they are to be saved, at an estimated cost of nearly $400 million.[20]

The results of surveys carried out to determine the size of the preservation problem in North America have been viewed with dismay in other parts of the world, and libraries in other countries have carried out similar research to determine the extent of deterioration in their collections. In the United Kingdom the situation has been determined to be of smaller magnitude, although still highly significant in terms of the total numbers of items in library collections. At the British Library approximately 14 per cent of items published after 1850 are estimated to contain paper in poor condition.[21] In Australia a survey of the research collections of the University of Sydney Library completed in 1990 indicated that 12.3 per cent were printed on paper which was very or extremely brittle,[22] and other surveys in that country indicate that the overall level of embrittlement is about 15 per cent. Of the 35 million pages of New Zealand newspapers published to 1985 an estimated 7 million pages (20 per cent) are on badly deteriorated paper and are in urgent need of microfilming.[23] As many as 40 per cent of the books in Indonesian libraries are estimated to be badly deteriorated.[24]

The figures reported above indicate paper deterioration only in percentages of total collections, and take no account of the variation in paper quality at different periods. As one example, the British Library survey noted above found that about 40 per cent of books published in the 1880s and 1890s were printed on paper that had become brittle, compared with only about 14 per cent of the total.

Causes of Deterioration

While the deterioration of library materials can be attributed to a large number of factors and their complex interaction, one factor alone has been, and will continue to be, responsible for a very high proportion of the damage. The culprit is the poor quality of the paper used from about the middle of the nineteenth century. It has resulted in deterioration on such a scale that the term 'bibliosuicide' describes the probable fate of most of the books published from about 1850 to the present time. Other factors, too, contribute their share of damage: increased and increasing use of collections, the introduction and use of new technologies in libraries, environmental factors and natural disasters are the major players.

The major problem is the poor quality of modern paper. Many social factors combined in the Western world during the nineteenth century to result in a dramatic increase in population, better education and the rapid spread of literacy. The consequent demand for paper caused traditional methods of paper manufacture, which produced stable and durable long-fibred paper with a long life, to be supplanted by mass-production methods based on materials other than the traditional rags, materials which have a built-in decay factor. From about 1850 most paper has been made from wood pulp, a cheap and renewable resource. However, wood pulp contains lignin, which has the undesirable properties of darkening paper when it is exposed to ultraviolet light and of breaking down cellulose (the essential building block in the structure of paper) into carbon dioxide gas over time. Paper made from mechanically ground wood pulp is the most vulnerable to decay, for during its manufacturing process the cellulose fibres in it are shortened and their capacity to bond together reduced. The result is weak paper.

The structural integrity of wood pulp paper is further reduced by additives introduced during the manufacturing process. These include rosin/aluminium sulphate as a sizing agent, necessary to reduce absorption of writing and printing inks, and bleaching agents, used to produce the white paper considered desirable for printing and writing. Such additives leave residual acids in the paper, which break the cellulose down to simpler molecules. This phenomenon is known as 'acid attack' and is one of the major reasons for paper deterioration. The breakdown of cellulose also occurs as a result of the paper's exposure to radiant energy in the form of light and heat. This is described as photochemical degradation.

Modern paper, then, decays rapidly because of its inherent structure. Its deterioration is hastened if it is stored in conditions where it is exposed to radiant energy such as light, heat and ultraviolet light. However, even if it were stored where the temperature was as low as possible and no light was admitted, the chemicals inherent in it would still cause deterioration and ultimately destruction.

Paper is not the only material in library collections which deteriorates. Other materials used in modern book production are at fault, sometimes to an almost equal degree. The material from which bindings are constructed – leather, cloth, paper, thread, glue – and the ink with which books are printed also have chemical properties whose interaction and reaction to the paper may increase the rate of deterioration. Book production has been the victim of the same pressures as paper manufacturing, with heavily increased demand from the middle of the nineteenth century. Hand in hand with this has gone a lack of emphasis on, or perhaps even a lack of awareness of, the essential requirements for permanence of the object and durability of the materials from which the object was constructed. The introduction of mass-production manufacturing techniques ('perfect' binding is a good example) to produce enough books to sate the increased appetite of the literate also meant that traditional craft-based processes (binding and printing, for example) lapsed. Standards of workmanship and quality were weakened as a result.[25]

Another significant cause of deterioration is increased use of library collections. Librarians have perhaps been too successful in one of their roles, that of providing information. In doing so they have considered items in library collections simply as sources of information and have not also considered them as physical objects; therefore, in the use of the collections little regard has been taken of the physical nature of the objects, their fragility and their handling requirements. Librarians have promoted use of and accessibility to their collections but have not considered sufficiently the preservation implications. Library staff and the users of the libraries consequently do not generally know how to store and handle the collections carefully in ways that minimize damage. The extension of leisure time and an increase in participation in post-compulsory education, particularly since 1945, have stimulated use of libraries, and this has increased the rate at which their collections deteriorate. Recent trends in librarianship, notably the growth of resource sharing and bibliographic networks, have also helped to accelerate the rate of deterioration.

Hand in hand with the deterioration caused by increased use has gone that caused by the introduction of new technologies into libraries. Here the most obvious example is the photocopier. Photocopying is, according to the eminent conservator Paul Banks, 'a prime example of the two-edged sword'.

While it is now difficult, if not impossible, to imagine libraries and their users functioning without photocopiers – not least as a tool for preservation – the act of photocopying is 'inherently at least somewhat stressful' to books and paper, 'and potentially disastrous'.[26] Photocopying is widely used as a legitimate preservation routine to preserve the intellectual content of items by making surrogate copies which are used to reduce wear of deteriorated originals. Unfortunately, the act of photocopying in most cases imposes on the item being copied high levels of mechanical stress (opening out the binding, for example) and light which speed up the rate of deterioration.

Other factors have also been responsible for deterioration. Chief among these are factors categorized loosely as 'environmental', and the major contributor here is air pollution. Modern industrialized cities typically have a high level of air pollution, whose major threat is to the paper in library collections. In particular, heavy concentrations of sulphur and nitrogen oxides in polluted air produce acids which hasten the process of paper deterioration. Dust and dirt particles may also cause mechanical damage, through abrasion of the paper with which they come into contact.

Disasters are another significant cause of damage to library collections, chief among them being floods, fires and earthquakes. Recent examples are, sadly, plentiful; two particularly disastrous examples in recent years are the fires at the Los Angeles Public Library in 1986, where 400,000 volumes were destroyed, and in 1988 at the Library of the USSR Academy of Sciences, where the total destruction of more than 400,000 volumes was reported. While some disasters come within the category of 'acts of God' and cannot be prevented, others can be avoided, or damage from them minimized, by appropriate planning and action. This is the subject of Chapter 6.

The last category of factors causing deterioration is best described as 'attitudinal'. Attitudes towards the book have changed from what was once a stance of respect towards the item – towards its intellectual content and also towards the craftsmanship of its manufacture – to what F.W. Ratcliffe has termed 'the paperback throw-away attitude to an article traditionally destined to be preserved'.[27] This is evident in standards of book construction, as already noted, and also, and perhaps equally dangerously, in the low standards of care and handling applied to books by their users and their custodians. And who can blame them, when all the evidence in bookshops, newsagents, service stations and everywhere else where books are now sold suggests that books can readily be replaced? But this is definitely *not* the case, and most books are not easily replaceable but rather must be conserved.

The second 'attitudinal' problem is present in many custodians of library and archives collections who have, suggests Guy Petherbridge, displayed 'an astounding insensitivity to the deterioration and destruction of historical, bibliographical and other significant features.' By not observing and understanding 'simple patterns of cause and effect in storage, exhibition and use' they have been professionally negligent by allowing destructive procedures to be continued. In addition, a lack of forethought has sometimes resulted in the application of inappropriate repair techniques which have caused more harm than good.[28] In a similar vein, planners of new library buildings have allowed standards of lighting and heating to be provided which, while good for users, take no account of the physical requirements needed to slow down the processes of deterioration.

Strategies to Address the Problem

As we have already noted, the magnitude of the preservation problem is immense. To provide methods of addressing the problem it is first necessary to develop policies which cover the nature and scope of the methods to be used rather than prescribe the precise methods themselves. What is needed, in other words, are strategies for the preservation of library materials.

Such strategies are actively being developed, examined and discussed in the preservation and library literature, and are being accepted finally as tenets. The first essential is agreement on clear definitions of preservation priorities, to determine what in our collections should have conservation attention devoted to it. Here some principles have evolved. The first of these recognizes the almost certain impossibility, given the magnitude of the problem and the quantity of deteriorated material, of physically saving all, or even most, items in our collections. Priorities for what can or should be preserved must, then, be established. These are often expressed purely in terms of what is physically possible. First to be salvaged should be materials not yet embrittled, as these require less attention and fewer resources to stabilize their storage conditions and handling. The second priority is to transfer to another, more durable, medium such as microfilm those items which are beyond recovery. Finally, an attempt should be made to contain the problem for items currently being produced by changing the nature of the materials they are made from. Paper, for example, should be made so that it is more durable, more stable and more permanent than what is made from mechanical wood pulp.

Strategies must be clearly related to the objectives of individual institutions. This is recognized in the IFLA *Principles for the Preservation and Conservation of Library Materials*. These note that the objectives of a preservation policy are to preserve the intellectual content of items, and/or to preserve the original physical form of items; they then state that: 'Not every library can, or will want to, preserve every item in its collection in its original form, and the establishing of policy priorities is a necessary prerequisite for any library undertaking such work.'[29] It is therefore vital that libraries have in place clear definitions of their function, role and service ethics, and also statements of their policies, for example collection policies, before a preservation program can be usefully implemented.

Another principle now accepted is that methods which treat material economically in bulk should be developed and applied in preference to methods which can be applied to only one item, or to a small number of items, at any one time. An example of this is the Library of Congress' research into a method of mass deacidification which is planned to treat one million books annually in a batch process. This is to be contrasted with existing methods of aqueous deacidification where books have to be disbound and each leaf treated separately, a time-consuming and expensive process.

A further principle to be established is that preservation is no longer the sole preserve of the conservator. The 'myth of the expensive expert', as one writer calls it, need not apply. Enormous advances can be made simply by altering existing library procedures to put into action the relatively simple notions of preservation. Take as one example the effect of minor changes in book return routines. Less damage would be caused to bindings if books were placed on a counter rather than returned through a book return chute. What is needed here is, first, time to put such routines into place throughout all aspects of library practice and, second, the willingness of staff at all levels who must be actively involved. Further requirements are the commitment by senior administrators of staff resources to the planning and development processes, and the reallocation of budgets to provide the initial and also the ongoing finance needed to maintain the routines. Additional staff will not necessarily be required, nor will major technical expertise. Improvements of this kind can be implemented readily in areas such as storage and handling routines, reproduction policies, and applying protective physical enclosures such as boxing or binding. In fact preservation is implicit in most library routines. What needs to be developed is an attitude of mind in all library staff, which will in turn inevitably have an impact on library procedures.

The collaborative nature of the preservation effort is another area where a clear message is being enunciated. All who have a stake in the preservation of library resources must cooperate; conservators and scientists must work together with librarians, archivists, administrators and policy-makers to plan and implement realistic strategies for coping with the problem.

One of the most important principles to be established has been that of distinguishing *preventive* conservation from *restorative* conservation practice. Preventive measures have recently assumed importance as the most significant and cost-effective way of addressing the preservation problem. The move has been from artisan-based conservation practices, based on traditional skills and attitudes, such as those of craft bookbinders, to a new discipline which has built on the traditional qualities of craftsmanship and high standards. The new techniques seek to provide protection for an object with the minimum of alteration (preferably none) to the item in order to prevent further deterioration, rather than to repair the item by renewing deteriorated segments in an 'authentic' style. For example, modern practice might determine that an eighteenth-century book with a deteriorated binding should not be rebound in the style of that period, but instead should be placed in a box which would protect the book and at the same time retain the original binding as evidence, rather than obscure or destroy it by rebinding. This attitude of minimal intervention is usually a more economical solution, important given the size of the preservation problem and the limited financial resources available to address it, and it also allows the possibility that new techniques and attitudes yet to be developed can be applied in the future if appropriate.

Another clearly expressed principle is that of the important role which education and training must play in addressing the issue. An understanding of the nature and extent of the preservation problem, the issues involved and the methods available to alleviate it is essential for personnel at all levels, from the lowliest library assistant to national decision-makers. This will be vital if the problem is to be addressed, as it must be, by introducing preservation awareness into all aspects of library management. For this approach to succeed, all library staff must be constantly kept aware of preservation.

Another issue is involved in education and training for preservation. In an ideal world it would be possible for all library preservation programs to be planned and implemented by fully trained conservators, preferably paper conservators. However, given the small number of paper conservators already qualified and likely to be trained in the immediate future, the way to ensure progress is to train librarians and archivists more adequately in the concerns, techniques and management of preservation programs. This has been carried out in a few library schools in the United States, the best-known being the one- or two-year program in preservation administration established initially at Columbia University in New York and now at the University of Texas at Austin. Making such education and training more widespread is the method that promises most success, given the magnitude of the problem.

There will always be many libraries and archives which will never be large enough to employ a professionally qualified conservator, although they may call upon the services of such from time to time, by employing a freelance conservator or by hiring the services of a regional cooperative conservation laboratory. The everyday work of these smaller institutions requires some knowledge of basic principles and simple technical processes in order to keep their collections intact and usable. For this reason all librarians and archivists need an awareness of preservation, best provided in their professional education. Another reason to provide all librarians and archivists with an awareness of the issues is to give some basis on which to assess the quality of the literature of preservation, which is ever-increasing in quantity (witness this book) and variable in quality.

Methods to Address the Problem

What specific methods are used to address the preservation problem? While these are fully described in later chapters, brief mention is made of them here. They can be grouped into four areas: those of a 'housekeeping' nature which can be implemented immediately in individual libraries and archives; those relating to disaster response planning; those relating to the transfer of information from a deteriorated medium to another medium; and those requiring cooperative action or the use of technology on a large scale.

The first group, the 'housekeeping' methods, affect all library routines. They include the introduction of preservation principles into all aspects of library procedures: training shelvers to handle books carefully and to notice damage which needs repair; replacing potentially damaging book return mechanisms with less harmful furniture; implementing a regular maintenance program for equipment such as microfilm readers, video recorders and sound cassette players; considering whether current binding procedures need to be replaced by methods which are more conservationally acceptable; introducing an ongoing and regular staff training program for preservation; preparing handouts for users which stress the importance of correct handling. The physical conditions in which the collection is stored should be assessed and modified as necessary. Here it is essential to set appropriate levels of heating, relative humidity and lighting, and to maintain them at constant levels. Any new building or refurbishing of structures housing library collections should be designed with a thorough awareness of preservation issues. The list is long and extends far beyond the points noted above.

Disaster response planning (known also by other names such as disaster planning, contingency planning, risk management) is now accepted as an important component of preservation management. Techniques are well formulated for assessing the causes of disasters in libraries, lessening the likelihood that they will occur, and minimizing the damage imposed should they happen. Effective techniques have also been developed for salvaging library materials after they have been exposed to fire and water damage.

Techniques also exist for the transfer of the content of deteriorated items in library collections to other more durable media. Procedures for microfilming are well established. Microfilming is likely to remain the main surrogate medium for library use for the near future, despite the current interest and increasing expertise in optical discs whose longevity is, however, still unproven in preservation terms. Other techniques have been developed and used in libraries for these purposes, some for a considerable number of years; among them are transcription from manuscript to typescript, photocopying and transfer to a digital form.

In the fourth category – methods requiring cooperative activity or the use of technology on a large scale – are included such concerns as efficient bibliographic systems, central registers of preserved copies, mass deacidification, the use of permanent paper and regional cooperation. The development of an efficient bibliographic system is an essential prerequisite for any large-scale conservation program to be fully effective and cost-efficient. Such programs, for example state- or nation-wide newspaper microfilming projects, require that all participants have ready access to bibliographic information. Those involved need to ascertain such details as the number of copies of an item, their location, whether a specific copy has been preserved, and the extent and nature of conservation treatments applied. Mass deacidification facilities, only now becoming commercially available, have required large cooperative research efforts over two decades to develop them, and as they become more widespread will require cooperation to ensure that they are used for the greatest preservation good. Some success can be seen with cooperative lobbying projects to encourage publishers to use permanent paper (that is, non-acidic and alkaline-buffered paper) for book production. Cooperation here has taken place among writers, publishers and librarians. Another proven cooperative preservation method is the establishment of conservation laboratories and centres which offer their services within a particular region or to a specific group.

A useful prediction of the strategies and methods likely to be most important in the next few years has been made by Diana Grimwood-Jones. She predicts that five areas will be the most significant:

greater standardization in methodology (in surveying collections and contingency planning); the key issue of selectivity, and increased integration of preservation with collection management policies; the fruits of research into mass treatment techniques; greater prominence of non-book materials, with their associated preservation problems and their increasing potential as primary publication or information storage media; and education in its broadest sense, involving decision-makers, conservators, library assistants, users and library school students: in fact anyone who handles information.[30]

The preservation problem is essentially a managerial one, and the methods available to librarians to address it are likewise essentially managerial: defining selection policies, establishing conservationally sound collection management policies, maintaining and housing the collections well, and educating staff and users. There is still a place, an important place, for treatment at the artefact or single item level. But the vast size of the problem means that our efforts must be directed towards improving the lot of the majority of items in our collections by implementing procedures and treatments which deal with our collections en masse.

Artefact versus Content Preservation

A key concept central to the preservation effort is that of distinguishing between the *intellectual* properties of an item and its *physical* properties. For example, a book's intellectual properties lie in the text and its meaning, while its physical properties are carried in its construction, materials and design. If the content (the intellectual properties) of a book is to be preserved, then photocopying or microfilming, or even reading the text onto a cassette tape, will suffice. For many items in library collections this kind of preservation is all that may be required, both for current use and in the future. If, however, the artefact itself (the book's physical properties) is to be preserved, then different methods will need to be applied to that item. It may need to have its paper deacidified then strengthened to improve its ability to be handled, its binding refurbished, and it may require enclosing in a custom-made archival quality box.

Artefact preservation is usually chosen when the item as a physical object has special value because it is old, it has beauty, it is rare, it has some historical significance, or it has a high monetary value. Such criteria can be difficult to define and apply to items in a collection. In some cases the artefact is preserved for its bibliographical significance. For example, although most users of newspapers are satisfied with a microfilm of the paper, the newspaper or printing historian will require evidence about such things as paper quality and size of page which can only be derived from the physical objects themselves. It may therefore be important to some users that at least a sample of the artefacts is conserved.

One of the key decisions to be made in a preservation program is what to conserve. To determine this on the individual item basis, it will be necessary to decide whether an item is to have only its intellectual content preserved (and so it may be microfilmed and the original discarded or allowed to disintegrate) or whether its physical fabric, the artefact itself, should be preserved. It will be necessary to ask the question: 'is the medium the message?' (to coin a phrase). There is not yet a clear consensus about when the content should be conserved in preference to the artefact.[31] The question has been aired for some time in the library literature. In his influential 1966 report Gordon Williams carefully examined the distinction between the 'physical' and 'intellectual' properties of a book. He noted that for some books 'the intrinsic physical characteristics of some of them also provide significant information about the text itself or its authenticity, or about the society that produced it';[32] and he strongly recommended the retention of an original copy of all significant books in a central storage facility.

While artefact conservation may well be appropriate for national heritage collections with a legislative and moral responsibility to retain objects for as long as possible (legal deposit collections, for example), it is probably not appropriate for most other libraries, whose aims are usually more immediate and are often defined in terms of availability to users. For most libraries the decision is more likely to be made purely in terms of the financial implications: what is the cheapest way of ensuring that the content of this deteriorating item is usable? Only infrequently will the question of whether the artefact itself has value and needs to be conserved be the major one to be answered.

The processes of artefact conservation have raised some ethical questions. The tenets first espoused by Roger Ellis are now generally accepted in answer to these questions.[33] He enunciates a philosophy of minimal intervention in such 'principles of archive repair' as 'before starting...ask..."How little need I do to this document to make it fit for use again?"' The importance of retaining the original condition, the integrity, of the object is emphasized:

Leave the nature and extent of [the] repair unmistakably evident; no process of repair may be used which could in any way damage or weaken the material of which the document is made; no process of repair may be allowed to remove, diminish, falsify, or obscure, in any way, the document's value as evidence.

Finally, the processes applied must be completely reversible: 'Never do anything which cannot be undone without damage to the document.'

Selection of Materials to Preserve

One of the major decisions to be made in any preservation program is what to preserve. The decisions made will determine the availability of the printed word and other library materials to coming generations. For libraries part of the decision is usually made at the initial stage of selection. The selection criteria applied in this process ensure that material relevant to the collection and useful or potentially useful is acquired, and by extension this material should be considered for preservation. This has typically been the case in research libraries.

Many other factors need to be in place so that these decisions can be made in the best way. Good bibliographic control is essential, at the local level to determine what is in the collection (so that, for example, an item for which a duplicate in better condition is held is not conserved), and at the national level (so that the national preservation effort is not diluted by treating several copies of the same item). Adequate bibliographic control of in-print items is also essential in order to ascertain whether a replacement – reprint or microfilm – is available and could be purchased in place of treating a deteriorated item.

Some of the questions involved in selection of items to be conserved are examined in more detail in Chapter 8.

Development of the Field of Preservation

Preservation of library materials is not a new concern. An early, but by no means the earliest, expression of concern was the publication in 1880 of William Blades' *The Enemies of Books*, in which the chapter headings are 'Fire', 'Water', 'Gas and Heat', 'Dust and Neglect', 'Ignorance', 'The Bookworm', 'Other Vermin', 'Bookbinders', 'Collectors'.[34] As it would take too much space to describe and examine all other writings here, only the more significant recent events, and particularly those in the United States, from where the lead in preservation has come, are noted.

It has been proposed that the 'modern field of library preservation' began in 1956 with the publication of an issue of *Library Trends* devoted to the conservation of library materials.[35] To the modern eye the contents of this issue overemphasize the subject of binding, six of the eleven articles being entirely or largely concerned with it. By 1959 Barrow's *Deterioration of Book Stock* had been published, bringing the paper deterioration problem to the library community's attention, and in the following years the Council on

Library Resources funded several research projects in the area of preservation. The most significant of these was Gordon Williams' report, *The Preservation of Deteriorating Books*, adopted by the Council in 1965.[36] His main recommendation, that a federally funded national agency accept the responsibility for preserving and retaining a 'last resort' copy of printed materials, was taken up by the Library of Congress.

The flooding of the Arno River and consequent damage of one million volumes in Florence's Biblioteca Nazionale Centrale was a turning point in the field of paper-based conservation. To salvage and conserve this material an international team of conservators worked in Florence to develop new techniques and refine existing methods. These became the basis of present conservation practice. The significance of the Florence flood has been examined in two writings.[37] It accelerated the development of conservation, encouraging discussion of the principles of conservation and of improved techniques, and raising awareness of library conservation problems internationally. It also led to the development of procedures for the mass treatment of water-damaged materials, an essential element of present-day disaster response planning.

The development of library preservation in the 1970s can be characterized as a period of continuing activity in many areas: refinement of conservation techniques and development of new methods; increasing research, for example into large-scale treatment methods such as mass deacidification; education and training of conservators and librarians; the establishment of preservation programs in individual libraries; and cooperative action such as the development of regional conservation centres.[38]

The 1980s saw an escalation of activity as the preservation problem became more apparent in libraries of all kinds in every country. Two influential reports were presented in 1984: in the United States the Council on Library Resources Brittle Books report, which established the extent of the problem and developed a national agenda for addressing it;[39] and in the United Kingdom the Ratcliffe report which, among other things, resulted directly in the establishment of the National Preservation Office, whose activities in promoting preservation awareness and initiating debate on preservation problems and solutions have been energetic and effective.[40] In 1986 IFLA (the International Federation of Library Associations and Institutions) launched a new Core Program, the PAC (Preservation and Conservation) Core Program, and regional centres to implement this program have been established in Tokyo (for Asia), Canberra (for Asia and Oceania), Caracas (for Latin America and the Caribbean), Leipzig (for Eastern Europe and German-speaking countries), and Sablé (for Western Europe, Africa north of the Equator and the Middle East). The international centre for the IFLA PAC program is the Library of Congress, Washington.

The Commission of the European Communities initiated a survey of member countries on library policies for preservation, and a report of this was published in 1988.[41] The film *Slow Fires* was made and shown on public television in the United States in late 1987. In 1988 the US National

Endowment for the Humanities nearly tripled its budget for preservation of library materials, to $12.5 million; in 1989 this was increased to $15 million and in 1991 to $22.6 million.[42] The Commission on Preservation and Access was established in Washington, D.C. in 1988 as an independent, non-profit corporation, having been set up under the auspices of the Council on Library Resources two years earlier. It has rapidly become a major player in promoting and developing preservation activities in the United States. Events in 1989 included the announcements of a new commercially available mass deacidification treatment and of the commercial availability of the Library of Congress' mass deacidification DEZ treatment.[43] There is no sign that the level of preservation activity will abate in the 1990s. As one example, the decade began with the establishment by the President of the American Library Association of a task force to examine preservation concerns.[44]

Two measures of the increase in preservation activities will illustrate the changes which have occurred over the last decades. In the United States five members of the Association of Research Libraries had preservation programs in 1978; by 1989 this had increased to programs in 107 libraries with a total of 1620 staff members involved in preservation activities.[45] In Britain an update in 1988 of the 1984 Ratcliffe report (based on data collected in 1982) indicated that positive changes had taken place. Some of these were: the number of institutions with a preservation policy statement had increased from two to seventeen, there had been an increase in conservation workshops, the number of conservation officers had doubled, and nineteen libraries (compared with two in 1982) had a disaster plan, with ten more in draft form.[46]

This is necessarily a very selective view of events, but it does indicate that preservation has now become a major concern of the library profession. As a result of these and many other activities and events, the perspective of librarians on preservation has altered considerably, from an activity that is primarily the concern of rare books and manuscripts librarians, to one which is an integral part of all aspects of library management.

Notes

1   John Feather, 'Preservation and Conservation: A Professional Issue for the 1990s', *New Zealand Libraries* 46, 2/3 (1989): 23.
2   Ina Bertrand, 'In Pursuit of the Kelly Gang', in *Finding and Keeping: Research Use of Audiovisual Materials*, ed. Marjorie Roe (Sydney: Library Association of Australia, 1987), p. 25.
3   Mary Lynn Ritzenthaler, *Archives and Manuscripts: Conservation; A Manual on Physical Care and Management* (Chicago, Ill.: Society of American Archivists, 1983), p. 9.
4   Christopher Clarkson, 'Conservation Priorities: A Library Conservator's View', in *Conservation of Library and Archival Materials and the Graphic Arts*, ed. Guy Petherbridge (London: Butterworths, 1987), pp. 235-236.

5   Diana Grimwood-Jones, 'Preservation,' in *British Librarianship and Information Work 1981-1985. Volume 2: Special Libraries, Materials and Processes*, ed. David W. Bromley and Angela M. Allott (London: Library Association, 1988), p. 270.

6   J.M. Dureau and D.W.G. Clements, *Principles for the Preservation and Conservation of Library Materials* (The Hague: IFLA, 1986), p. 2.

7   Commission on Preservation and Access, *Newsletter* 34 (May 1991): 2.

8   John Agresto, 'Preserving Our Heritage', *National Preservation News* (July 1986): 13.

9   Guy Petherbridge, 'Introduction', in *Conservation of Library and Archives Materials...*, *op. cit.*, p. 10.

10   Pamela W. Darling, 'Will Anything Be Left?: New Responses to the Preservation Challenge', *Wilson Library Bulletin* 56, 3 (1981): 181.

11   Michael Piggott, 'Conservation', in *Keeping Archives*, ed. Ann Pederson (Sydney: Australian Society of Archivists, 1987), p. 219.

12   Hilary Jenkinson, *A Manual of Archive Administration*. New and rev. ed. (London: Lund, Humphries, 1937), p. 15.

13   Sidney L. Jackson, *Libraries and Librarianship in the West: A Brief History* (New York: McGraw-Hill, 1974), p. 176. The same theme is discussed in Alex Wilson, 'For This and Future Generations: Managing the Conflict between Conservation and Use', *Library Review* 31 (1982): 163-172.

14   Council on Library Resources. Committee on Preservation and Access, *Brittle Books: Report of the Committee on Preservation and Access* (Washington, D.C.: Council on Library Resources, 1986), p. 16.

15   Commission on Preservation and Access, *Annual Report July 1, 1989-June 30, 1990* (Washington, D.C.: The Commission, 1990), p. 1.

16   William J. Barrow, *Deterioration of Book Stock: Causes and Remedies; Two Studies on the Permanence of Book Paper* (Richmond, Va: Virginia State Library, 1959).

17   Karen Lee Shelley, 'The Future of Conservation in Research Libraries', *Journal of Academic Librarianship* 1, 6 (1976): 15.

18   Gay Walker *et al.*, 'The Yale Survey: A Large-Scale Study of Book Deterioration in the Yale University Library', *College and Research Libraries* 46, 2 (1985): 111-132.

19   Randall Bond *et al.*, 'Preservation Study at the Syracuse University Libraries', *College and Research Libraries* 48, 2 (1987): 132-147 – 25 per cent needed repair, 86 per cent were on acidic paper, 12 per cent were highly brittle; Tina Chrzastowski *et al.*, 'Library Collection Deterioration: A Study at the University of Illinois at Urbana-Champaign', *College and Research Libraries* 50, 5 (1989): 577-584 – 37 per cent were brittle, and about 34 per cent were becoming embrittled.

20   Council on Library Resources. Committee on Preservation and Access, *op. cit.*, pp. 22-23.

21   Michael Pollock, 'Surveying the Collections', *Library Conservation News* 21 (1988): 4-6.

22   Robert J. Scott and Neil A. Radford, 'Assessing Collection Deterioration: The University of Sydney Survey', in Australian Library

and Information Association 1st Biennial Conference, Perth, 1990, *Proceedings* (Canberra: ALIA, 1990): pp. 231-243.

23 Ross Harvey, 'Nothing Left to Access?: The Problem of Deteriorating Newspapers', *Education for Librarianship: Australia* 5, 1 (1988): 22.

24 Jan Lyall, 'Library Preservation in Indonesia', *Asian Libraries* 1, 1 (1991): 65-69.

25 I am indebted for this concept to Guy Petherbridge, who expressed it in his 'Introduction', in *Conservation of Library and Archives Materials...*, *op. cit.*

26 Paul N. Banks, 'Preservation of Library Materials', in *Encyclopedia of Library and Information Science* 23 (New York: Dekker, 1978), p. 191.

27 F.W. Ratcliffe, *Preservation Policies and Conservation in British Libraries: Report of the Cambridge University Library Conservation Project* (Boston Spa: British Library, 1984), p. 5.

28 Petherbridge, 'Introduction', in *Conservation of Library and Archives Materials...*, *op. cit.*, pp. 4-5.

29 Dureau and Clements, *op. cit.*, p. 2.

30 Grimwood-Jones, *op. cit.*, p. 281.

31 Librarians could learn in this respect from archivists, who have developed the concept of intrinsic value. See 'Intrinsic Value in Archival Records', in *A Modern Archives Reader: Basic Readings in Archival Theory and Practice*, ed. Maygene Daniels and Timothy Walch (Washington, D.C.: National Archives and Records Service, 1984), pp. 91-99.

32 Gordon Williams, 'The Preservation of Deteriorating Books', Part 1, *Library Journal* (1 January 1966); 53.

33 Roger Ellis, 'The Principles of Archive Repair', in *Library Conservation: Preservation in Perspective*, ed. John P. Baker and Marguerite C. Soroka (Stroudsburg: Dowden, Hutchinson and Ross, 1978), pp. 316-324.

34 William Blades, *The Enemies of Books* (London: Trübner, 1880). Early preservation activities are noted in Larry McDonald, 'Forgotten Forebears: Concerns with Preservation, 1876 to World War I', *Libraries and Culture* 25, 4 (1990): 483-495; and Barbra Buckner Higginbotham, *Our Past Preserved: A History of American Library Preservation 1876-1910* (Boston, Mass.: G.K. Hall, 1990).

35 Pamela W. Darling and Sherelyn Ogden, 'From Problems Perceived to Programs in Practice: The Preservation of Library Resources in the USA, 1956-1980', *Library Resources and Technical Services* 25, 1 (1981): 10.

36 Gordon Williams, 'The Preservation of Deteriorating Books', Part 1, *Library Journal* (1 January 1966): 51-56; Part 2, *Library Journal* (15 January 1966): 189-194.

37 Sherelyn Ogden, 'The Impact of the Florence Flood on Library Conservation in the United States of America', *Restaurator* 3 (1979): 1-36; Peter Waters, 'The Florence Flood of 1966 Revisited', in *Preserving the Word: The Library Association Conference Proceedings, Harrogate 1986*, ed. R. Palmer (London: Library Association, 1987), pp. 113-128.

38   Darling and Ogden, *op. cit.*, describe these in more detail.
39   Council on Library Resources. Committee on Preservation and Access, *op. cit.*
40   F.W. Ratcliffe, *Preservation Policies and Conservation in British Libraries* (1984): see also F.W. Ratcliffe, 'Preservation: A Decade of Progress', *Library Review* 36 (1987): 228-236.
41   Alexander Wilson, *Library Policy for Preservation and Conservation in the European Community* (München: K.G. Saur, 1988).
42   *Library Journal* (15 November 1988): 16; *American Libraries* (September 1989): 719; Commission on Preservation and Access, *Newsletter* 34 (May 1991): 2.
43   *American Libraries* (May 1989): 389; *American Libraries* (September 1989): 721.
44   'Berger Calls for Coordinated Approach to Preservation', *Library Journal* (1 February 1990): 12-13.
45   Commission on Preservation and Access, *Annual Report, op. cit.* (Washington, D.C.: The Commission, 1991), p. 1.
46   Brenda E. Moon and Anthony J. Loveday, 'Progress Report on Preservation in Universities since the Ratcliffe Report', in *Preservation and Technology: Proceedings of a Seminar at York University, 20-21 July 1988* (London: National Preservation Office, 1989), pp. 11-17.

Chapter 2

Why Library Materials Deteriorate

Introduction

A knowledge of the structure of library materials is essential for all librarians who are concerned with preservation. This need be no more than a general knowledge of why library materials deteriorate. Such knowledge allows the practitioner to understand, for example, why some actions are effective and why certain activities must be carried out on a long-term basis to be effective. Better still is a detailed knowledge of the physical and chemical nature of the materials, but without some education in chemistry an understanding at this level is more difficult to acquire.

Equally as important for librarians is the need for many of those who are responsible for the management of library collections to change their perceptions. Books and all other library materials must no longer be seen only as items which are important for the information they contain and how it can be used, but also as physical objects governed by the same laws that affect all organic materials. This suggests strongly that all library education courses should have a compulsory preservation component and a course on the history of the book. Such courses have traditionally instilled a respect for the book (and by extension other library materials) which has been transferred into attitudes that take account of the physical requirements of books in libraries.

Deterioration is defined here as a loss of quality in any library material which decreases its ability to carry out its intended function.[1] Such deterioration is the result of two categories of actions on library materials: those caused by some inherent instability of the materials; and those caused by actions external to the material. The first category includes the acidic nature of some kinds of paper and the light-sensitive nature of the silver halide image-bearing layer of a photograph; the main elements of the second category are the actions of heat, humidity, light, biological agents (micro-organisms such as moulds, insects and rodents), atmospheric pollutants and humans. Disasters, another external element causing deterioration, are considered in Chapter 6.

Paper deterioration has long been a matter of concern for curators of library collections. Wessel gives a brief historical survey, noting that the earliest expression of concern dates from some 3000 years ago and relates to

Egyptian papyrus.[2] The longevity of paper was questioned in 1145 when Roger of Sicily decreed that all charters made on paper were to be recopied onto parchment. This suspicion was not dispelled in Italy until the fifteenth century.[3] A more recent expression of concern is that of the publisher John Murray, who in 1823 drew attention in the *Gentlemen's Magazine* to the poor quality of paper. The American Library Association established a Committee on Deterioration of Newsprint Paper which reported in 1913 and on other occasions during the next two decades.[4]

The problem of leather deterioration has, similarly, been a matter of concern over a long period. In 1900 a committee was established in London to investigate leather quality in response to observations that leather bindings were rapidly deteriorating. It concluded that books bound after about 1830 showed significantly greater deterioration than those bound before that date. It attributed the decay to the quality of the leather, particularly the tanning process ('modern leathers dyed with the aid of sulphuric acid are all to be condemned'), to modern binding practices and to the effects of gas fumes, tobacco smoke and daylight.[5]

Items in library collections are complex objects. They are usually constructed from a combination of many materials, each of which responds to external agents in a different manner. As just one example, a book may consist of paper, inks, boards, adhesives, thread and covering material. Each of these materials responds differently to heat or to high humidity. Heat may cause mechanical damage because the boards expand at a different rate from the paper. Furthermore, many varieties of one material may exist in one object; paper stock from several sources, for example, may be used in the manufacture of one book. The descriptions in this chapter are inevitably oversimplifications of these complexities.

Another point that must be kept in mind is that not everything that libraries collect was manufactured for permanent retention. Newspapers are the classic example of this. Despite the initial intentions of the manufacturers of these items, some libraries do want to preserve newspapers for a long period, while others do not. The objectives of the library itself are an important determinant here: research libraries are more likely to preserve items for long periods, whereas public libraries are unlikely to keep the same items beyond a short time.

THE MATERIALS: INHERENT CAUSES OF DETERIORATION

The Structure of Paper

Paper makes up by far the bulk of library collections. It will continue to do so in the foreseeable future, despite the rapid rise in popularity of information stored magnetically or mechanically as digital data. Paper is made by soaking vegetable fibres in water until they are softened (macerating them) and then draining the water off by using a sieve or fine screen. The result is a sheet of matted fibres – paper.[6] Most paper manufactured since the middle of the nineteenth century has been made from wood fibres, although cotton and esparto grass were also important sources of fibre for papermaking at various stages during this period. Because most paper which the librarian sees and deals with is made from wood pulp, the process of making paper from this fibre source is described here.

Wood is made up of plant cells which are joined together and strengthened by a material called lignin.[7] To make the fibres in wood usable for making paper the wood is first turned into pulp. There are two main wood pulping processes, one mechanical and the other chemical. In the mechanical pulping process logs of wood, having been stripped of their bark, are ground up in a purely mechanical process which involves no chemicals. In the chemical pulping process the wood is roughly chipped by a mechanical process, then the chips are heated under pressure with various chemicals in solution. Mechanically pulped fibres are made into paper which contains most of the ingredients of the original wood, lignin in particular. Lignin is an undesirable constituent of paper, rendering it weak and inclined to become brittle rapidly. However, mechanical pulping finds commercial favour because it gives a higher yield than does chemical pulping. While chemical pulping produces a lower yield, it results in stronger and longer lasting paper. This is explained by the longer, less mechanically damaged and consequently stronger fibres which are produced, and by the fact that in the chemical pulping process the harmful lignin is largely dissolved. The two processes are often combined in various ways, the resulting variants being known as chemithermomechanical pulping processes, which still produce paper with an unacceptably high lignin content.

To the pulp various materials are usually added. One is bleach, required to produce white or cream papers. The pulp or 'porridge', that is the suspension of fibres in water, is 'beaten' (or 'refined') mechanically to produce more flexible fibres which will make denser and stronger paper. The beaten fibres then pass on to the moving wire screen of the paper machine, to be formed into a continuous sheet which passes through presses and drying processes. Further substances are added during these processes, usually fillers (clay or chalk) to increase opacity, sizing to reduce the paper's ability to absorb liquid so that it can be printed or written on, and starch to increase strength.

Four main properties are required of paper that is to be printed on. It must be mechanically strong enough to allow handling in the printing, folding, binding and other related processes; it must have appropriate optical qualities of colour, brightness and opacity; its surface needs to be smooth; and it must be able to interact appropriately with liquids such as printing inks, that is, it must have the right degree of absorption. Of these, the property which most affects the deterioration of paper in libraries is strength. The tensile strength of paper is a result of the length of individual fibres and the strength of the bonds between fibres. Thus vegetable materials which have short fibres are less preferred for papermaking than are those with longer fibres, if paper strength is a desirable property.

Paper loses strength primarily as a result of chemical reactions which weaken and break the chemical bonds along the cellulose chains from which the fibres are made. These reactions are of two kinds: bonds breaking because of hydrolysis (involving water molecules) and because of oxidation (involving oxygen molecules). Cellulose, made up of hydrogen, carbon and oxygen and by itself chemically stable, requires other substances for the reactions to occur. For example, hydrolysis usually takes place because of the presence of acidic material in the paper. A major source of this acidic material is the alum (aluminium sulphate) used with rosin as a sizing agent; the acidity of paper after rosin sizing and alum have been added is 4.5 to 5.5 pH.[8] Acidity is also introduced into paper from atmospheric pollution (for example sulphur dioxide in the air), from the breakdown of lignin in the paper, and from organic acids introduced during the manufacturing process if the conditions have not been correctly controlled.

Oxidation, of less concern than acid hydrolysis in paper deterioration, results from the presence of small quantities of metals in the paper, for example copper and iron from papermaking equipment. Discoloration affecting paper's optical quality is mainly caused by the action of light on lignin. The resulting darkening of the paper is accompanied by brittleness.

Paper which will not deteriorate rapidly is made from long fibres and is free from acid, lignin and metallic elements. Such paper is being manufactured, and will be examined in more detail below and in Chapter 9. Paper which does contain acid and lignin can be treated by various processes to decrease its acidity and thereby prolong its life, but these processes are at present time-consuming and costly. Paper which has been deacidified remains weak, as the bonds broken by acid hydrolysis are not reformed, and another process must then be applied to strengthen the weakened paper.

The History of Papermaking

Readers will be aware that old paper, such as that on which books from the fifteenth, sixteenth and seventeenth centuries were printed, is in general still in excellent condition, whereas the paper on which today's newspaper is printed rapidly discolours and becomes brittle and is unlikely to last more than a few decades in normal library conditions. This brief history of papermaking concentrates on the introduction of new sources of fibres and on how new manufacturing techniques have affected the strength and permanence of paper.

Paper was made by hand until 1806, when the Fourdrinier machine was patented.[9] Handmade paper used rags, the cleaner the better, as its source of vegetable fibre. The rags were soaked in water and then beaten to flatten the fibres; the soaking swelled the fibres and promoted their chemical bonding, and the beating flattened fibres and caused the separation of fabrilles ('small hairlike fibres').[10] This beating was originally carried out with hand mallets, but mechanical stamping mills, usually water-powered, were introduced into European papermaking from the early twelfth century. Both hand-beating and early stamping mills produced long fibres. Into the vat containing the resulting thick suspension of fibres in water was dipped a paper mould, that is a fine wire screen, on which a layer of the slurry was deposited. The water drained out and the resulting fibre mat was placed on a felt blanket to dry. The paper sheet is formed through several kinds of bonding: mechanical bonding through the fabrilles tangling together, chemical (hydrogen) bonding of cellulose molecules, and surface tension between fibres. The sheets, at this stage between felts, were stacked and pressed, then removed from the felts and air-dried. Sizing was added by dipping the paper sheets into gelatin or animal glue.

Papermaking by machine is essentially the same process, but fully mechanized and carried out on a much larger scale. The paper is formed in a continuous sheet rather than in single sheets. A moving screen scoops up the slurry, which goes through various stages such as drying, calendaring (passing through rollers to give the paper a smooth surface), sizing and glazing. Machine-made paper is characterized by fibres which are aligned in the direction in which the screen moves, whereas hand-made paper has no grain. Machine-made paper is thus often weaker than hand-made paper because it folds and tears more easily with the grain.

Before the late eighteenth century papermaking was a hand process, using pure cellulose and clean water, and the result was a long-fibred paper with few additives which did not deteriorate quickly. This was to change. Increasing demand for paper led to greater mechanization of the papermaking processes. As already noted, cotton and linen rags were used as the source of cellulose fibres. The Hollander beater was first used by the Dutch, as its name suggests, in the 1680s. It used metal blades to macerate the fibres. Although this shortened the time needed to reduce the rags to an acceptable pulp, it resulted in shorter fibres and also introduced small particles of iron into the pulp and thence into the paper. These traces of metal introduced points where harmful chemical reactions could begin. Small metal particles were also introduced from the water used to make the pulp.

The increasing demand for paper required more and more raw material. One step taken to increase fibre supply was to use coloured rags, which had not formerly been used because of the difficulty of achieving the required whiteness with them. Many bleaching methods were tried, such as the use of chlorine in England in the 1790s, but such methods frequently introduced an acidic residue in the paper. In the mid-nineteenth century alum plus rosin replaced gelatin as the standard sizing material. Because it could be added directly to the water in the vats it was more economical than gelatin, but the consequence was the introduction of acid deterioration on a wide scale.

By the mid-eighteenth century it was evident that the rag supply would not be sufficient to satisfy the increasing demand. In the United Kingdom it was clear, for example, that there were serious problems in supplying enough rags to make paper for the newspapers, let alone for other purposes.[11] The massively increased demand for paper was a consequence of the growing population and improving levels of literacy, and was related to developments in the technology of printing presses and typesetting, and to faster and more efficient distribution systems such as railways and steamboats. The figures for paper use in the United Kingdom alone are illuminating (see Table 1).

Table 1. Paper Use in the United Kingdom, 1820-1859

Year	Weight (lbs)
1820	44,539,509
1830	63,686,802
1841	97,103,548
1850	141,032,474
1859	217,827,197

This translated into an almost four-fold increase in paper use per head of population between 1800 and 1850, from 2.5 to 8 pounds per head.[12] Initially rags were imported into England to meet the demand, but before long efforts turned towards finding new sources of fibre. In 1800 straw was used, and 1801 saw a patent for processing wood to make paper. New Zealand was the source of phormium tenax flax, some of which was exported to England around 1836 to be made into paper there.[13] Rags from mummies were exported from Egypt in the 1860s to the United States.[14] These sources were eclipsed later in the century by the use of the short-fibred esparto grass, grown in southern Spain and North Africa, which supplied much of the English market from the 1850s to as late as 1914.[15]

Wood had been identified as a possible source for cellulose long before its use became widespread, several patents for processes to extract its fibre having been registered in the first four decades of the nineteenth century. A process for making mechanical wood pulp was patented in Germany in 1840 and was gradually adopted throughout the world. Paper was first made by this method in the United States in 1867 and in England in 1870.[16] It was rapidly exported to British colonies such as Australia and New Zealand.[17] Economically viable chemical wood pulp processes were developed during the 1850s.[18]

Wood has been from the mid-nineteenth century the major source of cellulose fibre for paper, and almost all of the paper in our library collections is made from wood pulp. Wood consists of 'approximately 45 percent cellulose, 20-25 percent hemicellulose, 25-30 percent lignin, and less than 5 percent of other substances.'[19] The lignin, essential to the tree because it gives rigidity to its plant cells, is undesirable in paper because it is chemically unstable and readily deteriorates when exposed. The cellulose fibres of wood must be separated from surrounding substances so that they can form the bonds necessary to make paper. Fibre length is related to the type of tree pulped: softwoods (conifers) have longer fibres than hardwoods (deciduous trees). Most paper usually contains a blend of hardwoods and softwoods.

Mechanical wood pulp (also called groundwood pulp) releases the fibres by completely physical means: the logs are forced against grinding stones to reduce them to small particles, larger chips being screened out. Water is used in the grinding process. The resulting pulp thus contains everything except the water-soluble components of wood: in particular cellulose fibres (short, with reduced bonding properties) and lignin are present. Bleaches may be added to the pulp. Paper made from this pulp has a short life and is used for wrapping papers, newsprint and products not expected by the manufacturer or printer to have a long life.

In chemical wood pulp paper the substances which surround the cellulose fibres, including unwanted lignin, are dissolved by chemical means. The wood is first chipped and then 'cooked' at a high temperature and under pressure in a solution either of sodium sulphite (acidic) or of sodium sulphate (alkaline). The cellulose fibres are then washed to remove lignin and other undesirable substances. Paper made from chemical wood pulp is relatively strong, the fibres having been subjected to less mechanical bashing and therefore being longer and more durable, and contains less lignin than that made from mechanical wood pulp. Paper produced by the alkaline sulphate process is usually preferred in the preservation sense over that made by the acidic sulphite process, which results in shorter fibres and may leave residual acid in the paper. The sulphate process leaves an alkaline residue in the paper, a desirable attribute in paper which is expected to endure; it is, however, more difficult to bleach and is therefore considered unsuitable where whiteness is sought.

Commercial papermills currently use a wide variety of processes which combine aspects of both mechanical and chemical wood pulping processes.

Modern Paper and Its Permanence

Most paper made in modern times is impermanent. Its life is best measured in decades, sometimes as few as two or three, rather than in centuries. To last for longer than just a short period, paper must have permanence and durability. Permanence is 'the ability of the paper to remain stable and resist chemical action either from internal purities or the surrounding environment' and durability 'the degree to which paper retains its original strength, especially under conditions of heavy, sustained use'.[20] Permanence relates to the chemical stability of the paper, and durability to its physical strength.

If paper is to survive for any length of time in libraries, it must be sufficiently strong and stable to withstand the wear and tear imposed on it in library collections. While the use of an item and the length of its retention in a library collection may vary according to collection policy, it is fair to say that in general paper used in library materials must be both permanent and durable. Modern methods of paper manufacture can produce paper as permanent and durable as that made by earlier methods by using long fibres, by removing all chemical residues left from the pulping process, by using acceptable sizing and by removing all bleaches from it. As a general rule, paper for library use should be made from chemical wood pulp.

The most important measure of whether a paper is permanent is its pH, a measure of the acidity or alkalinity of a solution taken from it. pH is measured on a logarithmic scale from 0 to 14, with 0 being totally acidic, 14 being completely alkaline, and 7 being neutral. Acid-free paper has a pH of 7.0 or higher, and has no residual acid in it. As such paper may, however, become acidic through contact with pollutants carried in the atmosphere or by physical contact with acidic material – and we have already seen that acids are a major cause of paper deterioration – an alkaline reserve can be introduced into the paper. This buffer protects the paper by counteracting acids as they enter the paper from the air or from adjacent acidic materials. Alkaline reserve paper has a pH of about 8.5 to 10, through being treated with an alkaline substance such as calcium carbonate or magnesium carbonate. To resist the action of acids for 300 to 500 years, paper should have about 3 per cent precipitated carbonate by weight.[21] There have been moves to adopt the terms 'neutral' or 'alkaline reserve' rather than 'acid-free' for permanent paper, as acid-free paper is unlikely to stay acid-free for long in normal library conditions.

We have already seen that paper quality declined from the middle of the nineteenth century, owing mainly to the increased use of alum-rosin sizing and mechanical wood pulp which raised intrinsic acidity levels. Acid is also introduced into paper by residual chemicals used for bleaching, by some types of ink, air pollutants, and by acid transfer (or acid migration). Acid can move from materials with high acid content to those with lower or no acidity, either when in direct contact or when low acidity materials are enclosed with materials which have a higher acid content. A familiar example is the browning of an area of the endpapers when a newspaper cutting has been placed in a book.

Much acid comes from polluted atmospheres, with car exhausts a major source.[22] The effect of this acid on books is particularly noticeable in the discoloration and brittleness on the edges of pages. It is mainly caused by sulphur dioxide in the air reacting with metallic impurities in the paper to form sulphuric acid. Nitrous oxide, which reacts to form nitric acid, is also present in polluted atmospheres and has been identified as another source of deterioration of library materials.

Acidity weakens paper by breaking down the bonds between cellulose fibres and eventually the fibres themselves. The first of these processes is described by Wessel as 'hydrolytic and is chiefly an attack by hydronium ions on cellulose, the chief fibrous ingredient of paper. The rate of the deterioration increases with hydronium ion concentration, i.e., with a lowering of the pH levels of the paper as measured on a water extract.'[23] In the second process the cellulose, which is a complex molecule built up from carbon, hydrogen and oxygen molecules, tends to break down under certain conditions into its simpler components. The eventual product is carbon dioxide gas, which is of very little use as a carrier of information in libraries. Acid deterioration causes paper to become weak, brittle and stained.

The presence of lignin in paper is also not conducive to its permanence, as noted earlier in this chapter.

Although the problem of paper deterioration had been recognized long before the middle of this century, it was not until the 1950s that the causes were more fully identified and brought to the attention of the library community. In 1959 William J. Barrow, a scientist who had researched paper deterioration for most of his working life, published a monograph entitled *Deterioration of Book Stock: Causes and Remedies; Two Studies on the Permanence of Book Paper.*[24] He had tested 500 books published between 1900 and 1949 to establish the durability of the paper on which they were printed. Of the total sample of 500, 39 per cent were characterized by Barrow as very weak, 49 per cent as of low strength, only 1 per cent as of high strength and 9 per cent as of medium strength. Barrow developed and tested methods of stabilizing paper by washing it in an alkaline solution to deacidify it. He concluded that 'pure pulp and absence of ground wood is essential in manufacturing enduring book papers...the principal cause of deterioration seems to be acidity...[and] a pH of about 7 is desirable for maximum preservation.'[25] The implications of Barrow's conclusions for the lifespan of books in library collections were not lost on the library community, and as a result of his work efforts were made to explore the problem further and to encourage the wider use of permanent paper.

Poor quality paper may last as little as twenty-five years, whereas some paper has already lasted for about 2000 years.[26] As the permanence of paper is closely related to its acidity, studies of the pH levels of paper in books being added to library collections are a useful way to identify future problems. Testing of pH can be easily carried out by using pH pens which are, however, limited in their accuracy. More accurate results can be obtained by a variety of methods, one of which uses a pH meter to measure the acidity or alkalinity of a drop of distilled water applied to the paper. This is usually carried out in a laboratory.[27]

Three studies of pH levels in paper are noted here, the first examining current acquisitions of older French books and the second and third looking at acquisitions of more recently published material. In 1983 Rutledge and Owen released the results of a sample of books published in France between 1860 and 1914. This study was undertaken because of their concern that many recent acquisitions of French books from that period by the Wilson Library, University of North Carolina, were received in such a brittle condition as to be unusable. They hoped to identify publishers whose paper was of particularly poor quality and whose works they should therefore avoid acquiring. Their sample was restricted to books on French literature and history. They found that the more recent the paper, the more acidic and brittle it was likely to be, the worst years being from 1890 to 1914 when about 20 per cent of the paper was in bad condition, needing special care and likely to be damaged by ordinary usage. Seventeen per cent of the total were in bad condition.[28]

The results of the second study are more relevant to a greater number of libraries than are those of Rutledge and Owen's study, for it examined recently published books. It was a follow-up of McCrady's 1983 survey of books then being added to the Columbia University Libraries. The pH of the recent acquisitions in the 1983 study were: 41 per cent were alkaline (pH greater than 6.7), 16 per cent were close to neutral (pH 6.0 to 6.7) and 43 per cent were acidic (pH less than 6.0); 50 per cent of United States imprints were alkaline. In the 1988 follow-up, 35 per cent were alkaline, 11 per cent were slightly acidic and 54 per cent were acidic. However, of the United States imprints, 66 per cent were found to be alkaline, and of these 78 per cent of the 1987 and 1988 imprints were alkaline. This study noted that 'no alkaline papers were found in books from Africa, South and Central America, Eastern Europe, the Soviet Union, or Australia.'[29]

The third study, also of recently published material, examined 230 Australian-published monographs processed into the collections of the National Library of Australia during one week in 1991. The paper quality was of an encouragingly high standard: almost 60 per cent had a pH over 6.5 and less than 10 per cent tested positive for lignin. Of concern, however, were the findings that binding styles and methods of page attachment were largely unsatisfactory from a preservation point of view.[30]

The implications of these studies are not difficult to perceive: most books acquired by libraries are still printed on paper that will deteriorate within a short period, although there has been recent improvement in the paper quality of books produced in the United States.

Paper made at the present time covers a wide range of the permanence/durability spectrum. There is a very large amount of paper produced as newsprint which is not intended by its manufacturers and users to be retained beyond a short period, and no attention is therefore given during its manufacture to its permanence. On the other hand, considerable attention has been given recently to the manufacture of paper which is permanent and durable. The results of this are now being seen, for example, in the results of the survey of Columbia University Libraries' acquisitions already noted. One view that draws on the evidence of the survival of early handmade paper holds that only paper which is made from rags is permanent.[31] However, almost all permanent papers manufactured today are made from chemical wood pulp. Specifications for permanent/durable paper were developed by Barrow, and paper was first produced commercially to them in 1960. Specified, among other features, were that the paper must be free of ground wood and unbleached fibres and that the pH must be not less than 6.5 at the time of manufacture.[32] Modern permanent paper is now made to standards developed from Barrow's specifications. The manufacture and use of permanent/durable paper is further described in Chapter 9.

Other modern papers also appear in library collections. One is art paper, with its smooth, glossy surface heavily coated with china clay or chalk. As the inner fibre core is often of low quality and the paper is very susceptible to humidity, its leaves sticking together irretrievably when wet, special care is needed for items made from this paper. Recycled paper, of considerable importance in the environment-conscious 1990s, is also of special concern to libraries. Paper made from recycled fibres is usually less strong than that made from virgin pulp and is also more likely to be contaminated by other materials. Its use is not recommended in documents that are required to be kept for any length of time.[33] Thermal facsimile papers, at present most likely to be found in the library's administrative documents but which may eventually end up in manuscript collections accessioned by the library, will last only five years under optimum conditions.[34]

Ink

Ink is one of the main ingredients of printed and written library materials. Writing inks used in early manuscripts were made from carbon, usually lampblack, mixed with gum arabic. They were permanent and did not fade when exposed to excess light. Later writing inks, now known as iron gall or oak gall inks, contain ferrous sulphate which eventually oxidizes to form sulphuric acid and can burn the image out of the paper. It fades from black to brown and this, combined with its acidity, can lead to considerable loss of text. Since 1945 dye-based writing inks have replaced iron gall inks. Many of the inks present in library materials, particularly in manuscript collections, are pigments or dyes which dry by absorption into paper. Some are water-soluble and will run in very humid conditions, causing loss of text, and many are extremely light-sensitive.

Early printing inks were made from carbon (from soot or lampblack) mixed with boiled linseed oil. They produced a very stable image. Modern printing inks usually have additives, for rapid drying to reduce the possibility of setoff, which make them less stable.

Leather, Vellum and Parchment

Until the nineteenth century books were traditionally bound in leather, and leather is still used today for specialist and fine bindings. Early leather was vegetable-tanned by a lengthy process that left protective salts in the skins, which were consequently resistant to acid deterioration. New and faster tanning processes, developed from the late seventeenth century in response to the increased demand for books, produced leather which lacked the protective salts. This leather was particularly susceptible to deterioration from the sulphur acids of polluted air. Sulphur dioxide, which is readily converted to sulphuric acid, was also introduced into the leather during the tanning process. The effect of acid deterioration is the condition known as 'red rot', which turns leather reddish-brown and leaves it dry, porous and cracked or powdered. It is familiar to most librarians with nineteenth-century leather bindings in their collections.

Parchment and vellum may be present in some library collections, particularly in collections of manuscripts or of early printed books, where vellum in particular may be used as a binding material. Both are made from the skins of calves, sheep or goats, which are cleaned, soaked in a lime solution, scraped to remove hair, and then dried and stretched. They are strong and longer-lasting than leather and paper. However, they are very susceptible to changes in humidity, and considerable damage can result from swelling.

Cloth

Cloth is present in library collections as a book covering material in nineteenth- and twentieth-century bindings. Bookcloth was made in England from the late 1820s and quickly replaced leather as the chief covering material. It is usually woven cotton fabric impregnated with a filler to stiffen it. Starch was initially used as the filler, but because of its susceptibility to water damage and to mould and mildew has now been replaced by plastics, usually pyroxylin but sometimes vinyl. Vinyl, however, can cause problems when the plasticizers in it are released onto adjacent materials. Other materials suitable for use as book coverings, such as vinyl-impregnated paper, are being developed.[35]

Adhesives

Book bindings use adhesives, which may also be present in manuscripts and other library materials. Most adhesives deteriorate over time and lose their stickiness; they may also permanently stain the material they are applied to. There are many kinds of adhesive. Animal glues, traditionally used in bookbinding, are made from animal hides and bones. Gelatin, the main ingredient, breaks down over time and is a nutrient for insects. Animal glues have been largely replaced in bookbindings by PVA (polyvinyl acetate) glues, made from synthetic polymers with additives. They dry rapidly and do not provide a food source for insects, but their adhesion is difficult to reverse and their life span is not yet clear. Pastes are made from vegetable materials, usually wheat or rice starches, mixed with water. Their action is reversible with water. They are nutrients for insects and rodents and are susceptible to mould growth.

Other types of adhesive may be found, especially in manuscript collections or applied as well-intended but misguided repairs to books. These are usually pressure-sensitive tapes such as Sellotape or Scotch tape, made of plastic or paper tape with an adhesive layer. They are generally hard to remove and often leave permanent staining.

Photographic Materials

A wide range of photographic materials is held in library collections, including motion picture film and microforms of all kinds, as well as many kinds of photographic prints such as salted paper, albumen, collodion and gelatin prints. An exception is cellulose nitrate film, which is unlikely to be held in library collections because of the danger posed by its propensity to combust. If any is identified in library collections, expert advice should be sought as a matter of urgency.

Photographic images are formed by the action of light on a light-sensitive chemical compound, which is coated onto a support. This image-bearing emulsion is usually a suspension of silver halides on a layer of an organic viscous substance, usually gelatin but previously albumen (egg white), collodion or starch. In some forms of photographic material the image-bearing material in the emulsion may be made from metals other than silver, platinum for example, or from pigments or dyes. The support may be made from many possible materials, the most common being paper and film (acetate or polyester); glass and metal have also been used. The main types of prints likely to be in library collections are salted paper prints (used from the 1840s to the 1860s), albumen prints (1850s to 1920s, and the dominant print material in the nineteenth century), collodion prints (1890s to about 1910), and the dominant type, gelatin prints, which were introduced in the 1870s and are still used today.[36]

Photographs are structurally complex and are susceptible to many kinds of damage. The support, made of very different material from the emulsion, may be damaged – glass may break, plastic may shrink, paper may become brittle – and the image-bearing layer may be scratched or stained by mould. The support may separate from the image-bearing layer. In conditions of high humidity the two layers may expand at different rates and cause the photograph to curl. Inadequate processing of photographic materials is a common cause of deterioration. Residual fixer (thiosulphate) may be present because of inadequate washing during processing, and will continue to react with the silver in the image to form silver sulphide, causing tarnishing of the image.

Deterioration can often be attributed to the action of atmospheric pollutants on photographic materials. The hydrogen sulphide, ammonia, sulphur dioxide and ozone in polluted air result in oxidation, which causes the image to change colour and spots to form on the image, and eventually causes uniform fading of the image. These deteriorative processes are exacerbated by high temperature and humidity levels, high acidity levels, particularly in support materials, and storage in or with acidic materials.

Photographic materials are especially sensitive to the presence of sulphur. This is present in polluted air, as already noted, but may also come from rubber bands and from the fumes produced by some adhesives, insecticides and fungicides.

Optical Discs

The term 'optical discs' at present covers videodiscs, compact discs and various kinds of 'write once' erasable discs; it is very likely that new kinds will be developed at a rapid pace. Videodiscs became available in the late 1960s and were used in the early 1970s, but rapidly lost popularity with the advent of cheaper videotape recording machines. Compact discs were available in the mid-1980s, at first for recorded sound only but later for image and sound combined, and also for storage of digital information (as CD-ROMs). 'Write once' and erasable optical discs have recently become commercially available. Already there are many optical discs – largely CDs – in library collections, and their numbers will rapidly increase.

Videodiscs are made by a laser which burns minute holes into a glass master, which is then used to make a metal master from which plastic discs are stamped. An acrylic protective coating is applied. Compact discs are similarly produced by a laser which burns pits into a coating on a glass master from which a metal master is produced. This stamps a plastic base which is next coated with a thin layer of metal, usually aluminium, and is then covered with a protective lacquer layer. Optical discs are relatively robust, able to withstand heavy use and not easily harmed by scratches, surface blemishes and excessive heat and humidity. However, the aluminium used in their manufacture appears to have some susceptibility to oxidization, although the degree to which this is a problem has yet to be fully ascertained.[37] The archival life of optical discs has yet to be determined. In 1989 the archival life of write-once optical discs was estimated by manufacturers as ten years at least, although few were prepared to guarantee their discs for as long as this;[38] this estimate is now regarded as conservative, and a life of as high as 100 years for compact discs has been suggested. The evidence is not yet in.

Sound Discs

Sound recordings on vinyl discs (the standard 33-1/3 and 45 revolutions per minute records) and to a lesser extent shellac discs (78 rpm) are considered here. Sound recordings on magnetic media – reel-to-reel tapes and cassettes – are noted in the next section. Of those considered here, the most likely forms to be found in library collections are the long-playing microgroove discs usually pressed on polyvinyl chloride, and most often twelve-inch 33-1/3 rpm discs, although some collections will also contain seven-inch 45 rpm discs. These were first manufactured in the 1950s, became ubiquitous in a few years, and were only in the late 1980s overtaken by compact discs. They replaced shellac discs because they were more durable, had a longer playing time, and produced higher quality sound reproduction. Some collections may also have other kinds of sound recordings, such as wax cylinders, but these less widely held media are not discussed here.

Vinyl discs have a polyvinyl chloride base which contains plasticizers and other materials such as colouring, stabilizers and fillers.[39] Residue from the stabilizer, which is added because polyvinyl chloride is unstable at the high temperatures needed for the manufacturing process, remains after pressing and retards oxidization. Vinyl discs are considered to be relatively stable, with an estimated life of over 100 years in suitable storage conditions. Shellac discs are also stable, with the exception of those manufactured from incorrectly formulated shellac; the quality of shellac has been found to vary considerably.

Much damage to sound recordings relates to storage conditions. Physical stress is destructive; for example, incorrect shelving readily causes warping. While low temperatures slow the rate at which deteriorative chemical reactions occur, they also cause shellac to become brittle. Fungi on disc surfaces can cause pitting, which affects playback quality. Cycling (rapid fluctuations in temperature and relative humidity) causes expansion and contraction of the materials from which discs are made, which weakens the physical structure. This can lead to warping and distortion of sound quality. High temperatures can also cause warping. Dust is a particular problem because it can settle on the walls of the grooves which record the sound and directly affect reproduction quality. Manufacturers' packaging is another cause of deterioration, as acidic envelopes and jackets are often used.

Magnetic Media

In this section is considered magnetic tape such as that used to record computer data and sound. The description also applies to other magnetic data storage media, computer floppy discs being the most common example to date. Sound recording on magnetic tape started to become widespread in the late 1940s in the form of reel-to-reel tapes in various sizes, formats and speeds. While some libraries may still have reel-to-reel tapes in their collections, it is much more likely that the tape cassette, introduced in the 1960s and still a popular and common format, is strongly represented. Such cassettes are also used for computer data, although to a much lesser extent. With the increasing use of computers, library collections are encompassing more and more data stored in magnetic form, in reel, cassette or floppy disc formats.

Magnetic tapes are most commonly made of a magnetic layer of chromium or iron oxides on a Mylar (polyethylene terephthalate; other brand-names are Estar and Celanese) film base. A binder is used to adhere the magnetic information-carrying layer to the base. Cellulose acetate has also been used as a base for sound recordings.[40] Mylar is a very stable material (its life-span has been reckoned at over 1000 years) and the oxide layer moderately stable under normal storage conditions, but the binder is prone to deterioration. It absorbs moisture from the atmosphere and loses its adhesive qualities, so that the magnetic oxide is disarranged or falls off the film layer. Because the information is stored on magnetic tape in patterns formed by the magnetized particles, any loss or disarrangement of the magnetic oxide causes loss of information. Acetate-base tapes are much less stable than Mylar and should be dubbed to Mylar tape if long life is required.

As with most other library materials, fluctuations in temperature and relative humidity cause expansion and contraction of the materials of which magnetic media are constructed, resulting in a loss of oxide coating and distortion of sound quality (for sound recordings) and loss of data (for computer data tapes). Dust is a particular problem because it causes deterioration when dust particles become trapped between layers of tape and cause dropout (loss of data) in the region they alight on. Deterioration also occurs as a result of tape being wound on a spool. The magnetized oxide particles, which store information in the patterns they are aligned to, in time interact and realign themselves, and information is lost because the patterns which represented the information have been altered. This form of deterioration can be slowed by periodically rewinding tapes in the opposite direction from which they are stored. Strong external sources of magnetism may affect tape quality and should be avoided in storage areas.

Hardware is an important factor to be considered with magnetic tape media. It must be of good quality and well maintained to minimize the possibility of causing mechanical or other damage to the tape. With computer data storage media there is the question of hardware obsolescence. This question also arises with other media which require hardware to access their contents, but has been discussed up to now primarily in terms of computer technology. Although it is likely that magnetic computer data storage media will last for up to twenty years if appropriately stored and maintained (with regular rewinding, for example), the rate at which hardware has been developing means that it is very unlikely that the hardware to access the data will be available, unless it has been specially maintained as an operating museum piece. It may well be that a more appropriate solution to deterioration is to transfer the data from magnetic tape to whatever storage medium is current, rather than to put effort into preserving magnetic tape.

EXTERNAL CAUSES OF DETERIORATION

Introduction

Almost all materials in library collections deteriorate. Most are organic in nature and deteriorate because the molecules from which they are built up break down into simpler molecules. This process, entirely natural, can be slowed down but cannot be stopped. The rate at which materials deteriorate is determined by two factors: the first, the inherent chemical stability of the material, is examined above; the second is external actions which affect the material. While relatively little can be done to alter the intrinsic instability of materials in libraries (the main exception of paper has already been noted), much can be done to control the external factors. The external or environmental factors to be described here are temperature and relative humidity, light, atmospheric pollutants, biological agents and human causes.

Temperature and Relative Humidity

Temperature and relative humidity need to be discussed together because it is often difficult to separate their effects on the deterioration of library materials. Relative humidity is defined in terms of temperature, as 'the amount of water vapor in a volume of air expressed as a percentage of the maximum amount that the air could hold at the same temperature.'[41] The warmer the air, the more moisture it is capable of holding; therefore, if the temperature rises but no extra moisture is added to it, the relative humidity will decrease. The relationship between temperature and relative humidity is shown in Table 2.

Both the moisture content of the air and the temperature in library storage facilities are important. If they are too high, they speed up the rate at which chemical reactions take place and the rate of deterioration is thereby increased. One example is the deteriorative action of acid hydrolysis on paper: this process is both water- and temperature-dependent. If both the temperature and the relative humidity are too high, mould is more likely to grow.

Table 2. Relationship of Temperature, Absolute Humidity and Relative Humidity[42]

Temperature °C	Absolute humidity (g/kg)		
	20% RH	60% RH	100% RH
0	0.38	2.28	3.82
20	1.43	8.69	14.61
40	4.55	38.30	48.64
60	12.50	83.55	152.45

A rule of thumb decrees that for every 10°C increase in temperature the amount of chemical activity approximately doubles. Heat (and its absence, cold) is one the most important determinants of deterioration for two main reasons: it governs the rate at which chemical reactions occur; and it directly affects the physical structure of library materials. Heat evaporates water, and the absence of water causes brittleness in paper, leather and some plastics. When both the temperature and the relative humidity are too high, the two act together to encourage the growth of biological agents (moulds and fungi, for example) which damage materials. As a general guideline for preserving library materials, the lower the storage temperature the better.

Rapid changes in temperature are particularly damaging. They cause expansion of materials (if there is an increase of temperature) or contraction (if a decrease). When temperatures oscillate rapidly, the stresses on the materials can cause significant physical damage. If the water content in a room is fixed, a sudden lowering of temperature will cause a rapid rise in the relative humidity, and water may condense on the surfaces of items whose temperatures have dropped. In this way water damage such as staining can occur. One of the significant factors to control in order to reduce deterioration is, therefore, the speed at which temperatures change.

Because organic materials are hygroscopic (that is, they expand and contract as moisture levels rise and fall), paper, vellum and other library materials swell or shrink as relative humidity changes. (It should be remembered that changes in relative humidity are naturally concomitant with changes in temperature.) The changes in internal stresses in paper, as water is absorbed and released and the paper fibres expand and contract, will cause damage over time. A bound book, made of several materials all of which expand and contract at different rates, will be particularly affected by changes in relative humidity because conflicting pressures are exerted at different levels. Warped boards on a bound book are a visible indication of this. It is important to control the rate of change in relative humidity to lessen the deterioration of library materials.

Very high humidity levels are also harmful in other ways. They may cause water-soluble inks to run, and paper which is coated with china clay or chalk to stick. Very low humidity levels cause many materials to become brittle, so that paper breaks when handled, and book-covering materials may shrink, warping boards in the process.

The optimum levels of temperature and relative humidity in which to store library collections vary according to the kinds of material. While specific requirements are identified further in Chapter 4, it is possible to indicate general guidelines which are currently thought to strike the happiest medium for all materials in library collections. The two most important requirements are that the temperature should be kept as low as possible, and that it is essential to slow down the rate at which temperature and relative humidity change. For relative humidity, below 30 per cent is reckoned to be dangerous because it dries out the materials which become brittle, and above 75 per cent is unacceptable because the likelihood of mould growth increases considerably. Appropriate relative humidity levels should be maintained at about 47 per cent ± 2 per cent, and temperature levels should be maintained at about 20°C ± 2°. It must be emphasized that these are only general indications which are a compromise to accommodate all materials in library collections, that variations will be required to provide optimum storage conditions for some kinds of material, and that some authorities disagree with these suggested standards.

There will always be a need to compromise between the comfort of humans working in and visiting a library and the storage requirements of the collections. People will feel comfortable with a balance of temperature and relative humidity within a limited range of variation, while library materials also need a balance – but this will differ from human requirements and, furthermore, will vary from one kind of material to another. A practical compromise must be struck.

Light

Light is a form of radiant energy and as such is a source of the energy needed for chemical reactions such as the breakdown of complex cellulose molecules to simpler molecules in paper. Damage occurs in library collections when they are exposed to direct sunlight, fluorescent light and ultraviolet light. All objects which are exposed to direct sunlight are threatened; the effect of light on curtains will be known to readers in regions where there are high levels of sunlight. The shorter the wavelength of the light, the greater is the energy level. Of the usual sources of light, visible light has the longest wavelength, and ultraviolet light has the shortest. Ultraviolet light is the most harmful to library materials.[43]

Too much light affects paper in several ways. It speeds up the rate of oxidization and hastens chemical breakdown, it may bleach paper and inks and cause fading of the image, and if lignin is present, light will react with it to darken the paper (for example, the yellowing of newspapers). Photographs, part of which by definition are light-sensitive, are especially susceptible to deterioration by the action of light. The absence of light is generally unharmful, indeed positively beneficial, for all library materials.

One harmful effect on library materials has resulted from the changing requirements for light levels in library buildings. Wessel gives a particularly interesting illustration of this in a table which notes changes in lighting standards for different areas in a library over twenty-five years.[44] The differences can be seen by selecting two sets of figures for minimum illumination levels from his table (converted here from foot-candles to lux):

Reading rooms	1931	100 lux	1956	300-500 lux
Stacks	1931	15 lux	1956	100-300 lux

Wessel suggests that current illumination levels in libraries are higher still.

Preventing the deleterious effect of light on library collections is in principle straightforward: keep light levels as low as possible, and preferably keep collections in the dark! Specific methods of doing this will be noted in Chapter 4. The recent growth of awareness about the damaging effects of light as a result of interest in the greenhouse effect and in damage caused by increased ultraviolet levels should also be helpful in alerting users and custodians of libraries to light's harmful effects.

Atmospheric Pollutants

While air consists primarily of nitrogen and oxygen, it also contains small quantities of pollutants which are the cause of considerable damage to materials in library collections. This is especially true for collections housed in densely populated areas, which include almost all of the world's major libraries.

The pollutants present in air can be categorized in two main ways: by action they are either acidic, cause oxidization, are abrasive, or are disfiguring; and by form they are either gaseous or solid.[45] The most common gaseous pollutants are sulphur dioxide, nitrogen dioxide and hydrogen sulphide, all byproducts of the combustion of coal, petrol and the oil fuels used to operate cars and factories. Ozone, another gaseous pollutant, is produced by the action of sunlight on the nitrogen dioxide produced by car exhausts, electrostatic filters in some air-conditioning units and photocopying machines. Dirt, dust and solid particles such as sand and oily soot are the most common solid materials to cause damage.

Gaseous pollutants cause deterioration through acid attack or oxidization. Sulphur dioxide and nitrogen dioxide combine with water in the air, and the results, sulphuric or nitric acids, are harmful to paper and other library materials. (The process is not as direct as the preceding sentence suggests. Sulphur dioxide, produced from the combustion of coal, petrol and oil fuels, slowly reacts with air to form sulphur trioxide, and this in turn reacts with moisture in the air to form sulphuric acid.) The effects of acids on paper have already been noted. Leather, too, is highly susceptible to damage from acid. Ozone causes oxidization and embrittlement of paper and leather.[46]

Solid pollutants act on library collections in three main ways: through encouraging biological action, by their abrasive action, and by forming acid. If solid particles contain materials which provide nutrients, then fungi and moulds may grow, causing staining and discoloration. Oily soot can also disfigure in a similar manner. Solid particles – dust, dirt, sand – can abrade library materials: to a cellulose molecule the sharp edges of a dust spot must look very large and menacing. Such particles may also become embedded in paper fibres and cut them. Solid particles can scratch photographic materials, magnetic tape and indeed all library materials. Particles may adhere to the surfaces of library materials and, if they contain acidic substances, may alter the pH of the paper and cause deterioration, especially in moist conditions. In addition to the damage they cause to library collections, atmospheric pollutants may affect staff and patrons of the library adversely.

The major methods of controlling deterioration caused by air pollution are filtering of air intake into storage areas and regular cleaning. Increasing global awareness of the dangers of air pollution, especially that caused by the continuing burning of fossil fuels, may in time result in large-scale action which will reduce the quantities of pollutants in the air. Chapter 4 examines specific methods of controlling damage from air pollutants.

Biological Agents

Biological agents are a major cause of deterioration of library materials. Many living organisms, animal or vegetable, find nourishment in dead organic matter, which abounds in library collections: paper, leather and wood, for example, are food sources for bacteria, moulds, fungi (or mildew) and insects. Biological agents thrive in conditions where there is dust, inadequate ventilation, poor lighting and high temperature and relative humidity.[47]

Mould and fungi spores are always present in the air, and will start to grow wherever conditions are favourable. In general their requirements are warmth (about 25°C and higher), moisture (about 70 per cent relative humidity or higher), darkness and poor air circulation. Nutrients may also be required. Some fungi require nutrients which are found in leather, vegetable paste, cellulose, sizing or gelatin emulsions on photographs. Another source of nutrients may be found in solid particles present in polluted atmospheres.

Moulds weaken and stain paper. They can obliterate images on paper and on photographic materials if not halted, and they may react with trace elements in paper and with localized condensation within a book to produce the small brownish patches known as foxing. In the control of fungi and moulds libraries should aim at maintaining temperature and relative humidity at levels which discourage growth, and at removing dirt, dust and other solid particles. Control of relative humidity in particular is essential: there is little opportunity for mould or fungi growth below about 70 per cent, most grow well at a relative humidity between 80 and 95 per cent, and above 95 per cent growth is 'luxurious'.[48]

The insects which most commonly cause damage in libraries throughout the world are cockroaches, silverfish, termites, book-lice and beetles.[49] Spiders also cause damage indirectly, by supplying nourishment for living insects from the bodies of dead insects trapped in spiderwebs and from the dead spiders themselves.

Insects feed on organic substances such as cellulose in paper, pastes, glues, gelatin sizing, leather and bookcloth. They prefer warm, dark, damp, dirty and poorly ventilated conditions. Silverfish and book-lice need moist conditions. The presence of some insects should be taken as an indication that conditions in the library are inappropriate. As one extreme example, if wood-lice and weevils are noticed, then the conditions are too damp for book storage. A summary of the library materials damaged by the most common insects, and of the type of damage caused, is given in Table 3.[50] It should be noted that the damage caused by insects is usually irreversible. Holes eaten through books, or images eaten off photographs, or permanently fixed acidic fly-spots cannot be mended.

Table 3. Damage Caused by Insects Frequently Found in Libraries

Common Name	Type of Damage and Material Damaged
Cockroaches	Surface erosion with irregular outline. Paper, cardboard, leather, vegetable- and animal-based adhesives.
Silverfish	Surface erosion with irregular outline; much smaller than cockroach damage. Paper, cardboard, vegetable- and animal-based adhesives, textiles, photographs.
Book-lice	Tiny superficial abrasions, with irregular outlines. Paper, cardboard, vegetable- and animal-based adhesives.
Termites	Deep, crater-shaped holes...sometimes destroys whole volumes, leaving only the fore-edge and spine. Paper, cardboard, leather, vegetable- and animal-based adhesives, textiles, photographs.
Deathwatch beetles	Winding, circular tunnels. Paper, cardboard, leather, vegetable-based adhesives.
Skin beetles	Irregular borings and sometimes surface tunnels. Paper, cardboard, leather, animal-based adhesives, textiles.

Insects can be controlled in libraries by keeping the storage areas clean. As they are attracted by food particles and food wrappers, eating should be discouraged within libraries. Insects can be controlled or eradicated by fumigation and the use of insecticides. Once they have been eradicated, periodic inspections are required to see that they do not re-establish themselves. Low temperatures may also help to discourage them.

Rodents and other animals are the final category of biological agents to be described here. Rats and mice are the most likely to be present, although there may be specific regional pests: possums may establish themselves in the ceiling spaces of libraries in countries such as Australia and New Zealand, for instance. Animals cause damage by tearing up paper – mice to make nests, for example – and by the corrosive effects of their droppings. Birds should not be tolerated for similar reasons. Cats and dogs should not be encouraged in libraries because they provide nourishment for insects in the form of hair, secretions and dead parasites such as fleas. For the same reason plants should be discouraged.

Human Causes

A good case could be made for the argument that human involvement is the major factor in the deterioration of library collections. Involvement can be indirect: polluting the air or accepting poor manufacturing practices and inferior materials are examples. It can also be more direct: we abuse books, by deliberate pogroms (burning, looting, vandalism) and by less dramatic but equally harmful means (theft, careless reading habits, thoughtless handling). Damage caused by humans is examined here in four areas: population growth and increasing use of library material, attitudes towards libraries and books, new technologies, and abuse and mismanagement.

One result of the exponential growth in the world's population over the last three centuries is that more people are chasing fewer copies of books. This is particularly the case for the finite quantity of books produced before, say, the middle of the present century. Concepts of democracy have become more widespread in recent times, with one consequence being the greater accessibility of and greater need for information of all kinds, including that which is available in libraries. In more specific terms increased openness has meant the growth of open stacks in libraries and the active promotion of library use, making the contents of libraries more accessible and making them comfortable and attractive places. The inevitable consequence has been a rapid deterioration in the physical condition of the collections. A comparison can be made between, say, North American libraries and libraries in parts of Europe where the stacks are normally closed to the public, with less need to heat and light storage areas to make them comfortable for the public.

Heavier use of materials in libraries has also come about, perhaps illogically on the surface, because of the dramatic increase in the numbers of periodicals and books being published, the so-called 'information explosion'. One would expect that the increased number of items available for use might result, overall, in less use per item, but in library terms this has not occurred. Libraries have generally faced static or only slowly increasing budgets and have responded by developing subject specialization and resource sharing arrangements. This has meant that an item requested and not in a library's collection is borrowed from elsewhere; this item is exposed to heavy use in the process of 'going through the postal service, getting cut when the package is sliced open, being handled by 15 different people in the two libraries....'[51]

Changing attitudes towards books are another, less direct, cause of damage. Greater prosperity has meant that the cost of books has decreased relative to other commodities and services, and they are more likely to be marketed by the same techniques that sell supermarket items. Throwaway printed material is delivered every day to our letterboxes and is handed out in our city streets. The nett result is a lack of respect for the printed word, a contempt which is reflected in underlining of phrases in library books, tearing out of pages, and in the installation of book return chutes in libraries. Simple care of books and other library materials is no longer taught at schools or at library schools. The norm is now that library materials are handled by users in an unintentionally destructive manner, and the term 'users' here by no means exempts librarians.

We have noted earlier in this chapter that mass production techniques have had severely deleterious consequences on the quality of library materials, especially paper and leather. Equally damaging results can be seen in the way these materials have been combined in book production. One prominent librarian has gone so far as to state 'without equivocation' that modern techniques should be named 'current book production malpractice' and that their effect on libraries is 'absolutely devastating'.[52] One example – of many, sadly – is the typical modern paperback, where individual printed leaves of acidic paper made from ground wood pulp are glued to each other and to a light card cover by an adhesive. In a short time the paper discolours and becomes brittle, the adhesive cracks, pages fall out, often in clumps, and the cover bends and fails to offer any protection to the front and back pages. In earlier times libraries could choose the more durable hardcover version of a book over a paperback version. Now, the choice is often simply not available.

New technologies of all kinds have resulted in greater deterioration of library collections, imposed at a faster rate. Again the examples are almost legion. Central heating is one example: it has allowed temperature levels to be raised (although the constant heat it provides has replaced the perhaps more destructive gaseous byproducts of burning coal, wood and gas for heating and lighting). Air-conditioning is another, a boon if it runs all of the time and doesn't leak water onto the collections. Indoor plumbing is convenient, and indeed considered essential in today's world, but water pipes often run riskily through library storage areas. There will inevitably be leaks and water damage, probably minor but sometimes major. Photocopiers, without which many library users could not function effectively, cause considerable mechanical and light-related damage. Microfilming, the major conservation method in use at present, often renders the original bound volume useless by guillotining its spine. We drive cars and ride on buses, and the resulting air pollution contributes heavily to paper decay. While Luddite solutions are not advocated here, greater recognition of these causes of deterioration and of ways to minimize their effects will reap major benefits.

Finally, we can note abuse and mismanagement of library materials as major contributors to their deterioration. Both users and staff abuse library materials. Careless handling is one major cause: books are insecurely stacked on top of each other, or flicked over roughly to expose their inside back cover for date-stamping when being issued. Much photocopying is needlessly destructive with bindings being forced down hard onto the platen of the photocopier. Spilling coffee or drinks over books and leaving greasy marks from food are other examples, as are underlining of text, or writing on paper placed on top of the pages of an open book. Book return chutes cause considerable mechanical damage to bindings. Careless display techniques, with bindings being forced open and pages weighted down by heavy stones –

the list is seemingly endless. (All of the above examples were noted over a period of one hour in a library used by the author.)

Mismanagement is a separate but related cause of deterioration. Library policies can put materials at considerable risk. Again the examples are legion and are easy to observe. Lack of a regular effective cleaning program, causing mechanical damage from dirt and biological damage from rodents, is one example. The lack of a disaster preparedness plan and the use of inappropriate conservation techniques are two more.

Environmental control and informed storage procedures are important methods available to the librarian to counter deterioration of library collections. These are the subjects of Chapter 4. Routines to counter abuse of library materials and mismanagement of collections will be further described in Chapter 5. Damage to collections caused by disasters is dealt with in Chapter 6.

Notes

1   Based on Carl J. Wessel, 'Deterioration of Library Materials', in *Encyclopedia of Library and Information Science*, Vol.7 (New York: Dekker, 1972), pp. 69-120.
2   *Ibid.*, p. 75.
3   Lucien Febvre and Henri-Jean Martin, *The Coming of the Book* (London: NLB, 1976), pp. 30, 32.
4   Details of this and other expressions of concern in the United States are described in Lee E. Grove, 'Paper Deterioration: An Old Story', *College and Research Libraries* 26 (1964): 365-374.
5   Society of Arts. Committee on Leather for Bookbinding, *Report...* (London: G. Bell for the Society of Arts, 1905), pp.7, 9.
6   Dard Hunter, *Papermaking: The History and Technique of an Ancient Craft* (New York: Dover, 1947, 1978 reprint), p. 5.
7   This section is based largely on D.J. Priest, 'Properties and Problems of Modern Paper' [Paper delivered at the 53rd IFLA Conference, Brighton, 1987]. More detailed studies of paper-making can be found in Dard Hunter, *op. cit.*, and Verner W. Clapp, 'The Story of Permanent/Durable Book-paper, 1115-1970', *Restaurator*, Suppl. 3 (1972): 1-51.
8   *Preservation of Historical Records* [report of the] Committee on Preservation of Historical Records (Washington, D.C.: National Academy Press, 1986), p. 35.
9   Dates are taken from the Chronology in Dard Hunter, *op. cit.*, which also contains illustrations of many aspects of papermaking.
10 Mary Lynn Ritzenthaler, *Archives and Manuscripts: Conservation; A Manual on Physical Care and Management* (Chicago, Ill.: Society of American Archivists, 1983), p. 15. This section is based on Ritzenthaler's excellent account and on that given by Richard L. Hills, *Papermaking in Britain 1488-1988: A Short History* (London: Athlone Press, 1988).
11 Hills, *ibid.*, p. 121.

12   *Ibid.*, pp. 126-127.
13   Books printed on this paper are listed in the *New Zealand National* Bibliography to the Year 1960, ed. A.G. Bagnall, Vol. 1 (Wellington: Government Printer, 1980), entries 3689-3691.
14   Hunter, *op. cit.*, pp. 382-385.
15   Hills, *op. cit.*, Chapter 10 gives more detail.
16   *Ibid.*, p. 146.
17   Its use in New Zealand for newspapers published in 1871 was observed by me during a survey of New Zealand newspapers in 1983.
18   Hills, *op. cit.*, pp. 149-155.
19   Ritzenthaler, *op. cit.*, p. 19.
20   *Ibid.*, p. 20.
21   *Ibid.*
22   An excellent source of more detailed information about paper deterioration is Carl J. Wessel, *op. cit.*
23   *Ibid.*, pp. 99-100.
24   W.J. Barrow, *Deterioration of Book Stock: Causes and Remedies; Two Studies on the Permanence of Book Paper* (Richmond, Va: Virginia State Library, 1959).
25   *Ibid.*, pp. 52-54.
26   John C. Williams, 'A Review of Paper Quality and Paper Chemistry', *Library Trends* 30 (1981): 204.
27   pH pens are noted in *Alkaline Paper Advocate* 1, 4 (October 1988): 29; 2, 6 (December 1989): 62; 3, 5 (November 1990): 53-55; 4, 3 (July 1991): 28; and in *Abbey Newsletter* 14, 3 (June 1990): 45. The test method described is TAPPI T529 om-88 'Surface pH Measurement of Paper'.
28   John Rutledge and Willy Owen, 'Changes in the Quality of Paper in French Books, 1860-1914: A Study of Selected Holdings of the Wilson Library, University of North Carolina', *Library Resources and Technical Services* 27, 2 (1983): 177-187.
29   Bonnie Curtin, Elaine Harger and Akio Yasue, 'The pH of New Library Books: Monitoring Acquisitions at Columbia University', *Alkaline Paper Advocate* 1, 4 (1988): 30.
30   Communication to the author by Wendy Smith and Jan Lyall, Preservation Services, National Library of Australia, August 1991.
31   Ellen McCrady, 'Wood Is Good', *Library Conservation News* 20 (1988): 4-5.
32   Frazer G. Poole, 'Foreword', in W.J. Barrow, *Manuscripts and Documents: Their Deterioration and Restoration.* 2nd ed. (Charlottesville, Va: University Press of Virginia, 1972), pp. xv-xvi.
33   *Preservation of Historical Records* (1986), p. 35; Anne Picot, 'Waste Paper and Other Stories', *Archives and Manuscripts* 17, 2 (1989): 235-237.
34   Cheryl Jackson, 'A Short Research Project into the Permanence of Thermal Fax Papers', *Abbey Newsletter* 13, 8 (December 1989): 133-134, 136.
35   *Conservation in the Library: A Handbook of Use and Care of Traditional and Nontraditional Materials*, ed. Susan Garretson Swartzburg (Westport, Conn.: Greenwood Press, 1983), pp. 63-64.

36   For further information on the different types see Alice Swan, 'Conservation of Photographic Print Collections', *Library Trends* 30 (1981): 267-296, and James M. Reilly, *Care and Identification of 19th-century Photographic Prints* (Rochester, N.Y.: Eastman Kodak, 1986), pp. 69-72. Appropriate chapters in *Conservation in the Library* (1983) should also be consulted.

37   B. Fox, 'Tests Prove CDs Can Self-Destruct', *New Scientist* 119, 1620 (7 July 1988): 37.

38   D.R. Winterbottom and R.G. Fiddes, *Life Expectancy of Write Once Digital Optical Discs*, British Library Research Paper 66 (Boston Spa: British Library, 1989), p. 43.

39   This section is largely based on Jerry McWilliams, 'Sound Recordings', in *Conservation in the Library* (1983), pp. 163-184.

40   Detailed technical information can be found in Chapter 6 of *Preservation of Historic Records* (1986).

41   Ritzenthaler, *op. cit.*, p. 26.

42   Wessel, *op. cit.*, p. 86.

43   Wessel, *ibid.*, provides a more detailed explanation of the action of light on library materials.

44   *Ibid.*, Table 13, p. 114.

45   Wessel, *ibid.*, indicates the wide range of atmospheric pollutants and the chemical factors involved.

46   Mariona Herrera, 'Analysis of Ozone Concentration and Its Influence on the Archives of the Kingdom of Aragon, Barcelona', *Restaurator* 11 (1990): 208-216.

47   See Fausta Gallo, *Biological Factors in Deterioration of Paper* (Rome: ICCROM, 1985).

48   Wessel, *op. cit.*, p. 95.

49   Photographs and descriptions which allow identification are in Gallo, *op. cit.*, and in Norman Hickin, *Bookworms: The Insect Pests of Books* (London: Sheppard Press, 1985).

50   Based on Gallo, *op. cit.*, pp. 4-5.

51   Ellen McCrady, 'Why Collections Deteriorate: Putting Acidic Paper in Perspective', *Alkaline Paper Advocate* 1, 4 (1988): 31-32.

52   Paul H. Mosher, 'Book Production Quality: A Librarian's View; or, The Self-Destructing Library', *Library Resources and Technical Services* 28, 1 (1984): 15-16.

Chapter 3

Surveying the Library: Determining Suitability of Environment and Extent of Deterioration

Introduction

An early step in establishing a preservation program is to survey the library building or buildings and the collections. Once it has been acknowledged that a preservation problem exists, the next logical step is to find out more about the environment in which the library collection is housed, and to identify precisely what problems arise from that environment. This is a prerequisite to planning an effective preservation program, one which takes account of the particular needs of that library and its users and which uses the available resources to the best advantage. Two kinds of surveys are necessary. The first is a survey of the library's building or buildings and the physical environment within; and the second is a survey of the library's collections. The second kind of survey is noted in the IFLA *Principles for the Preservation and Conservation of Library Materials*:

> One of the first stages is to evaluate the number of documents in need of treatment in order to provide factual evidence. This needs to be tackled by conservation surveys based on random sampling methods to estimate the condition of the paper, whether the bindings need repair, the date of publication of the items and other factors such as country of publication, acidity of the paper, etc., in order to estimate the broad types of treatment required and the quantities involved. From this estimates can be prepared of the level of resources required to meet these needs.[1]

Reasons for Surveying the Library and Its Collections

Environment Surveys

The need to examine in detail the physical environment in which the library collection is stored and used should by now be well understood. In Chapter 2 were noted the effects of environmental factors on library materials, in particular the kinds of deterioration which result from excessive and fluctuating levels of heat, relative humidity and light. One of the most effective ways to preserve library materials is to control these environmental factors, so that the levels are maintained within limits which minimize damage and so that fluctuations are avoided as much as possible. The environment survey examines carefully all aspects of the physical environment, as a basis for determining whether library buildings and the environmental conditions within them encourage or obstruct the preservation of collections. This kind of survey is also an essential step in establishing a disaster response plan (see Chapter 6).

Condition Surveys
It is necessary to know as much as possible about the condition of the collections before planning an effective preservation program. Procedures have been developed which allow assessment of the physical condition and state of repair of the collections, and of the nature and magnitude of the problems therein. The data derived from the condition survey are important management information essential for adequate planning, resourcing and implementation of preventive and remedial preservation measures. This point is frequently made in the preservation literature: an example, describing the decisions necessary to establish a preservation microfilming program, states firmly that the first step is 'to survey a collection to determine whether microfilming is necessary to preserve brittle or poor-paper materials that may otherwise be lost.' These surveys should include 'reviews of the condition of the collection' and of whether there are alternative sources of replacements, such as reprints or microfilms from commercial sources, for the deteriorated items found.[2]

The preservation literature is similarly clear about the reasons why surveys are an essential first step. These reasons can usefully be examined at two levels: the national or large-scale level, and the local or institutional level. On the national level, surveys have been necessary over the last two decades to define more clearly the extent of the preservation problem. While it was recognized in some countries that there was a major problem, specific information was not available. What was known was based on estimates rather than on statistically valid samples. Valid data were provided by several surveys in the United States, in particular those at Stanford University and Yale University which are described later in this chapter. Such data were used to support successful funding applications for projects to raise awareness, nationally and internationally, and to develop methods to address the preservation problem cooperatively. However, the need for such surveys on the national level is now less important, at least in the United States. DeCandido makes this point in the results, published in 1989, of a survey of the United States History, Local History and Genealogy Collection of the New York Public Library:

> This survey and others like it have demonstrated sufficiently the size and importance of the preservation crisis. No more surveys are needed

to make that point. The true value of condition surveys in the future will be to give preservation administrators information to guide the formation of institutional preservation efforts and, perhaps more importantly, to give shape and direction to cooperative efforts.[3]

Such a statement cannot yet be made about the need for condition surveys to establish the size and nature of the preservation problem in most other countries. Although the nature of the problem is known and readily observable in these countries, its magnitude has generally not yet been ascertained clearly enough to describe the condition of library collections on a national basis with any certainty.

DeCandido's second point, that condition surveys are of considerable value at the institutional level, is certainly the case. Surveys are essential for planning, for securing resources and using them in the best way, and for other reasons noted below.

Condition surveys provide the facts and figures essential for good planning and administration. Only when the problem has been quantified and its nature categorized can it be realistically assessed. Quantification can indicate specific problem areas: for example, paper which is more embrittled in one storage area may indicate that the heat levels there are unacceptably high; scratching on microfilms may suggest that equipment maintenance is inadequate; high levels of damage to bindings in the circulating collection could indicate that the book return mechanism is inappropriate.

Once the problem has been quantified, preservation goals and priorities can be established. Questions can be asked such as: What patterns emerge? Do any groups of material, or storage areas, or formats of material pose a special problem? What is in good physical condition? Can any reasonable projections be made of rates of deterioration? The answers to these questions might suggest, for example, that a change from vertical to horizontal shelving would alleviate damage to the bindings of oversize items, that instead of binding some periodicals a subscription to the microform version could be taken out and the paper copies eventually discarded, or that books from certain publishers should not be purchased because they are printed on poor quality paper or are inadequately bound.[4] Short-term and long-term measures can be more realistically addressed using the results of a condition survey.

Condition surveys provide factual data which can be the basis of proposals to justify increased resource allocation for a preservation program, and can also be used to plan how best to deploy available resources. The data can be used to argue a case for increased resources, by alerting institutional administrations, parent bodies and funding agencies to the problem and to the consequences of inaction. The best use of limited resources can be made if problems are grouped together to use the time of the conservator most efficiently and to make economies in the purchase of materials. Examples include bulk purchasing of conservation supplies, and the development of and participation in cooperative projects designed to avoid duplication of effort and to reduce preservation costs. More specifically, Morrow explains,

Informed projections based on careful sampling can indicate the approximate number of items in each major condition category. This information will suggest the comparative need for this or that type of preventive or remedial treatment, thus enabling a library to allocate existing resources, and justify requests for additional support, in a responsible way.[5]

Among other reasons for conducting a condition survey is the need to establish a base for future comparison, as a guide to the progress and effectiveness of the preservation program. A less tangible reason is the involvement of most or all library staff members, to a greater or lesser degree, in such surveys. The increased awareness of preservation problems which results is beneficial to preservation of the collections. A typical result here is increased interest in and application of careful handling procedures. Another reason cited is that data from surveys can 'stimulate sensibly balanced research programs' into new or improved conservation methods and solutions to the preservation problem.[6]

Environment Surveys

The aim of an environment survey is to evaluate the suitability of the library building or buildings for collection storage. In order to do this it is necessary to pose and answer questions in four areas: 1) characteristics of the building itself; 2) the environment in the building; 3) building security; 4) stack areas and workrooms. Below are listed most of the main questions which need to be answered. A fuller listing is present in *Preservation Planning Program: An Assisted Self-Study Manual for Libraries* (1987), which should be consulted if a survey of this type is undertaken; Cunha's *Methods of Evaluation to Determine the Preservation Needs in Libraries and Archives* (1988) is also essential.[7]

The Building Itself
In what condition are the roof and walls? Do they leak? Does water accumulate on the roof? Are walls and roof insulated?

In what condition are the the the attic, basement and storerooms? Are they clean, or cluttered and dirty? Is the cellar wet or dry? Is there any evidence of rodents, insects or mould?

The Environment in the Building
Can the temperature and relative humidity be maintained at constant levels twenty-four hours per day, every day of the year? What machinery is available for this? Is it in good condition and well maintained? How effective is it?

If there is no machinery for positive control of temperature and relative humidity, what are the environmental conditions: a) in summer months; b) during periods when heating is required; c) during spring and autumn?

How are the effects of sunlight minimized, to control intensity and ultraviolet radiation?

What type of artificial lighting is present? What is its level? If it is fluorescent lighting, does it have ultraviolet light screens?

Are temperature and relative humidity levels regularly monitored? What method is used?

Building Security

What type of intruder alarm is fitted? Where is it connected to?

What type of fire alarm is fitted? Is it connected to the local fire brigade headquarters?

What kind of fire extinguishing system is fitted? Is it the most appropriate kind? Is it regularly maintained?

How many portable fire extinguishers are available? What kind are they? Are they regularly checked? Are staff trained in their use?

Are there any heating furnaces in or close to the building? How is heat transmitted through the building: hot water, steam, hot air? What are the age and condition of the heating and heat transferring system?

Stack Areas and Workrooms

These questions should be asked for each stack area and workroom:

What is the average temperature and relative humidity? How is it maintained?

Is the housekeeping adequate? Is it clean, or dirty and cluttered?

Is there any evidence of insects, mould or rodents?

Where are water and steam pipes located in relation to stacks or cases housing library materials?

Is there any evidence of excess heat: warping, splitting, cracking of materials?

Is there any evidence of excess moisture: mould, mildew, silverfish?

What type of artificial lighting is used? If fluorescent, is it screened to exclude ultraviolet (UV) light?

What is the condition of the electric wiring?

Is there any evidence of building leaks on walls or ceilings?

How many windows are there? What size are they? In which direction do they face? Are there any provisions for UV control or for reducing the intensity of sunlight?

Is there any evidence of light damage (fading) on the spines of books or on other items?

Is there any evidence of previous water damage, especially in basement and attic areas?

What type of shelving is present? Is it adequate for oversize items? Is there good air circulation around it? Is it free-standing? Is there any rust? Are there any splinters or sharp edges?

Are enough step stools provided? Are enough book ends provided? Is
   aisle space adequate?
Is there a well planned and supervised housekeeping program?
Are book returns present? Are they well designed? Are they locked
   when the library is open? Are they necessary?
Are there enough book trucks? Are they well constructed?
Are work surfaces and reading room tables large enough?
Is viewing and listening equipment adequately maintained?
Is there any evidence of damage to materials?

The answers to the questions put during the course of the environment
survey can be gathered by visual inspection, by interviewing staff and by
monitoring of temperature, relative humidity and light levels using
appropriate instruments. There may also be some existing records of
temperature and relative humidity. The results of the survey should
immediately indicate areas where improvements can be made. Typically,
regular checks of fire extinguishers could be started, monitoring of
temperature and relative humidity could begin, minor repairs could be carried
out to roofs, more step stools could be purchased, or book returns could be
cleared more frequently – the list of possibilities is long.

Some Important Condition Surveys

Condition surveys aim to evaluate the extent of deterioration of items in a
collection and the nature of that deterioration. Although examination of every
item in the collection is the ideal, it is possible only for very small collections,
and sampling techniques which establish a valid sample of the whole
collection are usually applied. Surveys may be conducted entirely by an
expert consultant, or may be carried out by library staff under the direction of
an expert. The major questions asked in condition surveys fall into three
areas: 1) preliminary information (for example, shelfmark, place and date of
publication); 2) the nature and condition of the primary protection (for
example, the binding of a book); 3) the nature and condition of the contents
(for example, pH and folding strength of paper in a book). Other questions
may also be asked, depending on the expertise and training of the surveyors:
for example, what conservation treatment is recommended for an item, or
what priority is placed on its treatment?
   Many condition surveys have been carried out over the last two decades
and the results of some of them have been briefly noted in Chapter 1. The
most influential, significant either for their importance in bringing the
preservation problem to wider attention or because of the methodology they
developed, are described further here.
   The seminal study, Barrow's *Deterioration of Book Stock* (1959), was
not a condition survey in the sense used here, as it did not examine the
condition of items in a particular collection. Its importance lies in the methods

Barrow developed to test the condition of paper, methods which are used in a modified form today in condition surveys. Studies in the two decades following the publication of Barrow's study produced results based on educated guesses rather than on any rigorous sampling techniques. For example, in 1973 the Library of Congress estimated that 34 per cent of its total collection of 17 million books were either completely unusable or irreparably damaged.

The 1977 survey of monographs in the circulating collections of the University of California Libraries did, however, apply more rigorous procedures for testing paper folding endurance, tear resistance, pH and groundwood content to a sample of 2280 items. This survey concluded that 'monographs published between 1850 and 1944...should be the target group for any preservation program for monograph collections'[8] and its methodology was shown to be valid for measuring the extent of deterioration. The 1979 condition survey carried out at the Green Library, Stanford University, was another important study in that it developed a standard survey tool. A random sample of 400 books was chosen from a total of 1.5 million items in the stacks and the condition of their paper, bindings, and boards and covers was assessed. Each category assessed was assigned a score, and a numerical total was calculated for each item. The category of paper deterioration was weighted to reflect more accurately the greater seriousness of this characteristic. This survey established that 32.8 per cent were in good condition, 40.8 per cent in moderate condition and 26.5 per cent in poor condition.[9] Because of the influence which this Stanford study has had on later surveys, its methodology is described more fully below.

The Yale survey of 1980 is the most significant of those whose results have been published to date, both for its methodology and its comprehensiveness. Over 36,500 volumes from the Yale library system's total collection (7.7 million volumes in 1982) were sampled in order to establish acceptable confidence limits. Fifteen questions were put for each item examined and the results analyzed. Because of the importance of this survey's methodology, it is described more fully below.[10] Another survey whose methodology has been used by others is that carried out at the Syracuse University Libraries in 1985. It was based on the Yale and Stanford methodology and assessed a randomly chosen sample of 2548 books and periodicals. The methodology, including a sample of the form used for gathering the data, and results are fully described in the published account of this survey.[11]

The Yale survey methodology was used for a more recent study at the New York Public Library, the results of which were published in 1989. Nine hundred and forty-five bound volumes were surveyed in the United States History, Local History and Genealogy Collection. Seventeen questions asked are listed in the published account. The final one is unusual: it asked whether anything obvious was evident which would indicate that microfilming was not an acceptable preservation option. Despite being a newish collection, with more than 40 per cent of items less than thirty-five years old, much of the paper was brittle. The results suggest that the transition of paper strength from strong to very weak happens rapidly somewhere between about forty-five and sixty-five years.[12] Another recent survey, at the University of Illinois at Urbana-Champaign, chose to use the Stanford methodology as being more applicable for a survey carried out at minimal cost by student assistants.[13]

A rare example of a condition survey carried out on the collections of a public library is that of the Wellesley Free Library, Massachusetts, in 1987.[14] This survey, based on the Stanford and Syracuse methodologies, sampled 0.003 of the collection. (This compares with 0.005 in the Yale survey and 0.002 at Syracuse.) Seven hundred and three items from a total collection of 225,000 were examined. One result of this survey was considered to have been especially beneficial. The Director of the Wellesley Free Library noted: 'Although the project was very demanding, the work was well worth it. Our community now sees the library collections as part of the capital assets of the town and have indicated a willingness to put significant funds into maintaining the collection.'[15]

Few British results have been published. One which has is contained in a report of an ongoing survey of part of the printed book collections of the British Library. A random sample of 5283 volumes from over 2.4 million in the Department of Humanities and Social Sciences was examined to assess the condition of bindings and to estimate the fold strength of the paper. It concluded that 14.28 per cent of all post-1850 books are printed on paper in a poor condition.[16] Books published between 1840 and 1939 in Trinity College Library, Dublin, were found to be in better condition than those in the British Library, with the highest percentage (16 per cent) of brittle paper located in books published in the 1860s. The reason for this was tentatively ascribed to cool storage conditions.[17]

Condition surveys from other countries suggest that the deterioration of library materials is similar in nature and scale, although the latter varies from country to country according to factors such as climate: material in tropical countries, for example, is more likely to be deteriorated than that in temperate climates. A 1983 survey of New Zealand newspapers published before 1940 found that 49 per cent (an estimated 7 million pages) of the total pre-1940 holdings of New Zealand newspapers in that country were in poor condition and that 15 per cent were in critical condition.[18] In Australia, of 2.4 million volumes in the research collections of the University of Sydney Library, 12.3 per cent were found to be printed on brittle paper and 73.1 per cent (1.74 million volumes) were printed on highly acidic paper.[19] More than 40 per cent of Indonesian books in the National Library of Indonesia need immediate preservation attention. Twelve per cent of volumes in West German research collections are unusable.[20]

Condition Surveys: Methodology

Condition surveys can be as detailed or as simple as the curator of the collection thinks fit. In some cases an item-by-item survey may be the most appropriate, but such instances will be infrequent: perhaps a small collection of items of considerable artefactual value would warrant such attention. More usually a sample will be selected to give an indication of the range of problems present and the quantities which will be affected by these problems.

As noted above, the 1979 Stanford survey was the first major study to develop and apply statistically rigorous techniques. One aim was to establish a methodology which could be consistently applied elsewhere, could assist in the development of nationwide statistics, and would at the same time be as economical of money and time as possible. The main elements of the methodology used at Stanford were: establishing a reliable sample with an acceptable confidence level (here 95 per cent with a 5 per cent tolerance level) selected by using random number tables; determining which elements of deterioration were most useful to examine and could be identified objectively by unskilled surveyors; developing a numerical score as a way to compare the level of deterioration of an item with that of other items; and running a training workshop for surveyors and pre-testing the sampling technique.

The categories of deterioration examined were paper condition, binding condition, and board and cover condition. Each category was assigned three grades:

1   good condition: needs no attention;
2   moderate condition: evidence of deterioration, needs some attention;
3   poor condition: rapid deterioration, needs immediate attention, should not be used.

Guidelines for applying these gradings were developed which were objective and easily applied with a minimum of training.[21] The gradings assigned were weighted by multiplying them with numbers which indicated the relative seriousness of different kinds of deterioration. For example, the grading assigned to indicate paper condition was more heavily weighted than the other categories 'because deterioration of paper is considered more serious than binding or board problems'. A numerical total for each item resulted.[22] The report of the Stanford survey is essential reading for all who are considering carrying out condition surveys of library collections.

The 1980 Yale survey examined a very large sample of books in order to derive results which were valid for the total large collection. Of the fifteen questions posed, the first eight were designed to allow more precise determination of the nature of the deterioration:

1   Is the primary protection (binding, box...) intact?
2   Is the leaf attachment (sewing, gluing...) intact?
3   Is the paper very brittle? [breaks after two double folds]?[23]
4   Is the paper very acidic [pH 5.4 or below]?

5   Is the printed area of all pages intact?
6   Is the book mutilated (i.e., damaged by humans or animals)?
7   Is the book damaged by environmental factors (i.e., fading or water damage)?
8   Does the volume require immediate treatment (replacement, reproduction, repair, rebinding)?

The next set of questions was intended to help explain why deterioration had occurred:

9   What is the country of publication?
10   What is the date of circulation?
11   Is the book circulating or non-circulating?
12   What kind of primary protection (binding, box, wrapper) does the book have?
13   What kind of material covers the joint (the outer hinges)?
14   How are the leaves of the book attached?
15   What is the width of the gutter (inner margin)?[24]

The importance of a pilot study to identify and correct problems, for example with the wordings of questions or with applying the random number tables, was emphasized in the Yale survey, as was the importance of training the surveyors. The published report of this survey is, like that of the Stanford survey, essential reading before planning and carrying out a condition survey.

For those conducting surveys of larger collections, further guidance is available from the Association of Research Libraries' self-study method published in *Preservation Planning Program: An Assisted Self-Study Manual for Libraries.*[25] The first stage recommended in this approach is to compile an inventory of all holdings, in order to establish a general summary and an overall picture of the library's collections. The Preservation Planning Program's manual provides a 'Sample Inventory Format' (p. 69) which suggests these categories:

physical types (bound volumes, unbound serials, newspapers, microforms, etc.);
estimated number of items;
ages or date range;
estimated use (heavy, etc.);
notes (special considerations).

Much of this information may already be available in statistics collected for other purposes, such as for annual reports or for national statistics collecting programs.

The inventory will provide a general idea of what is held. The next step is to select parts of the stock which, when assessed in greater detail, will provide quantitative data about the nature of deterioration present in the collections and about its extent. The selection of parts of the total stock should aim to be as representative of the whole as possible. It should include collections of old as well as of newer materials; it should cover all physical formats which are represented in significant numbers; it should include materials from areas where the library has a special collecting commitment; and materials heavily used should be selected, as well as those for which there is less demand. There may also be a need to select special areas of the stock for inclusion in the survey, for example materials about which users of the library have expressed concern about physical condition.

The Preservation Planning Program notes that condition surveying should be part of an ongoing preservation program. Sampling, although it is capable of producing reliable and accurate data, cannot produce comprehensive results. Comprehensiveness can come only from putting together the results of many samples. Comprehensiveness may also be possible for small and specialized areas of the collection: it could be thought necessary, for example, to assess the condition of every item within a collection of material which was published in the city or state in which the library is located, or of manuscripts which belonged to the institution's founder. The self-study approach described by the Preservation Planning Program does not prescribe a specific methodology, so guidance should be sought from the Stanford or Yale studies or from other published studies.

The Program continues by emphasizing the final stages, analysis of the results and their implementation. In the analysis stage questions such as these should be asked: Do patterns emerge from the data? Are there any surprises? How do the results compare with other libraries? Do any particular formats, collections or groups of material have particular problems? What groups of material are in good condition? What might be the cause, and do these causes suggest any actions which could be applied to material in poorer condition? The manual suggests further questions to be addressed. From the results of this analysis, steps which will aid in preserving the collections can be identified. These can usefully be separated into short-term solutions, longer-term solutions and areas requiring further investigation.

It may not be necessary to develop and implement a survey of a sample of the collection in order to assess the condition of the stock. Another possible way of assessing physical condition is to integrate the data-gathering process into other library routines. For example, condition reports could be completed as part of the routines of accessioning new items (perhaps most relevant for secondhand or antiquarian material added to a collection) or before reshelving. It is unlikely, however, that such methods could be readily incorporated into the routines of any but the smallest libraries.

Methodologies which are less detailed have also been developed. These are based on the same principles as the surveys already described, but use less complex procedures for selecting the random sample and pose fewer questions to be answered for each item. One example is that used to assess the condition of printed books in the British Library's Department of Humanities and Social Sciences.[26] Here a sample size of 5283 was chosen from an approximate total of 2.486 million items. A selection of shelfmarks which would provide a wide range of examples was made, and then random number tables (which are reproduced in the published description) were used to select shelves within those shelfmarks and a distance along each shelf from which to select a book for assessment. The data recorded did not provide detailed information about types of binding, binding materials or pH readings, but rather were intended to generally indicate the binding condition and paper strength. For each item were noted the shelfmark, date of publication, country of publication, number of pages, condition of the paper and condition of the binding. Paper condition was determined by a double fold test (described as poor if it broke on 1 to 3 double folds, fair on 4 to 5 folds, good if it survived 5 folds) and the condition of binding was described as poor, fair or good. A personal computer software package was used to analyze the results.

A similar, simple methodology was published by the National Preservation Office at the British Library.[27] It provides suggestions on how to select an adequate number of items to sample, and random number tables with directions on how to use them to select items are given. It suggests noting the following: call number, date of publication, country of origin, number of pages, condition of paper (assessed as good, fair or poor for volumes considered to be valuable, or by the number of double folds), signs of mould, signs of insect attack, type of binding.

A word of warning is in order to conclude this chapter. There is a danger in taking the results of condition surveys at face value without also taking account of the place of the collection within the library and of the library's collection development policy. A survey may establish, for example, that 20 per cent of books in a collection are brittle, but the conclusion that 20 per cent of books in the collection need conservation treatment will probably not also be valid. Each brittle item needs to be assessed in terms of the collection development policy. Any one of a wide range of treatments may be possible, ranging from inaction (no treatment to be applied to a low use item which is not in the library's primary collecting areas), through discarding and replacement by a commercially produced microfilm copy, to a full treatment by disbinding, paper deacidification and strengthening, and rebinding.

Notes

1   J.M. Dureau and D.W.G. Clements, *Principles for the Preservation and Conservation of Library Materials* (The Hague: IFLA, 1986), p. 4, no. 13.

2   *Preservation Microfilming: A Guide for Librarians and Archivists*, ed. Nancy E. Gwinn (Chicago, Ill.: American Library Association, 1987), pp. 8-9.

3   Robert DeCandido, 'Condition Survey of the United States History, Local History and Genealogy Collection of the New York Public Library', *Library Resources and Technical Services* 33, 3 (1989): 281.

4   This section is based on the following, where more examples will be found: Pamela W. Darling and Duane E. Webster, *Preservation*

Planning Program: An Assisted Self-Study Manual for Libraries, Expanded 1987 ed. (Washington, D.C.: Association of Research Libraries, Office of Management Studies, 1987), pp. 64-65. Another excellent guide is Merrily A. Smith and Karen Garlick, 'Surveying Library Collections: A Suggested Approach with Case Study', *Technical Services Quarterly* 5, 2 (1987): 318.

5   Carolyn Clark Morrow, *The Preservation Challenge: A Guide to Conserving Library Materials* (White Plains, N.Y.: Knowledge Industry Publications, 1983), p. 6.

6   Christopher Clarkson, 'Conservation Policies: A Library Conservator's View', in *Conservation of Library and Archival Materials and the Graphic Arts*, ed. Guy Petherbridge (London: Butterworths, 1987), p. 238.

7   This section is based on Mary Lynn Ritzenthaler, *Archives and Manuscripts: Conservation; A Manual on Physical Care and Management* (Chicago, Ill.: Society of American Archivists, 1983), pp. 66-67; Darling and Webster, *op. cit.*, Chapter 5, especially pp. 53-54. The most useful source, however, is George M. Cunha, *Methods of Evaluation to Determine the Preservation Needs in Libraries and Archives: A RAMP Study with Guidelines* (Paris: Unesco, 1988).

8   Richard G. King, Jr, 'Deterioration of Book Paper', in *Advances in Library Administration and Organisation* 2 (Greenwich, Conn.: JAI Press, 1983), p. 121.

9   Morrow, *op. cit.*, p. 179.

10 Gay Walker *et al.*, 'The Yale Survey: A Large-Scale Study of Book Deterioration in the Yale University Library', *College and Research Libraries* 46, 2 (1985): 111-132.

11 Randall Bond *et al.*, 'Preservation Study at the Syracuse University Libraries', *College and Research Libraries* 48, 2 (1987): 132-147.

12 DeCandido, *op. cit.*

13 Tina Chrzastowski *et al.*, 'Library Collection Deterioration: A Study at the University of Illinois at Urbana-Champaign', *College and Research Libraries* 50, 5 (1989): 577-584.

14 Anne L. Reynolds, Nancy C. Schrock and Joanna Walsh, 'Preservation: The Public Library Response', *Library Journal* (15 February 1989): 128-132.

15 Letter to Sandra Cassano from Anne L. Reynolds, 2 October 1989.

16 Michael Pollock, 'Surveying the Collections', *Library Conservation News* 21 (1988): 4-6.

17 Paul Sheehan, 'A Condition Survey of Books in Trinity College Library Dublin', *Libri* 40, 4 (1990): 306-317.

18 Ross Harvey, 'The 1983 Survey of New Zealand Newspapers', *New Zealand Libraries* 44, 7 (1984): 117-120; D.R. Harvey, *Survey of New Zealand Newspapers: Final Report* (Wellington: Trustees of the National Library of New Zealand, 1983).

19 Robert J. Scott and Neil A. Radford, 'Assessing Collection Deterioration: The University of Sydney Survey', in Australian Library and Information Association 1st Biennial Conference, Perth, 1990 *Proceedings* (Canberra: ALIA, 1990), p. 231.

20   Akio Yasue, 'IFLA's PAC: A Worldwide Network for Preservation and Conservation', *Asian Libraries* 1, 1 (1991): 62.
21   These guidelines are explained in Sarah Buchanan and Sandra Coleman, *Deterioration Survey of the Stanford University Libraries Green Library Stack Collection* (1979), in *Preservation Planning Program Resource Notebook*, comp. Pamela W. Darling; rev. ed. Wesley L. Boomgaarden (Washington, D.C.: Association of Research Libraries, Office of Management Studies, 1987), pp. 196-197.
22   Buchanan and Coleman, *ibid.*, pp. 195, 197-198.
23   A double fold is made by folding a piece of paper once in one direction and then folding it back to its original position.
24   Walker *et al.*, *op. cit.*, p. 113.
25   Darling and Webster, *op. cit.*, Chapter 6.
26   Michael Pollock, *op. cit.*
27   'Conservation Survey – Methodology', in *Preservation: A Survival Kit* (London: National Preservation Office, 1986?).

Chapter 4

Controlling the Environment

Introduction

This chapter and the two that follow consider the major methods used in carrying out preventive preservation, with one important exception – the promotion and use of permanent paper, which is considered in Chapter 9. Preventive preservation, as its name implies, encompasses all those actions which have some effect on preventing deterioration of library materials from the moment they are added to a library collection. Preventive preservation is to be distinguished from conservation, which has already been defined in Chapter 1 in terms of methods and techniques which make deteriorated items stable or usable. These methods and techniques are examined in Chapters 7, 8 and 9.

Every recent writer on the preservation of materials in libraries and archives notes the areas encompassed by preventive preservation. Three definitions are given here to delineate the concerns and to emphasize by repetition their importance. In the words of Joyce M. Banks, preventive preservation

> involves safe housing and handling of materials and includes the provision of optimum environmental conditions; the provision of adequate stack space and suitable storage containers for fragile materials; training programs for staff to ensure that materials are handled in ways which will minimize mechanical wear and tear; establishment and enforcement of use regulations to prevent damage to holdings during consultations and exhibitions; increased conservation awareness among colleagues, staff and the general public; organization and co-operation in preservation microfilming projects; support and encouragement of conservation research; and participation in disaster planning.

Banks establishes eight 'Principles of Preventive Conservation':

1. The library should aim for the best total conservation environment.

2.   Stack areas should be equipped and maintained to ensure that suitable storage facilities and conditions are provided.
3.   All library staff should be trained to handle materials in ways which will minimize mechanical wear and tear, and staff should ensure that patrons use materials with care.
4.   Librarians and staff should work to raise conservation awareness.
5.   Preservation microfilming projects should be encouraged and supported where established microfilming standards are respected.
6.   Exhibition regulations should be prepared to cover in-house displays and conditions for lending materials for displays outside the institution.
7.   A disaster plan should be prepared and reviewed at regular intervals.
8.   A suitably trained librarian should be appointed and have authority to implement a conservation program based on these principles.[1]

This chapter addresses the first two of these principles, that is, the provision of the best environment.

Mary Lynn Ritzenthaler has neatly summarized what the environmental concerns are for archives, and her statement is equally applicable to collections of library materials.

The ideal physical environment for archival materials includes controlled temperature and relative humidity, clean air with good circulation, controlled light sources, and freedom from mold, insect, and rodent infestation. Good housekeeping practices, security provisions, and measures to protect collections against fire and water damage complete the range of environmental concerns.[2]

Another statement, from A.D. Baynes-Cope's *Caring for Books and Documents,* is intended for curators of small collections but is equally applicable for curators of larger ones. In his common-sense style Baynes-Cope notes:

The basis on which the proper storage of books and documents is founded is, quite simply, good housekeeping taken to its fullest extension....
The main things to consider are as follows:
1.   The buildings must be sound in all respects.
2.   The rooms used as a store must be sound in all respects.
3.   The room must be easy to keep clean and inspect thoroughly.
4.   The free circulation of air is probably the most important single factor in the climatic condition of the safe storage of books.
5.   Every effort should be made to ensure an even climate, changing as slowly as can be managed, throughout the room.
6.   The room is better cold than warm.[3]

Temperature and relative humidity, light, air quality, pest management, housekeeping, storage materials and equipment, security and building design are examined here. In each category the examples given are not intended to be comprehensive, but to illustrate the principles involved. Environmental requirements for specific materials are noted at the end of the chapter.

Temperature and Relative Humidity

Ordinarily the warming of libraries...appears to be considered as merely for the comfort and convenience of the public and the employés. A greater mistake cannot well be made, for in reality the conservation of the costly treasures which the buildings contain depends, to a large degree, upon the heating facilities; but they must be rightly applied and regulated. (J.G.O. Tepper, 1900)[4]

The importance of temperature and its control for the preservation of materials in libraries has been clearly recognized for many decades. It was explained in Chapter 2 that on the whole the lower the temperature and relative humidity, the longer paper-based materials will retain their strength. Low temperatures and relative humidity also inhibit the growth of biological pests. Fluctuations in temperature and relative humidity, especially rapid fluctuations, are another cause of deterioration. The control of both temperature and relative humidity is, therefore, a vital part of preventive preservation. This section is concerned primarily with conditions for paper-based material; conditions suitable for other formats in library collections are noted at the end of this chapter.

While there is considerable agreement about the range within which desirable levels of temperature and relative humidity should fall, there are some differences about precise levels. The IFLA *Principles for the Preservation and Conservation of Library Materials* suggest that 'A suitable compromise for conditions in storage areas can generally be found in the temperature range of 16°C to 21°C and a relative humidity between 40 and 60 per cent.'[5]

For temperature levels, North American recommendations are usually slightly higher than those for Britain and Europe, typically about 21°C for United States reading rooms compared with about 18°C for European. For example, Britain's National Preservation Office recommends a temperature not exceeding 18°C, with those between 13 and 18°C being acceptable, compared with Ritzenthaler's suggestion of 67°F (20°C) ± 2°F.[6] By comparison, 21°C is reckoned to be too cool for reading rooms in tropical areas, where outside temperatures are usually higher and readers sitting in temperatures of about 21°C will feel cold. The desirable level to aim for is flexible within the range suggested by the IFLA *Principles,* but should be as low as can be tolerated.

There is also the possibility of maintaining storage areas at lower temperatures, for example special materials in cold storage rooms. An example of this is the National Library of Australia's cold storage room, with an associated acclimatization room, where master negative microfilms and other materials are stored. The cold storage room operates at 8°C ± 1°C and 30 per cent relative humidity ± 5 per cent, and the acclimatization or conditioning room at 16°C ± 1°C and 50 per cent relative humidity ± 5 per cent.[7] What needs to be kept in mind is the need to condition items, that is, to let them come up to the temperature of the reading room gradually, a process which can take hours or even days if the storage room temperature is extremely low. Cooling down to the temperature of the storage area takes a similar length of time, to avoid the possibility of condensation as the temperature drops. Another potential difficulty of cold temperature storage is the greater cost of maintaining temperatures lower than those usually found in libraries. Temperatures in cold storage rooms can be as low as -29°C. Cool storage rooms, where staff can work for short periods, are also used; temperatures in these are around 13°C.[8]

There is less agreement about relative humidity levels. The IFLA *Principles* recommend that they be maintained at between 40 and 60 per cent. Ritzenthaler recommends that a relative humidity of 47 per cent ± 2 per cent be maintained, while the suggested level for the United States National Archives is 40 to 50 per cent.[9] Levels lower than about 35 per cent are generally considered to be too damaging to books, and those above about 70 per cent too risky because of the increased likelihood of mould growth, although this commonly held view has recently been challenged.[10] A level somewhere between 40 and 60 per cent is practical and economical for most air-conditioning systems to maintain.[11]

Some standards have been established for temperature and relative humidity levels in libraries and archives. For paper-based materials the United States National Bureau of Standards recommends 18-24°C and 40-45 per cent relative humidity for immediately accessible books, 10-13°C and 35 per cent relative humidity for less frequently used material, and -29°C for cold storage.[12] The British Standard for storage of archival documents recommends for paper and parchment 13-18°C and 55-65 per cent relative humidity, and suggests different ranges of temperature and relative humidity for materials other than paper.[13]

It will have been noted that recommended temperature and relative humidity levels usually specify allowable fluctuation limits. Constant levels are essential in order to avoid damage such as that caused by physical stress when rapid changes in relative humidity occur, and by the increased rate of acid attack on paper at high temperatures. Levels can usually be maintained by the use of air-conditioning, which must be reliable and must run all of the time. It is probably preferable to have a constant high temperature without an air-conditioning unit than to have a unit which fails frequently or which is only run during the library's opening hours. The IFLA *Principles for the Preservation and Conservation of Library Materials* again state the requirements for stability well:

Long-term stability of temperature and humidity conditions is another important consideration. Large and frequent fluctuations in environmental conditions should be avoided. Any changes in the environmental conditions within the range of temperature and humidity levels suggested...should be small and gradual. This need for stability emphasises the seriousness of any failure in air conditioning systems. Fluctuations in humidity may lead to dimensional changes in some library materials. These changes can introduce stresses that may lead to cracks and/or distortions.[14]

It follows that suitable means of monitoring temperature and relative humidity must be available, so that fluctuations can be noted and problems can be addressed. Monitoring is especially important in the first year after new air-conditioning equipment has been installed, until the correct balances have been worked out and a full cycle of seasonal changes has been experienced. Equipment to monitor temperature and relative humidity levels ranges from the relatively simple, such as a thermometer and a sling psychrometer to measure relative humidity, to the more sophisticated recording thermohygrograph and the use of fully automatic electronic sensing equipment, which can be linked with the regulation of the air-conditioning system. The different kinds of monitoring equipment and their use are described in Ritzenthaler's *Archives and Manuscripts: Conservation.*[15]

While the temperature and relative humidity levels suggested above are desirable goals, their attainment may not always be possible. In practice, the best that many libraries can hope to achieve will be limited by such factors as the local climate, financial resources or the lack of availability of technical resources. The ideal levels, however, must always be kept in mind and aimed at.

Stable temperature and humidity levels are usually maintained in libraries by the use of mechanical air-conditioning systems. The Association of Research Libraries in the United States, in fact, notes in its 'Guidelines for Minimum Preservation Efforts in ARL Libraries' that some specified materials should be housed in an environment which is controlled by a mechanical air-conditioning system which has 'at least...cooling, humidity control and particulate filtration.'[16] Air-conditioning engineering is complex and it is beyond the scope of this book to explain it. The preservation librarian does, however, need to have some knowledge of such things as the relationships between dew points, humidity levels and temperatures, of building design and layout and their effect on the maintenance of environmental conditions. An excellent introduction is that given by Timothy Padfield in 'Climate Control in Libraries and Archives'. One point should be noted: a major cause of dissatisfaction with air-conditioning systems in libraries stems from setting limits too precise to be maintained. In fact, no evidence was found in a 1986 study that there were benefits to be derived from controlling temperature levels to ± 1°F (0.5°C) rather than ± 2°F (1.1°C) or even ± 5°F (2.8°C), or of controlling relative humidity to a closer level than ± 5 per cent.[17] To avoid dissatisfaction, an understanding of what air-conditioning systems can realistically be expected to achieve (here Padfield assists greatly) is necessary. In addition to the air-conditioning other factors to be considered in maintaining stable temperature and relative humidity levels are the building's design, the internal layout of the building and the microclimates around items in the collection.

Air-conditioning may not always be a feasible means of achieving acceptable climatic conditions in libraries. Its costly installation may perhaps only be afforded for part of the collections, for example rare books or other special materials collections. Other means are available. Some are noted in the IFLA *Principles for the Preservation and Conservation of Library Materials*:

> simpler measures may be of use in limiting the extremes of temperature and humidity such as the following:–
> a) ensure good air circulation by appropriate use of fans and windows
> b) use of dehumidifiers to reduce humidity in badly affected areas of book stack
> c) use of insulation methods to reduce heat gain and use of blinds to keep out direct sunlight
> d) ensure buildings are properly maintained to keep out dampness during rainy periods.[18]

The concept of 'passive climate control' is noted by Padfield as effective in controlling temperature and humidity levels without mechanical air-conditioning. Here the two main principles are to put items in 'a set of nearly airtight and close-fitting enclosures', and to 'prevent rapid temperature change around the collection'.[19] Enclosures (boxes or even simple envelopes, for example) around the items ensure that a microclimate is created around the item, which delays the effects of changes in temperature and relative humidity on the item and therefore buffers it. On a larger scale such actions as insulating ceiling spaces and walls, stacking books closely, keeping book stacks away from outside walls or plant rooms where a furnace may be installed, and building libraries with thick walls help to lessen the effects of sudden temperature changes, in particular the detrimental effects of water condensation resulting from sudden drops in temperature.[20] Storage in an inner room without windows or external doors allows for good climate control. Such simple actions as using heavy curtains and blocking up windows can also be effective, although adequate air movement must be maintained.

Many other measures could be listed. These range from long-term but simple actions such as painting buildings with pale-coloured light-reflecting paint and planting trees near buildings to reduce heat gain, to shorter-term, but mechanically more complex, actions such as using free-standing humidifiers and dehumidifiers during seasonal changes in temperature and humidity. The area of climate control without using air-conditioning is one where lateral thinking should be encouraged and where unconventional methods can achieve good results. Plenderleith notes a case where old fire hoses were placed in window boxes to absorb excess humidity and stabilize both temperature and relative humidity levels.[21]

There is no doubt that maintaining temperature and relative humidity at steady and appropriate levels must be a top priority for the preservation of library materials. Although compromises will probably be necessary – as Padfield notes, 'people have a great tolerance for low relative humidity with little tolerance for low temperature, while books have a great tolerance for low temperature with little tolerance for low relative humidity'[22] – every attempt should be made to stabilize temperature and relative humidity at appropriate levels in all areas of the library. Building structures and limited budgets may mean that the best that can be achieved is still short of the ideal, in which case the aim should be to achieve 'a moderate environment...that isn't too hot, isn't so humid that mold grows and insects thrive, and whose temperature and relative humidity don't fluctuate to extremes.'[23]

Light

Light levels, like temperature levels, need to be kept as low as possible in all library areas. The effects of light on the deterioration of library materials have been noted in Chapter 2. To summarize, light provides energy to speed up the rates at which the chemical reactions causing the breakdown of materials occur. Ultraviolet light has the most detrimental effect.

Measures to limit light levels are relatively simple to implement. The ideal is, of course, darkness, but it is hardly practicable in libraries except in low-use storage areas. Storage areas may be fitted with time switches so that when there is no one in them they are not lit. It may be possible to reduce the number of lights, particularly fluorescent lights, and to replace incandescent bulbs with others of a lower wattage. Direct sunlight should be avoided if possible, and can be reduced by using protective blinds inside and awnings, shutters or even trees outside windows. Skylights can be covered or whitewashed. Windows can be treated with film which excludes ultraviolet light (this, however, needs regular replacement) or can be painted with UV-absorbing paint. Fluorescent light tubes should be fitted with diffusers and filters to exclude ultraviolet light. Some types of fluorescent tubes emit less ultraviolet light than others and should be considered as replacements for existing tubes.

Recommendations for lighting levels and total exposures are given in various sources. There is general agreement that ultraviolet levels should not be allowed to exceed 75 microwatts per lumen.[24] Stack lighting should not exceed 50 lux, and exhibited materials should be lit by no more than 50 lux, while reading rooms can be permitted higher levels, up to 100 lux.[25] Most libraries, especially smaller ones, are unlikely to have equipment to measure light levels. For these, the general guidelines – no direct sunlight, light levels kept as low as possible, length of exposure kept as short as possible, and reduction of ultraviolet levels – should provide sufficient protection from deterioration caused by light.

Air Quality

The causes of gaseous and solid air pollutants and their role in the deterioration of library materials are noted in Chapter 2. Both need to be controlled in order to avoid damage to the collections, although total elimination is very expensive and is usually not aimed at.

Gaseous pollutants can be controlled only by cleaning the air which is taken into the library building, the filters or adsorption system usually being part of the air-conditioning system. In areas where air pollution is heavy such control measures will be especially needed to protect collections containing materials intended to be retained for as long as possible. Collections containing primarily high use material which is not intended for retention (public libraries, for example) may not warrant such measures.

Solid particles can also be reduced by filtering air coming into the building as part of an air-conditioning system. In a typical system the air might pass through a series of fibre filters ranging from coarse to fine. Electrostatic filters are not recommended because they generate ozone, itself a pollutant.

Standards have been established for air filtering systems. A wide range of United States standards is given in *Preservation of Historical Records*, and British Standard BS5454: 1989 notes recent British suggestions.[26] The National Preservation Office in Britain suggests that 'when economically feasible, incoming air should be filtered (to eliminate 95% of dust particles of 2 μm diameter or more).'[27]

As with the control of temperature and relative humidity, much can be done to protect against air pollutants if an air-conditioning system is not economically feasible. For example, windows and doors can be adjusted so that they seal tightly, and can be provided with sealing strips. Hinged windows are more dustproof than are sliding windows. Filters over windows which are opened can be made from air-conditioner filter material.[28] An effective and regular cleaning program in the library (noted later in this chapter) is an essential method for reducing deterioration caused by airborne pollutants, as also is the minimizing of pollutants being generated in the building by such processes as smoking or cooking.

Pest Management

The kinds of damage caused by biological pests, mainly moulds, insects and rodents, are noted in Chapter 2. Library collections are a veritable warehouse of foodstuffs for these pests, and have the added advantage of offering benevolent surroundings that are not subject to extremes of climate. The most effective control measures are temperature and relative humidity regulation, already noted, and regular cleaning, noted later in this chapter. Control by fumigation methods is noted below and in Chapter 7. Other methods are also noted here.[29]

Important procedures for controlling insect pests are those relating to building maintenance. Regular removal of vines and ivy, and removal of plant debris from the exterior of the building will help control cockroaches. Eliminating damp spots, for example those caused by leaky pipes, will help to keep silverfish, which need free water, under control. Regular inspections of all areas of the building should be made to locate and destroy rodent nests and to detect the presence of beetles. Some measure of control of insect pests is also possible through outfitting the building with door and window screens. Carpets, which provide hiding places for insects such as silverfish, could be removed.

A second set of control measures can be loosely classified as methods not needing pesticides. These include the placing of silica gel in areas where silverfish are present: silica gel is a desiccant which dries out the moisture which silverfish need. Another method is the laying of mousetraps. Mechanical traps should be used in preference to toxic chemical baits, which allow the mice to die in walls, floors and ceilings and thus provide food for other insect pests such as carpet beetles. Freezing is being used increasingly as a means of eliminating insects from books. Infected books, or those about to be added to a collection, are sealed in polythene bags and then placed in a blast freezer at a low temperature, for example -30°C for three days.[30] Experiments have taken place using microwaves, for example domestic microwave ovens, but there are numerous problems associated with this method and it is not recommended at present.[31] Commercial gamma irradiation facilities, such as those used to irradiate foodstuffs and medical supplies, have been tested, but again this method is still in the experimental stage.

Chemical controls such as fumigation, and the application of pesticides and fungicides, usually offer only temporary relief of the problems they are intended to control. For example, when a chemical spray is applied, only the mould which is present is killed, and after a short time new mould spores will drift in and begin to grow if the conditions are right. Similarly, fumigation in an enclosed chamber has no residual mould control effects, although it should kill the mould already growing on the items fumigated. Parker goes so far as to state that 'much of the fumigation that is done in libraries is not warranted.'[32] Considerable expertise is required to apply chemical control methods, there can be health risks associated with their use, and legislation strictly limiting the use of once-common chemicals has been enacted in recent years. For these reasons it is very strongly recommended that expert advice is sought before any fumigation or other application of chemical control measures is carried out. Recent research into the use of inert gases such as argon, carbon dioxide and nitrogen may offer promising and low-cost alternatives to the use of toxic chemical pesticides.[33]

Far more effective in controlling mould and mildew growth is to change the environmental conditions which were responsible for the growth in the first place and which, if left unchecked, will encourage further growth. Chemical treatment may be necessary as the first step to kill the growth present; Chapter 7 notes some methods of carrying this out. Temperature and relative humidity levels should be monitored and altered where necessary. In particular, control of relative humidity is essential, by the means noted above and by others such as using fans to keep air moving and to lower moisture, by applying water-sealant paint to floors and walls in damp areas, and by removing ornamental waterfalls and fountains or altering the temperature of the water used in them. Removing planted areas, and keeping the number of hanging plants to a minimum, will help to reduce the quantity of water released into the air. Removing plants and dried plant arrangements will also help to control insect pests by reducing sources of food available for insect pests. Other methods are being used or tested: success has been reported with the use of freezing to kill insects and their larvae.

Current practice is to avoid chemical controls wherever possible. Instead, reliance is placed on a program of integrated pest management which incorporates environmental control, good housekeeping, the use of freezing of affected material, and ongoing inspection and monitoring to detect the presence of pests and harmful environmental conditions.

Housekeeping

Effective housekeeping regularly carried out is second only to maintaining stable temperature and humidity levels as the most effective preventive preservation method. Regular cleaning impedes deterioration of materials in libraries by reducing dust which causes mechanical damage and acid deterioration and by reducing the nutrients available for biological pests. Another less direct effect is that of the example which a clean and obviously regularly maintained collection sets for users, who are less likely to upset its orderliness.

Cleaning of items in the collections should be carried out by staff trained for the purpose. Contract cleaners can be used for cleaning floors and other areas of the storage areas, but not for cleaning items in the collection. Contract cleaners should be under clear instructions not to touch library materials. Training of library staff in appropriate cleaning methods is necessary. Using library staff members rather than contract cleaners also has the advantage of allowing stack cleaning to be carried out during normal working hours: this allows for increased security as fewer personnel have access to collections and restricted areas, and the possibility of inadvertently throwing out important materials is lessened.

Cleaning methods appropriate for library collections have two aims: to remove rather than redistribute dust; and to monitor the condition of the collections on an ongoing basis. Dusting is carried out with treated cloths to which dust adheres, rather than with feather dusters which merely spread it around in different places. Low suction vacuum cleaners fitted with a cheesecloth filter and soft brush should be used instead of regular commercial vacuum cleaners.[34] Careful handling of the items being cleaned can lessen considerably the normal wear and tear caused by use. Special attention should be paid to thorough vacuum cleaning of the perimeters of all rooms, as these are the areas where silverfish live, and of all floor areas and especially carpets, where carpet beetles may be present. Special attention should also be paid to areas where food is prepared and eaten: these should in any case be entirely separate from storage areas and staff workrooms, as any food scraps left are a powerful attraction to rodents and insects.

The monitoring aspect of a housekeeping program is every bit as important as the cleaning itself. Regular examination of the collection and its storage facilities allows for early observation of problems, such as the incursion of biological pests, of excess humidity or of chemical damage. In addition to the ongoing cleaning program a less frequent (but still regular, probably annual) inspection should be made of all areas in the building, including areas not normally accessed such as false ceilings, attics and cupboards. The purpose of this inspection is again to monitor conditions to provide early warning of problem spots. Thorough vacuum cleaning should be carried out to pick up and remove dead insects and other organic debris, which provide food sources for biological pests and can also block drainage pipes, resulting in water damage of buildings and collections.

The results of a regular cleaning program are both the obvious – reducing damage caused by dust and biological pests – and the less apparent. As Ritzenthaler notes, 'an atmosphere of orderliness and cleanliness is a positive impetus to maintain good conditions, and creates a positive impression with visitors and donors.'[35]

Handling

Careful handling of all materials in library collections, by staff and by users, is an essential ingredient in a preventive preservation program. It is discussed in more detail in Chapter 5.

Storage Materials and Equipment

Inadequate storage materials and equipment cause deterioration of library materials through mechanical damage and chemical damage. The former occurs, for example, when equipment is poorly designed so that items lack adequate support; the latter can occur, for instance, when storage materials release acidic gases and cause acidic reactions.

All equipment used to house library materials must be appropriate for the task. It must allow storage in the correct positions: upright for most bound books and vinyl sound discs, flat and supported over all of its surface for large bound volumes, flat and protected in a box for unbound paper sheets, and so on. It must provide protection from 'dust, distortion and mishandling'.[36] It should be designed and constructed in such a way that it does not damage any items in the collection: there should not be any sharp edges on shelves or on bookends to cause mechanical damage, and the surfaces of reading desks should not have any projections which could damage items.

All materials from which library equipment is made, and all materials which are added to library collections, must be constructed of substances which are not harmful to the collections. To give some examples, the paint used on library shelving should not release gases which cause acid deterioration of paper, all envelopes or boxes in which items are enclosed must be non-acidic and preferably alkaline buffered, and spools and cans used to contain microfilm should be constructed of chemically inert substances.

Shelving is the equipment most obvious in library storage areas. It must be strongly made and non-combustible. Shelves should be deep enough to support fully all items placed on them. There must be no protrusions or sharp edges on which items can catch and tear. The ideal construction material is metal, usually baked enamel. The lowest shelf should be raised from the floor at least ten centimetres so that damage from water on the floor, from floods or overenthusiastic mopping, for example, is avoided. Wooden shelves and cabinets should, if possible, be avoided, as they can release acidic materials. If they must be used, they should be sealed with several coats of a polyurethane varnish, or lined with heavy polyester sheets or acid-free board. As already noted, the location of the shelves is important: not against outside walls, parallel with the air flow to promote good ventilation, and with aisles of sufficient size to allow easy movement and careful handling of items. They should be kept clean and regularly inspected for signs of rust, or if wooden for dry rot or woodworm.

It is also essential that shelving fully supports the items on it. 'Good posture for books promotes physical well-being', to quote Merrily Smith's graphic if slightly moralistic words.[37] If there is insufficient support for books, spines become weakened or broken. Unbound material is much more prone to staining and damage to edges if unboxed and unsupported, and books shelved with edges protruding are more likely to suffer from damaged corners and boards. Each shelf should be slightly larger than the items to be stored on it, both to give support and to allow for air to circulate around the item. Book-ends are necessary for support. They must be large enough and strong enough to support fully the items upright, and must be carefully designed so they do not damage items which are roughly shelved.

Large bound books and unbound sheets need special shelving and equipment, as well as special handling. Care should be taken not to mix items of different sizes, as this can easily result in lack of support to larger items with consequent damage such as warping. Large bound items should be horizontally shelved, ideally individually, although two or perhaps three items may be stacked on top of one another if they are not heavy. Unbound sheets should be stored flat in boxes, or wrapped in acid-free paper or enclosed in envelopes (made of polyester or acid-free card) in drawers. Maps usually fall into this category. Very large unbound sheets, some maps for example, may be stored horizontally after first being wrapped around acid-free cardboard cylinders.

Of other equipment in libraries, book return areas and mechanisms deserve special mention. Most in common use have an enormous potential for damage. If they are a flat surface, such as a table or counter, they must be kept clear so that piling up is avoided. Book return chutes and spring-loaded bins should be avoided whenever possible, because of the damage they cause by abrasion and bumping to bindings and edges of books. Tables and reading desks must be large enough to support items fully and provide room for the user to work comfortably, and should have a surface which is flat and has no protrusions. Special care should be taken when selecting viewing and reading equipment (video players and microfilm readers, for example) to ensure that it does not damage the tape or film, and preferably that it cannot cause damage when incorrectly adjusted. Showcases for exhibiting items should be of substantial construction so that they cannot be moved or tipped over accidentally, and should be fitted with security locks. Constant appropriate temperature, relative humidity and light levels must be able to be maintained within them. Further details of the requirements of exhibition furniture can readily be found in writings on library preservation.[38]

Security

Security in libraries is an important aspect of preventive preservation. It is primarily concerned with the prevention of damage from fire, water and theft, and may also take account of natural disasters such as hurricanes or earthquakes, depending on which phenomena can be expected in a particular region. Building design plays a large part in security, and this is noted in the following section of this chapter. Reference should also be made to Chapter 6 where disaster response plans, which in part cover ground similar to this section, are described. This section is concerned with the security of library collections rather than of library personnel, whose safety should be the first priority.

Fire
The likelihood of fire can be reduced by taking care with fitting out the library building. Fire doors can be installed and care taken to see that electrical wiring and electrical services ducting do not pass through storage areas, in order to reduce the possibility that fire will spread through them to the collections. Materials and equipment should be non-flammable and when heated should not give off toxic fumes harmful to library materials or to readers.

Regular checking and maintenance of the building and of fire detection and suppression equipment are essential. Potential sources of fire can be listed and frequently checked; these sources include electrical wiring, lighting and power connections, kitchen facilities and chemical stores. Portable and fixed fire extinguishing equipment should be well marked and all staff should be instructed, on a regular basis, in its use. Smoking in any part of a library building should be very strongly discouraged. In particular, smoking in storage areas must be banned and this ban enforced vigilantly.

Current thinking about fire suppression devices for libraries favours the use of automatic sprinkler systems, especially those which contain no water pressure in the pipes until they are activated by smoke. Automatic fire detection and alarm systems (smoke and heat detectors) should also be fitted. Regular maintenance of detection, alarm and suppression systems is vital. This is an area where many standards have been established, and they are regularly updated; each country sets its own standards. Halon and carbon dioxide gas extinguishing systems have proved expensive to install and maintain, are dangerous to human life when in operation, are environmentally unacceptable, and are now rarely recommended.

Water

Water damage, while still destructive and best avoided if at all possible, is preferable to fire damage in library collections. Salvage techniques for water-damaged materials have over the last two decades been refined to a point where most materials can be salvaged and returned to a usable condition. (They are noted in Chapter 6.) For this reason water damage from a sprinkler system is preferable to fire damage, which either destroys library materials completely or damages them so badly that restoration to a usable state is difficult or impossible.

Building maintenance is the most effective measure which can be taken to prevent water damage. Sources of water, such as pipes – in central heating or air-conditioning systems, as well as in water pipes to bathroom, kitchen, laboratory or workroom facilities – need to be checked regularly and maintained. (Water pipes should not, if possible, run above stacks.) Gutters and downpipes need to be kept clear, and any damaged roofs or windows repaired as soon as they are noticed.

Theft and Mutilation

The measures taken to guard against theft of library materials and their mutilation are an important part of the security program in most libraries. Such measures will not be appropriate in all kinds of libraries: company libraries, for example, which serve a small and known clientele will probably not need to take such measures as are described here, nor perhaps will some public libraries, except for any special collections they may own. However, most libraries, in addition to the expense of replacing stolen and mutilated material, can ill afford the levels of anger and frustration which these problems engender in users.

There should be as few exits and entrances to a library building as possible. Emergency exits, for example those required by legislation for rapid exit in fires and other emergencies, should not allow access to, or egress from, the collections under normal circumstances. Secure areas (special stack areas, for example) need appropriate security measures such as locks, physical bag checks or security passes. Reading rooms, especially those where special materials such as rare books are used, may need to be supervised to prevent theft and to minimize damage caused by careless handling. To prevent theft from the collections such measures as physical bag checks, or electronic and magnetic systems of the tattletape kind, can be instituted.

Recent major thefts from libraries have prompted increasing recognition by librarians that theft and mutilation of library materials is a more significant problem than has previously been acknowledged. This has resulted in security being considered as an integral part of the library's preservation program. Marie Jackson, reporting on a national conference on library security held in England in 1991, summarizes the advice speakers gave on that occasion. Clearly not all actions are appropriate for every kind of library.

1. Review your

    – *collections*
        buildings and their design – doors, windows (reduce to minimum, brick up redundant doors, install window bars); locks; alarms; and perimeters (view should be 'open'; cut back shrubbery and install exterior lighting; remove ledges, put anti-climb paint on drainpipes)
        storage
        transportation
        book detection systems
        exhibitions and displays
        safeguards on lending
        ownership stamping
        reporting thefts and exchanging information

    – *policies with regard to users/readers*
        admissions and exclusions
        cloakroom facilities
        reading room procedures
        invigilation/CCTV [closed circuit television]
        access to closed stacks
        amnesty

    – *policies with regard to staff*
        training and awareness
        security staff
        staff passes
        staff use of collections
        searching of staff bags

2.   Create an air of calm, efficiency and confidence
      have staff and visitor badges
      have digital locks on staff rooms
      challenge strangers
      remove unattended bags
      make deposit of bags and coats compulsory – in 'automatic'
      cloakrooms
      internally secure fire exits
      draw curtains or blinds at night
      have as large a staff presence as possible and regularly walk the
      public areas
      organise the space in the library to maximise the ability of staff to
      overlook public areas
      consider putting up warning signs about theft and damage
      mark IT [information technology] equipment visibly and
      indelibly.[39]

Security in library buildings has a well developed literature of its own, and
the reader should refer to it for more information.[40]

Building Design

As the IFLA *Principles for the Preservation and Conservation of Library
Materials* state boldly, 'library buildings should be designed as far as possible
to meet conservation requirements.'[41] They go on to note that a wide range
of matters is of concern: how the building is oriented on the site, what
materials it is made of, how massive is its construction; all of these and many
more are to be considered in the design of a library along sound preservation
principles. Some examples will suggest the factors to be considered.

Building design can have a great impact on the maintenance of constant
and appropriate temperature and humidity levels. Passive environmental
control can be achieved by such means as burying or partially burying storage
areas underground, or by using materials with high thermal resistance.
Traditional building methods in subtropical and tropical areas, such as the
thick limestone walls of Maltese buildings, have often allowed library
materials to be stored in excellent conditions; they are discussed by Helmut
Bansa.[42] Existing buildings can also be renovated to provide more
acceptable conditions, for example, heat conduction through a roof can be
reduced by installing a ventilated attic space.

Given that damage from light is a major cause of deterioration in library
materials, the planning of new buildings should incorporate a minimum
number of windows. Biological damage can also be reduced through the
design of new buildings or the renovation of existing ones. Floors are
important here. They should be continuous and sealed, without cracks to
harbour foodstuffs for insects or the insects themselves. Walls should not
have shelving attached to them, as this can create pockets of stagnant air

where mould and insects can breed, even in buildings in which the levels of temperature and humidity are otherwise acceptable.

Some security features are legislated for in the construction of new buildings, for example, standards for building materials and types of allowable construction may be prescribed in building codes in areas prone to earthquakes.[43] The possibility of theft can be minimized by designing buildings to reduce the number of entrances and exits, both conventional (doors) and unconventional (windows, service ducts, sewers). Fire risk can be minimized by avoiding large open spaces and staircases in libraries, both of which act as chimneys during fires, by isolating any book return system from the rest of the library, and by reducing the combustibility of fittings and furnishings. The possibility of water damage can be reduced, for example, by ensuring that drainage sumps are not present in areas where library materials will be stored.

These examples illustrate only a handful of the considerations pertaining to preservation which need to be taken into account in the design of library buildings. A more comprehensive list appears in Cluff's 'The Role and Responsibility of the Library in Preservation and Conservation'.[44]

Storage Requirements of Specific Materials

The sections above note environmental requirements for the storage of paper-based library materials. Other types of materials commonly found in library collections may have different optimal storage requirements. The British Standard, *Recommendations for Storage and Exhibition of Archival Documents*, notes that materials other than paper should generally be stored at 13-16°C and a relative humidity of 50-60 per cent, unless different levels are given in the sections relating to specific materials.[45]

Table 4 lists some of the suggested levels of environmental conditions for formats commonly represented in library collections. There is some variation depending on the authority cited, but in general the optimal ranges should be clear from the levels given here. All authorities note that fluctuations in temperature and relative humidity must be kept to a minimum. Some authorities do not note desired air conditions, but it can be assumed that, where nothing is specified, the requirements are for the same conditions as for paper (see the section 'Air Quality' above in this chapter).

Environmental Control in Tropical and Arid Climates

Most of the literature on environmental control is based on conditions in temperate climates. Only in recent years have the specific conditions which apply in tropical and arid climates and the special preservation difficulties these impose been addressed.[46]

Table 4. Storage of Specific Library Materials

Name of Material	Temperature (°C)	Relative Humidity (%)	Other Conditions
PHOTOGRAPHIC MATERIALS (EXCLUDING MICROFORMS)			
General	20	35-40	
Black-and-white photographic paper prints	15-25	30-50	
	15-20	30-50	
Colour negatives[47]	-18 to -12	25-30	
	-18	25-35	
	0		
	10		
Motion picture (safety-based)[48]	20 ± 2	40 ± 5	filtered air, dark if possible
Motion picture (safety-based, archival collections)[49]	10	50	
Photographic film (safety processed, active collections)[50]	< 21	< 60	
	< 21	30-60	
Photographic film (safety processed, archival collections)[51]	< 21	varies: e.g. silver-gelatin layer, cellulose ester base 15-50	
	< 21	30 varies according to type of base	
Slides (active collection)[52]	21.5	25-45	
Slides (archival collection)[53]	-18 to -12	25-30	
Stills[54]	20 ± 2	40 ± 5	filtered air, dark if possible
For both negatives and prints: 'essential to identify the process and materials employed' and seek specialist advice			
Triacetate and polyester-base films (archival collections)[55]	< 16	30-40	air purification
MICROFORMS			
General[56]	21 ± 5	0-60 ± 5	
	20	45-55	
Archival[57]	< 21	20-40	non-fluctuating
Medium-term[58]	< 25	30-60	non-fluctuating

MAGNETIC STORAGE

General[59]	18	35-45	
	20	40	
	4-16	0-60 (except polyester tape: 35-45)	
Audiotape[60]	18 ± 2	40 ± 5	filtered air, dark if possible
	21 ± 3	50 ± 10	
Computer tape[61]	18-22	35-45	
Computer tape (archival collections)[62]	10	20	
Computer (active collections)[63]	10	50	
Videotape[64]	18 ± 2	40 ± 5	filtered air, dark if possible
	20	55	
	< 23	30-55	

OPTICAL DISCS

Optical discs[65] 'should be stored in accordance with the manufacturer's recommendations'

Videodiscs[66]	18-24	40-55

SOUND DISCS

General[67]	20 ± 2	45 ± 5	filtered air, dark if possible
	21 ± 2	50 ± 10	
	10-21	40-55	

Preservation of library materials in non-temperate climates differs from that in temperate climatic zones in degree rather than in kind. Temperatures and relative humidities will almost certainly be higher, the latter on occasion – in monsoons or wet seasons – being very high indeed. Fluctuations of temperature between night and day may be severe, for example in desert regions. Harsh winds may suddenly arise, blowing large quantities of sand into the library. Ambient light levels may be high. In addition to these natural impediments to preservation, most libraries situated in tropical or arid zones will be located in developing countries which typically do not have access to resources at the levels considered necessary in developed countries. Such countries may also lack a stable political environment, which could put library collections in danger of damage or even destruction during periods of civil unrest. This section notes briefly some of the issues and procedures which may need to be taken account of by libraries located in non-temperate zones.

Standards developed for temperature and relative humidity levels may be very difficult to attain in tropical and arid climates, where levels such as 20°C and 45 per cent relative humidity may appear to be very cold and very dry. It may only be possible to achieve such levels by using sophisticated and costly air-conditioning equipment which needs expensive fuels (often imported) to run it. In such cases the general principles, rather than the specific standards, should be adhered to: temperature and relative humidity levels can be higher than the standards suggest, but every attempt must be made to avoid fluctuations in them.

Light levels may also be higher and contain more ultraviolet content in these regions. It is important to limit the exposure of library materials to light, and solutions to this need not be expensive or complex: curtains and blinds, for example, are as appropriate in these climates as they are in temperate zones. Atmospheric pollutants, too, can be limited by some of the same methods as used in temperate climates, for example by sealing doors and windows.

Pest management is likely to assume greater importance in non-temperate climates. To take one example, high humidity levels mean that the likelihood of mould growth is considerably increased. Insects in these regions may be more voracious than their counterparts in temperate zones – termites may munch through both the material in libraries and the very fabric of library buildings. An integrated pest management program is the best current solution, with a heavy emphasis on good housekeeping practices and constant monitoring.

It is in the area of building design that the greatest preservation challenges lie for libraries located in tropical and arid zones. As already noted, traditional building methods are likely to offer the most appropriate models. Examples of library buildings from developed countries are unlikely to be suitable, relying as they do on the availability of cheap energy to operate sophisticated air-conditioning systems. Local building designs, developed over centuries to provide comfortable dwellings for local conditions, are more likely to provide the best methods for constructing buildings which house library collections adequately.

Other aspects of preservation also need to be addressed when considering libraries in tropical and arid climates, although – as with environmental control – they differ in degree rather than in kind. Disaster planning is perhaps the most obvious example, as natural disasters are likely to be more extreme (cyclones and earthquakes come to mind) and their consequences more dire. These and related matters are noted in following chapters.

Notes

1   Joyce M. Banks, *Guidelines for Preventive Conservation* (Ottawa: Committee on Conservation/Preservation of Library Materials, 1987), p. 9.

2   Mary Lynn Ritzenthaler, *Archives and Manuscripts: Conservation; A Manual on Physical Care and Management* (Chicago, Ill.: Society of American Archivists, 1983), p. 30.

3   A.D. Baynes-Cope, *Caring for Books and Documents*. 2nd ed. (London: British Library, 1989), p. 40.

4   J.G.O. Tepper, 'The Relation of the Heating Arrangements in Libraries, Museums, etc. to the Conservation of Books, Specimens, etc....', in Library Association of Australasia, *Transactions and Proceedings of the Library Association of Australasia...Adelaide... 1900* (1901), p. lxxi.

5   J.M. Dureau and D.W.G. Clements, *Principles for the Preservation and Conservation of Library Materials* (The Hague: IFLA, 1986), no. 25, p. 7.

6   'Storage and Display', in *Preservation: A Survival Kit* (London: National Preservation Office, 1986?), p. 1; Mary Lynn Ritzenthaler, *op. cit.*, p. 30.

7   Jan Lyall, 'Cooperative Preservation Programs in Australian Libraries', in *Preservation of Library Materials: Conference Held at the National Library of Austria, Vienna, April 7-10, 1986*, ed. Merrily A. Smith (München: K.G. Saur, 1987), Vol. 1, p. 91.

8   Siegfried Rempel, 'Cold and Cool Vault Environments for the Storage of Historic Photographic Materials', *Conservation Administration News* 38 (1989): 6-7, 9.

9   *Preservation of Historical Records* [report of the] Committee on Preservation of Historical Records (Washington, D.C.: National Academy Press, 1986), p. 27.

10   'The Advantages of Low RH', *Abbey Newsletter* 14, 4 (1990): 59; 15, 2 (1991): 20-21.

11   Excellent discussions of air-conditioning systems are Timothy Padfield, 'Climate Control in Libraries and Archives', in *Preservation of Library Materials*, Vol. 2 (1987), pp. 124-138; and Timothy Walsh, 'Air-Conditioning for Archives', *Archives and Manuscripts* 8, 2 (1980): 70-78.

12   *Air Quality Criteria for Storage of Paper-Based Archival Records*. NBSIR-83-2795, quoted in Padfield, *op. cit.*, p. 137.

13   *Recommendations for Storage and Exhibition of Archival Documents*. BS5454: 1989 (London: British Standards Institution, 1989).

14   Dureau and Clements, *op. cit.*, no. 26, p. 7.

15   Ritzenthaler, *op. cit.*, pp. 33-34.

16   *Preservation Planning Program Resource Notebook*, comp. Pamela W. Darling; rev. by Wesley L. Boomgaarden (Washington, D.C.: Association of Research Libraries, Office of Management Studies, 1987), p. 261.

17   *Preservation of Historical Records* (1986), p. 25.

18   Dureau and Clements, *op. cit.*, no. 28, p. 7.

19   Padfield, *op. cit.*, p. 134.

20   Some possibilities are noted in Hugo Stehkämper, '"Natural" Air Conditioning of Stacks', *Restaurator* 9, 4 (1988): 163-177.

21   H.J. Plenderleith, *Preservation of Documentary Material in the Pacific Area: A Practical Guide* (Canberra: Australian Government Publishing Service, 1972), p. 9.

22   Padfield, *op. cit.*, p. 132.

23   Merrily A. Smith, 'Care and Handling of Bound Materials', in *Preservation of Library Materials*, Vol. 2 (1987), p. 51.
24   Dureau and Clements, *op. cit.*, no. 29, pp. 7-8; Joyce M. Banks, *op. cit.*, p. 10; ANSI Draft Standard *Practice for Storage of Paper-Based Library and Archival Documents*, Z39.XX-1984, section 3.4.
25   Dureau and Clements, *op. cit.*, no. 29, pp. 7-8; Banks, *op. cit.*, p. 10.
26   *Preservation of Historical Records* (1986), pp. 26-27.
27   'Storage and Display', in *Preservation: A Survival Kit* (London: National Preservation Office, 1986?).
28   Helen Price, *Stopping the Rot,* 2nd ed. (Sydney: Australian Library and Information Association, New South Wales Branch, 1989), p. 5.
29   This section relies heavily on Thomas A. Parker, 'Integrated Pest Management for Libraries', in *Preservation of Library Materials*, Vol. 2 (1987), pp. 103-123.
30   Norman Hickin, *Bookworms: The Insect Pests of Books* (London: Sheppard Press, 1985), pp. 159-160. See also Peter Lawson, 'Freezing as a Means of Pest Control', *Library Conservation News* 20 (1988): 6; and Eleanore Stewart, 'Freeze Disinfestation of the McWilliams Collection', *Conservation Administration News* 32 (1988): 10-11, 25.
31   Jerome Brezner and Philip Luner, 'Nuke 'em!: Library Pest Control Using a Microwave', *Library Journal* (15 September 1989): 60-63.
32   Parker, *op. cit.*, p. 117.
33   Kymron B.J. deCesare, 'Safe Nontoxic Pest Control for Books', *Abbey Newsletter* 14, 1 (1990): 16.
34   Some cleaning techniques are illustrated in Carolyn Horton, *Cleaning and Preserving Bindings and Related Materials*. 2nd ed. (Chicago, Ill.: American Library Association, 1969), pp. 5-8. See also *Preservation Planning Program Resource Notebook* (1987), pp. 136-141, 143-144.
35   Ritzenthaler, *op. cit.*, p. 35.
36   Dureau and Clements, *op. cit.*, no. 33, p. 10.
37   Smith, *op. cit.*, p. 46.
38   For example, 'Storage and Display', in *Preservation...* (London: National Preservation Office, 1986?).
39   Marie Jackson, 'Conference Reports', *Library Association Record* 93, 6 (June 1991): 394, 397. Another helpful checklist is in *Basic Conservation of Archival Materials: A Guide* (Ottawa: Canadian Council of Archives, 1990), pp. 46-48.
40   For example, *Security for Libraries: People, Buildings, Collections*, ed. Marvine Brand (Chicago, Ill.: American Library Association, 1984); Timothy Walch, *Archives and Manuscripts: Security* (Chicago, Ill.: Society of American Archivists, 1979); Terri L. Pedersen, 'Theft and Mutilation of Library Materials', *College and Research Libraries* 51, 2 (1990): 120-128; John Morris, *The Library Disaster Preparedness Handbook* (Chicago, Ill.: American Library Association, 1986).
41   Dureau and Clements, *op. cit.*, no. 35, p. 11.
42   Helmut Bansa, 'The Conservation of Library Materials in Tropical and Sub-Tropical Conditions', *IFLA Journal* 7, 3 (1981): 264-267.

43 An example of a library built to withstand earthquakes is described in Anne M. Cox, 'Three Faults, No Flaws', *American Libraries* (April 1990): 304, 306.

44 E. Dale Cluff, 'The Role and Responsibility of the Library in Preservation and Conservation', in *Conserving and Preserving Library Materials*, ed. Kathryn Luther Henderson, William T. Henderson (Urbana-Champaign, Ill.: Graduate School of Library and Information Science, University of Illinois, 1983), p. 191.

45 *Recommendations for Storage and Exhibition of Archival Documents*. BS5454: 1989 (London: British Standards Institution, 1989).

46 A selection of recent sources is: Helmut Bansa, *op. cit.*; Jan Lyall, 'Library Preservation in Indonesia' in ALIA 1st Biennial Conference, Perth, 1990 *Conference Proceedings* vol. I (1990): 453-462; Philip C. Aziagba, 'Deterioration of Library and Archival Materials in the Delta Region of Nigeria', *International Library Review* 23 (1991): 73-81.

47 Nancy Schrock Carlson and Christine L. Sundt, 'Slides', in *Conservation in the Library* (1983), pp. 103-128; *Keeping Archives*, ed. Ann Pederson (Sydney: Australian Society of Archivists, 1987), p. 235; Dureau and Clements, *op. cit.*, no. 79, p. 24; no. 80, p. 24; *Recommendations for Storage...*, BS5454: 1989, *op. cit.*

48 *Conserving and Preserving Library Materials* (1983), *op. cit.*, pp. 106-109. Temperatures have been converted to °C.

49 Eileen Bowser, 'Motion Picture Film', in *Conservation in the Library*, ed. Susan Garretson Swartzburg (Westport, Conn.: Greenwood Press, 1983), pp. 139-153.

50 Klaus B. Hendriks, 'Storage and Handling of Photographic Materials', in *Preservation of Library Materials*, Vol. 2 (1987), pp. 55-66; *Recommendations for Storage...*, BS5454: 1989, *op. cit.*

51 *Ibid.*

52 Carlson and Sundt, *op. cit.*

53 *Ibid.*

54 *Conserving and Preserving Library Materials* (1983), *op. cit.*; Dureau and Clements, *op. cit.*, no. 79, p. 24; no. 80, p. 24.

55 Dureau and Clements, *ibid.*

56 Helga Borck, 'Microforms', in *Conservation in the Library* (1983), pp.129-138; *Keeping Archives* (1987), p. 235.

57 *Storage of Microfilm*, Australian Standard AS 3674-1989.

58 *Ibid.*

59 *Keeping Archives* (1987), p. 235; *Preservation of Historical Records* (1986), p.64; *Recommendations for Storage...*, BS5454: 1989, *op. cit.*

60 *Conserving and Preserving Library Materials* (1983), *op. cit.*; Jerry McWilliams, 'Sound Recordings', in *Conservation in the Library* (1983), pp. 163-184.

61 *Recommendations for Storage...*, BS5454: 1989, *op. cit.*

62 Susan B. White and Allan E. White, 'The Computer', in *Conservation in the Library* (1983), pp. 205-219.

63 *Ibid.*

64 *Conserving and Preserving Library Materials* (1983), *op. cit.*; Susan G. Swartzburg and Deirdre Boyle, 'Videotape', in *Conservation in the Library* (1983), pp. 155-161; Alan Calmes, 'New Preservation

Concern: Video Recordings', *Commission on Preservation and Access Newsletter* 22 (April 1990): 6.

65   *Recommendations for Storage...*, BS5454: 1989, *op. cit.*
66   Judith Paris and Richard W. Boss, 'Videodiscs', in *Conservation in the Library* (1983), pp. 189-203.
67   *Conserving and Preserving Library Materials* (1983), *op. cit.*; McWilliams, *op. cit.*, pp. 163-184; *Recommendations for Storage...*, BS5454: 1989, *op. cit.*

Chapter 5

An Attitude of Respect: Careful Handling and the Education of Users and Librarians

Introduction

This chapter is about *attitudes* of respect towards the objects in library collections. Three aspects are examined: the importance of careful handling of items in library collections; teaching users of libraries to have respect for the collections; and the need for librarians to learn respect for the materials in their care as an essential part of their professional education. All of these are important in preventive preservation. Appropriate handling of library materials, that is, protecting materials from the excesses of physical stress which careless use can impose, will help to ensure that they remain usable for as long as possible. Careful handling is an essential part of preventing deterioration of library materials from the moment they are added to a library collection. However, careful handling does not come naturally to either the clientele of libraries or those employed in them and must be taught.

HANDLING

This section is concerned with the role of careful handling of materials in libraries, and the effect which this has on preservation of the materials. Other aspects of care and handling are noted elsewhere in this book: providing protective enclosures for library items (for example, boxing and binding) is examined in Chapter 7; stack maintenance is noted in both Chapter 4, where routine cleaning procedures for storage areas are examined, and in Chapter 7, where stack refurbishing programs are described.

The materials collected and preserved in libraries are intended to be used. This self-evident statement contains an inherent conflict, that of use of the materials versus their preservation, which is the central quandary of the preservation librarian. Banning use completely of an item in an advanced state of deterioration will almost certainly prolong its life, but this is at the expense of rendering it unusable – which is not what library preservation is about. Restricting use of that deteriorated item to those who can indicate that they have a real and demonstrable need to use it will also prolong its life, but this solution only addresses part of the problem. The item will also need either to have conservation treatment, for example its binding and paper strengthened to withstand handling, or it will need to be copied, for example by microfilming it, and the copy used as a surrogate for the original item.

If use of library materials is the key reason for the existence of libraries, librarians have a duty to make sure that library materials in their custody are handled as carefully as possible in order to prolong their life. This care with handling should start from the moment an item enters the library. The major source of damage to library materials is probably the handling they receive from *both staff and the library's users*. Apparently insignificant practices such as correctly removing a book from its shelf or not opening a tightly bound volume too far have a cumulative effect which actually saves money, money which might otherwise be spent on the repair and rebinding of damaged items.

The reality of the situation is that librarians and users by and large do not, as Merrily Smith notes, 'have a genuine concern for the physical survival of library materials' and will not handle them carefully.[1] She also notes that most librarians and users of libraries are at best 'oblivious' to the effects of poor handling and at worst 'don't care'. Only a few moments of observation in almost any library will be needed to convince the reader that Smith's statements are perfectly correct. The challenge for those concerned with preservation is to alter the handling habits of librarians and users to practices which are less harmful. The following section in this chapter describes means of user education in preservation, and the concluding section examines the place and significance of preservation education and training for librarians.

Staff attitudes may well be the key to making careful handling the norm rather than the rare exception in the library. The attitudes of the library's senior management are most important. If there is a commitment at the top level to preservation as an integral part of the library's 'mission', especially if this is complemented by providing resources for preservation programs, then library staff will respond positively. There will be an incentive to practise good handling and storage techniques as part of the preservation 'push', which will in time result in library staff showing care more naturally in their day-to-day handling of library materials. These attitudes will demonstrate to the users by example what acceptable handling is, and this in turn will have an effect on the physical condition of the collections. In such ways as these attitudes can be changed and handling practices can be altered from destructive to beneficial.

Although many examples are given in the following sections, the list is by no means comprehensive; rather, the examples are intended to be indicative and to illustrate the principles of handling.[2]

General Handling

Library materials should be protected from external causes of deterioration. These causes – water and direct heat, for example – are not likely to be present when the materials are housed in the library, but may become a problem either while they are being used in the library or, more likely, out on loan. Library materials should be protected from dirt, water, food and drink, direct heat and undue physical stress. Hands are one source of dirt, as any public librarian with a collection of car manuals can verify, or as any library employee who has been involved with moving shelving will testify. Similarly, dirty clothing, for example work clothing such as soiled dustcoats, can pass dirt onto library items. Library materials should not be allowed to come into contact with water. This is most likely to occur when items are on issue, possibly on a wet day or if they are dropped into the bath or the dog's water-bowl at home.

Drink and food are also to be avoided. Their effect on books and other materials is usually serious: greasy stains and water stains are just two of the possibilities, resulting in illegibility of the text and a decrease in the item's attractiveness. Liquids of any kind – correcting fluid is one often seen in the hands of library users – should not be used near library materials. Smoking should also be avoided, as it can burn paper and leave disfiguring, unattractive deposits. Direct heat – from sunlight or from a radiator, for example – is to be avoided because of the effects (discussed in Chapter 2) on paper deterioration and the increase in physical stress associated with rapid heating and cooling. Light, too, is harmful. Physical damage, most often to the bindings of books, is caused by rough handling of any kind: throwing books during domestic disputes or when children play is abhorrent, but less dramatic actions such as dropping books even a short distance, or stacking them so that they topple onto the desktop or floor, are also damaging.

Library users who can honestly state that they are not guilty of any of these breaches of the principles of careful handling are very rare creatures. One has, of course, very little direct control over items out of the library on loan (here the temptation is to suggest that spot checks should be carried out on borrowers' homes, but the reality is too uncomfortably totalitarian to accept), although a small measure could be instituted by establishing penalties such as fines for seriously damaged items. Greater control over items being used in the library is possible, by monitoring reading rooms or stack areas, and by curbing the worst excesses of careless handling.

Careful handling of library materials in the general sense of respecting the physical nature of that material is also frequently ignored. Corners of pages should not be folded down, as this weakens the paper which will eventually break off, nor (ideally, although this is less likely to be observed) should folded pages be straightened out without specialist attention, to avoid placing undue stress on the paper. Fingers should not be licked before turning pages. Places should be marked in books only when essential, and then only by using a bookmark of thin card or paper, preferably only one per book. Too many bookmarks, and bookmarks which are too thick, can damage bindings. Paperclips are definitely unacceptable as bookmarks, rustmarks being only one consequence of their use. Similarly, bacon rashers or other food items (whose use has been observed by public librarians) must not be used as bookmarks.

Bindings serve to protect the text and paper within them from physical damage but are not themselves indestructible. New or newly rebound books should be carefully opened in order to flex the hinges of the binding, first from one end then from the other: gentleness is the key. An insert found in a book published early this century and attributed to 'Modern Bookbinding' – no further details of its source are given – entitled 'How to Open a Book' begins:

> Hold the book with its back on a smooth or covered table; let the front board down, then the other, holding the leaves in one hand while you open a few leaves at the back, then a few at the front, and so on, alternately opening back and front, gently pressing open the sections till you reach the center of the volume. Do this two or three times and you will obtain the best results. Open the volume violently or carelessly in any one place and you will likely break the back and cause a start in the leaves. Never force the back of the book.

Books should not be left casually open face downwards, for example over the arm of a chair, as this will weaken and eventually break the spine. Bindings should not be forced in any way. Books can be kept open during use, for example during the cataloguing process, with book snakes (usually constructed from dried beans in a soft fabric cover) or by using a book stand, rather than by placing other books on them and possibly straining their spines. Leaning on an open book can damage the spine and binding, and placing the paper on which one is writing on top on an open book is unacceptable.

The paper within the book is, like its binding, also susceptible to damage. No rubber bands or metal clips should be used with paper, as these can cause acidic decay, stains, rusts and cuts. No pressure-sensitive tapes should be used, as adhesives stain paper, and in any case almost always fail by losing their stickiness. 'Post-It Notes' are manufactured from adhesive paper and leave adhesive on the surfaces to which they have been stuck. Marginalia of any kind, indeed any annotations or underlining, must be strongly condemned. At their worst they obscure or even destroy text, and at their best are distracting.

Shelving

Care taken in shelving library materials achieves two important aims. The first and most obvious is that damage to the items is avoided, for example, tearing of paper caused by forcing a book against a book-end; the second, much less tangible, is the effect of tidiness on users, who will tend to maintain the neat and tidy status quo.

Careful and non-harmful shelving practices which must be learned include how to take a book off a shelf. This should be done by nudging back the two books on either side of the one to be taken from the shelf, grasping it by the middle of the book and not by the headcap (the top of the binding), and pulling or lifting it from the shelf. To reshelve, move the book-end to loosen the whole row of books and make space for the book to be placed back on the shelf, and then adjust the book-end again so that the books are upright but not too tight. Books must not be jammed in.

Books and their binding are best shelved upright, unless they are very tall or wide, in which case they should be housed flat. Leaning books place undue strain on the spines, sewing and edges, and contribute to unnecessarily rapid deterioration; simply keeping books upright is helpful. Books should not be shelved on their fore-edges as this causes the text block to pull away from the covers of the book. Book-ends come into play here: they are essential for the good posture of books on shelves. They should not have sharp edges which could damage both books and people; they should not be dirty or rusty (they can be repainted if necessary); they should not slide on the shelves (rubber strips can be glued to their bases); and they should be high enough and deep enough to give as much support as possible.

The shelving itself needs attention. As noted in Chapter 4, it must not be constructed with sharp edges or corners which could cause damage, and should not be located in areas of potential danger to the materials. It should in addition be fully supported, so that it will not topple in the slightest earth tremor or when the lower shelves are empty and it becomes unbalanced. The space vertically between shelves should allow enough headroom (that is, room above the books) so that the possibility of damage to the top of tall items when they are shelved is minimized. Enough shelving should be provided so that all items can be shelved, rather than placed on the floor or on other unsuitable surfaces. Compact shelving should be operated smoothly and slowly so that its contents do not move, and nothing should be shelved in it that extends over the edge of the compact shelves.

The less tangible result of attention to careful shelving practice is that of tidiness, an effect which will be transmitted unconsciously to the users who will then tend to maintain it. In the words of the author of a *Binding and Physical Treatment Manual* at Columbia University:

> People's natural tendency is to leave things as they found them, or more so. If books are haphazardly sprawled on shelves, users are likely to be pretty casual about handling them. But if they're upright in neat rows, users will tend to keep them that way, and may even straighten up a toppled row if it is a conspicuous exception to overall neatness. The trick, then, is to give enough time to tidying up to create an overall impression of straight lines and right angles so that readers will be inclined to perpetuate the arrangement. A sign or two beseeching assistance in keeping order may also be useful.[3]

Library Materials in Transit

If environmental conditions are right, library materials can come to relatively little harm when standing on the shelves. Once they are moved, though, the possibility of damage increases considerably. For this reason special attention needs to be paid to moving any library materials, both within and outside the library. Procedures which minimize the potential for damage to the materials should be established and regularly monitored, as should any machinery used for transport, such as book-trucks. All staff who are involved in moving materials should be trained in the best procedures for moving materials.

The practices most frequently mentioned in the preservation literature for transporting library materials are the following. To avoid dropping items, only as many as can be comfortably managed should be carried at any one time; some writers suggest that three is the maximum number for books. If any more than this are to be transported, a box or book-truck should be used. Book-trucks need to be well designed to minimize the possibility of damage. They should, for example, have wide shelves with protective rails and wheels of large diameter. Book-ends may need to be used on book-trucks; no books should be placed on their fore-edges. They should not be overloaded, to avoid unbalancing them and thus causing spills. Special care needs to be taken when packing and unpacking books for inter-library loan. Such matters as removing staples from a jiffy-bag before unpacking, and wrapping books in protective materials so that corners are not bumped, are important.[4]

Circulation

Items being circulated are especially vulnerable to damage. Although little direct control of material is possible once it has been issued, as noted above, staff handling procedures can be instituted which minimize damage and which suggest to users that care is necessary. For example, any date due slips, bar codes or other labels on which pressure is put during the charge-out procedure should be positioned on the text block rather than inside the back cover; for items where this is not done or is not possible, staff should provide support before stamping or using a light-pen. Another procedure is to provide users with plastic bags when it rains, obviously to protect the item from water and, at a more subtle level, to suggest to the borrower that the item has value and is worth taking care of.

Book return mechanisms and procedures need careful assessment to make sure that the minimum amount of damage is caused. The convenience of the book-drop to patrons has to be balanced against the often considerable damage caused to material returned through it. If a book-drop has to be used, damage can be minimized in several ways. It can be closed during the hours that the library is open, so that materials are returned to the circulation desk where they are placed on the desk, which should be frequently cleared. Chutes or slides should be cleared as frequently as possible. Correct placement of depressable book-trucks or depressable bins, so that any overflow spills gently onto an adjacent truck or bin, can minimize damage.[5] If the installation of new book-drops is unavoidable, they should be designed so that materials drop only a short distance and so that bumping of items against one another is minimized.

Appropriate Furniture and Equipment

It has already been noted that furniture and equipment in libraries should not damage the materials in the collections. One further point needs to be made. Enough, and appropriate, furniture and equipment should be provided to ensure that handling of library materials is as easily and comfortably carried out as possible. In this way any awkwardness in handling which may readily lead to damage, for example reaching up to a high shelf rather than using library steps, can be avoided; users feel more secure and comfortable and are less likely to lose balance and drop items and perhaps to damage themselves as well. This principle applies equally to other furniture such as book-stands or lecterns to support rare books, large or sloping tables for large bound volumes, and adequate lighting in reading rooms.

Photocopying

The careful handling of materials being photocopied and the appropriateness of photocopying machinery are considered here; photocopying as a process for preserving the intellectual content of library materials is discussed in Chapter 8.

Paul Banks comments that 'photocopying is a prime example of the two-edged sword.' The ease of preserving intellectual content of library materials, but at the same time imposing considerable stress on the material, has already been noted in Chapter 1. Banks, writing in 1978, noted that one possible way to reduce damage caused by careless handling during photocopying was to offer staff to do the copying at the same price as that charged for coin-operated machines; the staff would be trained in careful handling techniques.[6] This is unlikely to be an attractive solution a decade or more later, given the cost of staff time and the all-pervading use of photocopying by library users in all types of libraries. The possible exceptions are small libraries where little photocopying occurs, and special collections within larger libraries. Banks' solution, however, highlights the main cause of damage during photocopying: careless handling.

Bindings suffer most of the damage caused by photocopying. Spine damage results from pushing down on the binding to force the pages flat so that text near the inner margin can be reproduced. Also damaging is the failure to support that part of the book which is not face down on the photocopier's platen (the transparent copy surface). Damage can be caused by flipping the book over when copying sequential pages, by paper being inadvertently, or deliberately for that matter, bent, and by copying from fragile brittle paper. Large bound volumes are particularly at risk, and indeed many libraries do not allow them to be photocopied. If possible, an alternative method of copying should be offered if photocopying is not allowed; microfilming or other photographic copies are the usual processes available.

One method of reducing damage caused by photocopying is to alter the binding specifications, taking particular care to reduce the size of volumes and to keep the inner margin (binding or gutter margin) as wide as possible. This is discussed in Chapter 7.

Photocopying machines themselves are another cause of damage. Damage results from excessive light, including ultraviolet light, excessive heat, and from inappropriate design which forces materials into stressful positions. Of the photocopiers most generally available, those which have a platen extending right out to the edge of the machine are preferable. This allows the half of a bound volume not being copied to extend down the side of the machine (adequately supported, of course) so that the binding does not need to be opened fully nor the spine pushed down.

The British Library has been active in recent years in developing and making available new photocopiers and new methods of copying. Three of these have been developed: the overhead photocopier, the image digitizer, and electroluminescent copying.[7] The overhead photocopier, marketed as the Archivist, uses a V-shaped cradle to hold the bound volume being copied. This cradle is operated by compressed air to raise and lower the book to the glass scanning window, from which the image goes optically to a normal office photocopier. The Archivist allows copying to within 8 millimetres of the gutter of bound volumes up to A4 size, without the binding needing to be opened to anywhere near 180 degrees.

The image digitizer has a cradle mechanism similar to the overhead photocopier, but the image on the page is converted to a digital electronic signal which can then be stored, displayed on a screen or sent to a printer or to another destination. This allows copying to within 3 millimetres of the gutter. The process gives off no ultraviolet light or heat. The electroluminescent copying method uses a thin, flexible sheet lamp which glows all over when electrically energized. This sheet is inserted into the book together with a sheet of photographic paper, the lamp is illuminated briefly, and the photographic paper captures the image on the page and is developed in the usual manner. This process emits no heat and no ultraviolet light at all. It is especially suitable for books with fragile bindings which cannot be opened far without causing damage.

The costs of these new photocopiers are high: in 1985 the overhead photocopier was £6900 and the image digitizer £20,000 or more. Equipment needed for the electroluminescent copying process cost about £200. Recently released photocopiers have taken note of preservation needs. One example, the Xerox 5042, has a platen the end of which is angled at 35 degrees to allow better copying of inner margins without requiring force on the spine, and has an optional foot-switch which leaves both hands free for more careful handling of materials. Despite their high costs, to help to avoid damage during photocopying, libraries need to supply the most appropriate photocopiers they can afford.

Microform and Other Non-Book Media

All library materials, in whatever medium, require careful handling in order to prolong their usable life. Microform (microfilm and microfiche) is noted here as one example of a non-paper medium which is already heavily represented in library collections and which is likely to increase its representation, given the current emphasis on microfilming as an appropriate preservation medium. As well as normal careful handling, microform requires some particular handling procedures. It should be handled only by its edges, for if its image is touched there is a strong possibility that it will lose definition and perhaps even total legibility. Rubber bands must not be used near microforms, as they emit gases containing sulphur which have a deleterious effect on the photographic image.

   All microform reading and printout equipment must be kept clean and regularly maintained so that the possibility of scratching and other mechanical damage is minimized. In particular, all parts of the equipment which come into contact with the microform must be thoroughly cleaned at frequent intervals, at least weekly but perhaps even as much as twice per day if the equipment is in heavy use. A frequent source of damage to microfilm is the difficulty some users have in threading microfilm onto the equipment. This can be minimized by placing clear instructions on or near each microfilm reader or reader/printer.

   This point about regular maintenance of equipment is one which applies equally strongly to equipment used to access other media: audiotape and videotape playback equipment are perhaps the most likely pieces of equipment to be found in libraries. Other media may also require special handling and storage in addition to what should be the usual careful handling. As examples, special care is required with compact discs and CD-ROMs so that they are not scratched or marked by fingerprints; and magnetic media such as computer discs and tapes should not be stored near strong magnetic fields. Further information concerning the handling and storage of non-paper materials can be found in many sources.[8]

Rare and Special Materials

Rare and special materials need extra handling precautions because of their scarcity, difficulty of replacement, or significance in cultural, historical, association or other terms. The most important precaution is the need for constant supervision of readers, to ensure both the security of rare items and that they are carefully handled. Ink and pens are usually prohibited and soft lead pencils required for use with special materials. White cotton gloves are often supplied to users: as well as offering protection to the item from natural oils, perspiration and dirt on hands, they have the psychological effect of reinforcing the message that special care in handling the item is expected. Special handling may be required for rare bound volumes, as on older bindings the joints are often weak. Such volumes should not usually be opened further than is required to read the text comfortably. To encourage this kind of care in handling supports, for example of high density foam or wooden stands should be available, as should weighted book snakes.

The first part of this chapter has identified the reasons why careful handling is an essential requirement of a library preservation program and has described handling techniques which minimize the possibility of damage to library materials. How to get these procedures established as common practice by users of libraries is the concern of the next section.

USER EDUCATION

User education is of major importance in any library preservation program. Care and proper handling are essential elements of preventive preservation; they must be carried out all of the time by all who handle library materials, both staff and users. The education of users in careful handling techniques is described here; education and training of library staff are noted subsequently.

It has already been noted that more damage is likely to occur to materials in library collections when they are in use than during storage, and this especially holds when materials are out on loan and so out of the direct control of library staff. Involving users in careful handling of library material is therefore vital. Involvement is necessary in two ways: the first is constant care when handling; the second is by alerting library staff to damage which the user observes.

Education of users in preservation is not an activity which is likely to meet with immediate success. Several factors militate against its rapid acceptance. Attitudes, probably ingrained ones at that, need to be changed, and this is never easy to do. Darling and Webster have described this factor succinctly:

> We live in a time and place where shared resources are rare. We are used to owning things, and treating them as we see fit. The idea that a borrowed book is the property of many, and the right to consult it a privilege, does not necessarily come naturally to the modern reader. Nor, then, does a sense of responsibility for ensuring that library materials are passed on from reader to reader in unchanged condition. Occurrences of highlighted text and marginalia, for example, are sometimes so common as to appear to be legitimate study aids.[9]

These authors also note that proper care and handling of library materials are not taught at school and are generally not widely known, and that careful handling takes more time than more harmful procedures: for example moving books by carrying only three at a time is more time-consuming (and more potentially harmful) than finding and filling a box or book-truck. In addition, general frustrations with library services (and in many cases who can blame library users, for we as librarians have often set lamentably low standards of catering for their requirements) can result in 'revenge' being taken against library materials. Finally, user education – unlike education of staff – cannot usually be made mandatory.

Despite the difficulties of educating users in careful handling of library materials, the potential benefits are great and well worth the effort. A user, for example, who has seen a photograph of damage to bindings caused by a full book return is more likely to return his books to the circulation desk, if that facility is offered; a genealogist who has been made aware of the destruction of rare directories caused by heavy use is more likely to be careful when consulting a directory and will understand why photocopying of it is not allowed.

A possible first step in a user education program in preservation is to mount a preservation awareness campaign. An approach which is likely to have some success in the present economic climate is to present the monetary implications of preservation action. The costs of acquiring, accessioning and storing items in the library could be presented, together with the financial consequences of their deterioration, for example the costs of locating and acquiring a replacement copy or of making a surrogate copy such as a microfilm, and the costs of repair techniques. Other ideas which could be used are noted below.

Two general points are worth making. User education activities need to be presented in as appealing a manner as possible, and any suggestion of dwelling tediously on the subject or of finding fault must be avoided. User education is not a one-off exercise, because a library's users are constantly changing, as new borrowers join a public library or there is a fresh intake of first-year students. A user education program needs to be permanently maintained, with implications for continuing financial and personnel resources.

Awareness of the General Public

Before starting a user education program in preservation in a specific institution, the matter of the general public's awareness of the preservation problem should be considered. Public awareness must be an essential component of any program which will successfully address the preservation problem. While there is, internationally, increasing concern with 'conservation' as related to both our cultural patrimony and to our natural surroundings, and this will continue to increase in coming years, there is still much to be done in informing the public of the specific problem of preserving library materials. This has been clearly understood by the writers of various major reports on library preservation in recent years. The 1986 report of the Brittle Books program notes that 'wide understanding of the preservation problem is necessary if sufficient and continuing financial and institutional support is to be secured.'[10] Two years later Alexander Wilson's report for the European Community noted:

> The raising of awareness among the library profession, scholars, governors and potential funders of libraries, and indeed among the general public, must be a priority objective at this time of general indifference and ignorance on the subject in the European environment.... Without awareness there will not be the means to effect change.[11]

There is a general agreement that top administrators, politicians and decision-makers must be targeted, as well as the general public, to convince them of the urgency of the preservation problem and the extent of the resources which are required.

Raising of public awareness can be addressed in many ways. Films such as *Keeping Your Words* and *Slow Fires*, which was shown on public television in the United States, are available on videotape, and their wide screening is one method.[12] Establishing a central organization to coordinate promotional activities, like the British Library's National Preservation Office, is another. Publications, short courses, widely distributed handouts and meetings all have some effect.

An innovative method of raising public awareness, and at the same time raising funds for conservation activities, is the British Library's Adopt a Book Appeal. In this program members of the public and corporate institutions donate £200, or part thereof, to conserve fully a book in the British Library's collections. Donors receive a certificate with their name and the details of the book their donation has helped to conserve.[13] Handouts of various kinds have also been used to effect. For example, the British Library's National Preservation Office issued a four-page A4 format publication which contains sections on 'General Hints on the Care of Books and Documents', 'Some Further Reading', 'Courses' and 'Some Suppliers of Conservation Materials'. A badge which depicts a well-known hedgehog character and the slogan 'Nei til sure bøker!' ['No to acid books!'] has been used to good effect in Norway to publicize the need for permanent paper.[14] The AICCM (Australian Institute for the Conservation of Cultural Material) has distributed widely a brochure entitled *Paper Here Today...Gone Tomorrow* on the same topic.

The Example Set by Library Staff

The importance of library staff setting a good example for users to follow in care and handling of library materials can never be overemphasized. This is especially so in a library which lends materials, where, because of the lack of direct control of material on loan, the example set by staff becomes more important than it is, say, in a closed access research collection. Staff should be willing to speak up and intervene with firm guidance when they see library materials being poorly handled. Also important is access to a repair facility so that if a book is judged to be too damaged to be issued, it can be quickly restored to a usable condition. As already noted, the general ambience of a library – including its cleanliness and tidiness – has an effect on how carefully users handle library materials.

Formats and Forums for User Education Activities

Possibilities for user education activities are many and varied. They can include the distribution of bookmarks, brochures, flyers and other handouts; printed messages can be tipped into problem volumes (for example, newspaper volumes may have a note about brittle paper and the need for careful handling); messages on book wrappers, messages appended to standard library handouts (such as maps of the library and bibliographies) can reinforce the impact of posters, signs and exhibits; audiovisual programs can be used in orientation sessions; a preservation awareness week can provide a strong focus; regular diagnostic clinics to which items requiring conservation can be brought could be held; plastic bags can be distributed on rainy days.

Forums in which user education can be pursued include staff newsletters, student newspapers, alumni newsletters, local newspapers, publications of the parent organization (for example, of the local city or town council, or of the university), bibliographic instruction programs, users' guides to the library, users' guides to the care of personal book collections, student orientation activities, formal academic course work, library tours, meetings of university or college staff (for example, faculty meetings, university senate meetings) and library friends' groups. The levying of penalties against students and staff in academic libraries who destroy library materials might be considered.[15] Talks to professional and service groups and publication, especially in non-professional and general publications, are other possible forums.

General Awareness Programs for Library Users

There is a wide range of possible programs for raising awareness of library users about the preservation problem, from the more traditional posters and bookmarks to the unconventional, for example comics whose heroine is dedicated to the fight against acidic paper and mishandling of books.

Posters with a simple and general preservation message can be used to effect. Examples are illustrated in *SPEC Kit* 113 and the *Preservation Planning Program Resource Book*.[16] The latter source includes illustrations of posters from the Hilton M. Briggs Library, South Dakota State University, with the theme:

PLEASE. RESPECT YOUR LIBRARY. DON'T DAMAGE OUR BOOKS

and

PLEASE. RESPECT YOUR LIBRARY. NO FOOD OR DRINKS.

Some simple and effective posters from the British Library, aimed at staff members but some of which are easily modified for library users, are illustrated in this book.

Bookmarks have been used in awareness raising campaigns and as a constant reminder to users of the problems. *SPEC Kit* 113 is an excellent source of ideas.[17] Illustrated here are bookmarks with legends such as:

Stanford University Libraries are committed to the CONSERVATION of LIBRARY MATERIALS. Please Help By: 1. Handling our many materials with care. 2. Removing books from shelves without pulling them at the top of the spine. 3. Abstaining from food and drink while using library materials. 4. Refraining from the use of paper clips and marking pens on books. 5. Photocopying, if necessary, without pressing bound materials flat. 6. Reporting damage so it can be repaired.

and

USE A PENCIL TO TAKE NOTES   INK CAN STAIN BOOK PAPER AND IS DIFFICULT TO REMOVE   Help preserve our library collections, the key to the Columbia tradition.

In a different but related category are signs which can be attached to relevant materials or which can be displayed as posters. For example, microform areas and storage cabinets could have displayed in and on them the message: 'One finger on a microform can blot out a whole page; handle by the edges only', and bound volumes of newspapers could have this message attached to their covers: 'Most of the newspapers in this collection are old and brittle; please be careful about turning the pages.'

Books are like lovers. they need

handling!

Poster prepared to remind staff at the British Library of the need for careful handling of library materials. Reproduced by permission of the British Library. (This poster was produced for internal use and is not available from the British Library.)

Poster prepared to remind staff at the British Library of the need for careful handling of library materials. Reproduced by permission of the British Library. (This poster was produced for internal use and is not available from the British Library.)

Life can be
ROUGH

Don't
take it out
on our books!

Poster prepared to remind staff at the British Library of the need for careful handling of library materials. Reproduced by permission of the British Library. (This poster was produced for internal use and is not available from the British Library.)

CAN A STICK OF CELERY BE USED AS A BOOKMARK?

That's a crunch
question.

It's certainly
long enough,
but may take up
an unacceptable
amount of space
in your bookcase.

It will also place
rather a strain
on the spine
of your book.

Books are
surprisingly
fragile,
and need careful
handling.

Please remember:

**A book should be
opened gently,
and supported
while being read.**

**Particular care
should be taken
not to force
a book open when
photocopying or
to make it
easier to read.**

**Your place should
be marked by
nothing thicker
than a bookmark.**

Stick the celery –

use a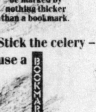

Issued by the National Preservation Office, The British Library, Great Russell Street, London WC1B 3DG. Telephone 01-323 7612

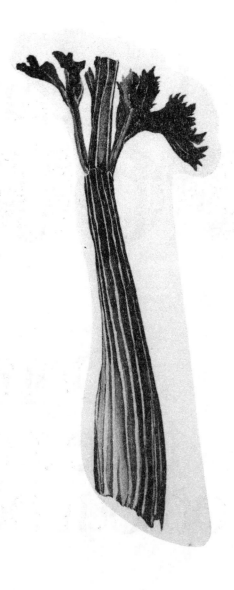

Bookmarks which promote preservation awareness. (Originals in colour.)
Reproduced by permission of the National Preservation Office, British
Library.

A BACON BOOKMARK?

Stranger things
have been used!

But we don't
recommend it.

Books are like people —
vulnerable to
grease and dirt,
cuts and scratches.

Unlike people,
a good soak and
a bit of sticking plaster
can be a disastrous
remedy for books.

Please treat them
with care,
and follow these
few simple guidelines:

**Keep inks, glues
and adhesive tape
well away.**

**Avoid getting them wet.
If they do,
let them dry slowly,
away from direct heat.**

**Don't use them as
a doorstop,
an armrest,
or to stand on.**

Save your
bacon — use a BOOKMARK

Issued by the National Preservation Office, The British Library, Great Russell Street, London WC1B 3DG. Telephone 01-323 7612

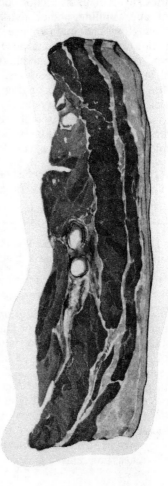

*Bookmarks which promote preservation awareness. (Originals in colour.)
Reproduced by permission of the National Preservation Office, British
Library.*

Comprehensive user guides to handling have been prepared in some libraries. One lengthy example is that of the Stanford University Libraries.[18] It contains sections on book handling (shelving, book-trucks, support and handling, photocopying, book returns, circulation staff), non-book handling and maintenance (storage and handling, copying and production) and book maintenance (environment, treatment of books by readers, repair). Another, and shorter, from Yale University Library and aimed at its research collections, is divided into sections on care and handling, shelving, photocopying, microforms, at-home use of library materials, repair (that is, not to be attempted).[19]

Less conventional examples include a questionnaire devised for the University of British Columbia Library.[20] It poses eleven facetious multiple-choice questions, such as:

1. I remove books from the shelf by pulling the top of the spine and am pleased to hear the sound of tearing, especially with a new book.
_____always   _____frequently
_____sometimes   _____never

4. I mark my place in a book with a rusty paperclip or a wet lettuce leaf unless I have a slice of bacon handy.
_____always   _____frequently
_____sometimes   _____never

A comic book entitled *The Librarian* has a female superhero who 'fights the never ending battle against acidic paper, book vandalism, and the destruction of books.'[21] A probably not often repeated display was that at the Montana State University Libraries in 1987.[22] Here a mouse was placed together with a book in a display case (locked) in the Library. Before a fascinated audience of library users, Miss Bianca took only a short time to reduce the book to shreds to make a nest. The final example is from the Harvard Law School Library, whose users may buy 'a small plastic bag filled with the brittle and crumbled remains of one page from the library's collections'.[23] There is obviously considerable scope for imaginative thinking in this area of user awareness programs in preservation!

User Education and Orientation Programs

Some categories of libraries have a captive audience which can provide a useful forum for imparting the preservation message. The libraries of educational institutions usually have certain times of the year when students visit for orientation tours or to participate in user education programs. Such programs can include segments covering aspects of preservation such as care and handling of library materials, in addition to the more usual contents. Opportunities also exist in library sessions at other levels, such as those sometimes held as part of some undergraduate classes or, more often, during sessions for postgraduate or research students.

Public libraries do not have the same opportunities, but might consider offering a brief session on care and handling of library materials, perhaps as part of an optional tour of the library offered to the new borrower when they sign up. Other kinds of libraries will have to seize opportunities where they find them.

Many sample handouts about preservation which are used as part of orientation or user education programs are given in the *SPEC Kits*. An example is the 'Care and Handling' sheet handed out to all freshmen at Princeton University during library orientation. It covers basic handling, shelving and care of books.[24]

Programs Based on Reading Room Regulations

Research libraries often require their users to apply for a reader's pass or ticket, frequently after an interview, and this provides an excellent opportunity to get across or reinforce the preservation message. A graphic example is the oath, whose origin lies in the early seventeenth century, which readers at the Bodleian Library, Oxford, are required to swear:

> I hereby undertake not to remove from the Library, or to mark, deface, or injure in any way, any volume, document, or other object belonging to it or in its custody; not to bring into the Library, or kindle therein any fire or flame, and not to smoke in the Library; and I promise to obey all the rules of the Library.

More usual is the requirement that readers sign a statement to the effect that they have read and understood a list of regulations, usually including some about care of the materials, which are to be observed in the library.

The following selection of reading room regulations is from the Alexander Turnbull Library, Wellington, New Zealand:

4. Do not bring into the Library anything likely to damage the collections:
    (a) smoking, eating, and drinking are forbidden;
    (b) pens, ink, correcting fluid etc. are not permitted in the Reading Rooms. Pencils for taking notes are available at the Enquiry Desks....
5. All Library materials must be handled with care:
    (a) clean hands are essential;
    (b) do not lean on, fold, or mark Library materials in any way, for example – by taking notes on top of a book, or licking fingers to turn pages;
    (c) do not open volumes on top of each other or turn them face down on the desk;

        (d)   no tracing is permitted.

6.   Some items are too fragile for use:
        (a)   if available, copies will be issued to readers....

10.   The Library does not photocopy original paintings, drawings and prints, fold-outs in books, large flat sheet items, newspapers and other large volumes....

14.   The Library's photographer can copy most items....[25]

A less formal example is from a sheet placed in the reading room at the Hocken Library, University of Otago, Dunedin, New Zealand:

CARE OF ITEMS   Please take all reasonable care, particularly when using newspapers, and archives and manuscripts. So, please do not:
Use fountain pens
Turn opened volumes face down
Insert bulky markers between pages
Write on the top of opened volumes....[26]

EDUCATION OF LIBRARY STAFF

Much of the preceding section is entirely relevant to this section, which notes the need for and place of education and training about preservation for library staff. Indeed, the point is made above that an essential element of an effective user education program for preservation is the example set by the library staff; it follows that all employees of the library must have some knowledge of preservation principles and of acceptable storage and careful handling of the materials in their care. This knowledge is imparted in two main ways: training of library staff, usually in-house; and education of librarians, usually at the schools of library and information studies. Both are considered below.

The answer to the question: 'Why should all library staff be taught preservation?' is simple: they are all involved in preservation activities, preservation being defined as 'the activity that attempts to keep what you want and need for as long as you want or need it.'[27] All library staff, in no matter what kind and size of library, are involved: public and school librarians are, for instance, not exempt, as they have to cope with the effects of heavy use, have to apply repair techniques, and may need to administer a rebinding program. Library staff handle library materials constantly and need to know how to store safely, handle, and transport these materials. The possession of knowledge about preservation is, purely and simply, a matter of being an adequately trained member of the library's staff.

In-House Training

What, then, should all library staff learn? An essential minimum is the same training in careful handling of library materials that library users receive. But much more is required. A general knowledge of the nature and extent of the preservation problem is very useful in order that staff members can put the handling skills – which can often be more time-consuming and may appear to require more effort – into some kind of context so that such knowledge will help to explain the reasons why care is necessary. It may also be necessary to teach some new skills to staff, for example, some basic 'running repair' skills, or the ability to recognize when a repair is needed (such as when a hinge needs tightening on a binding), or when the item needs the attention of a conservator. Another skill which it may be necessary to teach is how to deter readers from damaging library materials through poor handling.

The methods noted earlier in this chapter to educate users in preservation matters can also be used for training library staff. Other methods of training which could be used are lectures given by experts in preservation, the screening of videotapes to raise general awareness levels (such as *Keeping Your Words* or *Slow Fires*[28]) or to illustrate specific handling techniques, articles in staff newsletters, and encouragement to attend conservation workshops. Three audiences can be identified. Present staff members may need retraining and their level of awareness raised. New staff members will require a formal orientation program in preservation. All staff will need continual reminders, both formally and informally.

Examples of material used in staff training sessions are readily available in *SPEC Kit* 113. One is the University of Connecticut's 'Preservation Education for Library Staff', aimed at all new staff members. This describes a two-hour session, held regularly throughout the year, which gives a general introduction, shows a slide-tape presentation, *The Care and Handling of Books*, provides a discussion of this, describes treatment options, and concludes by focusing on the library's preservation program. Also illustrated in the same source and from the same university is a one-page handout for library staff entitled *Care of the Library's Collections: A Role for Everyone*. A similar handout from the University of Michigan is given. A more detailed manual is *Preservation Guidelines for Circulation and Stack Maintenance Personnel* which covers:

A. Circulation Area: Bookdrops, Charge/Discharge, Placement of Security Strips, Problem Books
B. Transportation of Books: Hand-carrying, Book trucks, Unloading book trucks
C. Shelving: Position and placement of books, Oversized volumes
D. Care and Maintenance in the Stacks: Vacuuming and dusting.

Education of Librarians

Educating librarians about preservation is now widely recognized as an essential element of any plan to address the preservation problem. One of the major recommendations of the Ratcliffe report was that more teaching of preservation in library schools should be pressed for, and this has been rapidly acted on in the United Kingdom in the few years since that report.[29] The situation is the same in the United States: at the end of 1989 preservation education courses were offered at thirty-one library schools accredited by the American Library Association.[30] Other countries such as Australia have followed suit.

Preservation education courses for library professionals are typically in one of three formats: the course is included as part of a compulsory course, often on library administration, in a first professional qualification; it is an optional course of about one semester; or it can be a separate qualification, such as the one- and two-year courses in preservation administration formerly held at Columbia University in New York and now taught at the University of Texas at Austin.[31] The general opinion of the place of preservation in education for librarianship courses is expressed by John Feather, who considers that

> conservation is as much a problem for management as an amalgam of scientific competency with technical and artistic competencies.... To accumulate these skills in a single person is not always possible; it is nevertheless certain that the librarian, aside from his training in administration, must have a familiarity with these points of view and with the historic [bibliographical] point of view.[32]

A complementary view is expressed by another British writer who considers that librarians must be educated to a level of preservation awareness 'to the point where conservation questions become a normal part of library administration, an essential element of library planning, and a component of stock maintenance which is just as important as deciding which books to purchase.'[33] For those who wish to establish a preservation course in a library school plenty of guidance is now available. Sample syllabi have been published, such as that by Peter Havard-Williams; more detailed curricula are given in the Unesco publication, *A Model Curriculum for the Training of Specialists in Document Preservation and Restoration*.[34]

It is also essential to offer continuing education opportunities in the preservation of library materials, for there will be those whose qualification was obtained before preservation was considered necessary knowledge for inclusion in library education programs, and who have since realized that they need to know something about it. There will also be those who are seeking to update or build on knowledge about preservation already obtained. There are many ways in which continuing education in preservation can be offered. One is by running short courses. Other opportunities for continuing education will be found in local seminars and workshops. There are also possibilities in reading the considerable body of literature (with, of course, a critical eye to evaluate its worth), in joining professional organizations concerned with conservation or subscribing to their publications, and by studying bookbinding.

Research into preservation has a place, and indeed is often noted as another essential ingredient in the 'mix' of solutions to the preservation problem. There is a need for new solutions, both technical and administrative. While the development of technical solutions is usually not within the purview of librarians, but is rather in the hands of scientifically trained conservators and research scientists, there is a place for research by those being educated and by the educators themselves. The next few years should see more research published as the place of preservation in library schools becomes more established and more research is undertaken by students enrolled for higher degrees.

Notes

1   Merrily A. Smith, 'Care and Handling of Bound Materials', in *Preservation of Library Materials: Conference Held at the National Library of Austria, Vienna, April 7-10, 1986*, ed. Merrily A. Smith (München: K.G. Saur, 1987), p. 45.

2   A good source of descriptions of handling procedures is Section 3, 'Protection of Library Materials', in *Preservation Planning Program Resource Notebook*, comp. Pamela W. Darling; rev. ed. Wesley L. Boomgaarden (Washington, D.C.: Association of Research Libraries, Office of Management Studies, 1987); another is 'Basic Preservation Procedures', *SPEC Kit* 70 (January 1981). Also useful is Jane Greenfield, *The Care of Fine Books* (New York: Nick Lyons Books, 1988).

3   'Basic Preservation Procedures', *SPEC Kit* 70 (January 1981), p.18.

4   More practices are listed in Joyce M. Banks, *Guidelines for Preventive Conservation* (Ottawa: Committee on Conservation/Preservation of Library Materials, 1987), p. 19; Susan G. Swartzburg, *Preserving Library Materials: A Manual* (Metuchen, N.J.: Scarecrow Press, 1980), pp. 23-24; and Paul N. Banks, 'Preservation of Library Materials', *Encyclopedia of Library and Information Science* 23 (New York: Dekker, 1978), pp. 197-199. Containers in which to transfer books are noted in Robert DeCandido, 'Out of the Question', *Conservation Administration News* 43 (October 1990): 22-23; 44 (January 1991): 44-45.

5   Illustrated in *SPEC Kit* 70 (1981), p. 11.

6   Paul N. Banks, *op. cit.*, p. 191.

7   This account is largely based on H. Wilman, 'Document Delivery without Damage', *Interlending and Document Supply* 13, 4 (1985): 112-115.

8   Two such sources are Klaus B. Hendriks, 'Storage and Handling of Photographic Materials' and Harald Heckmann, 'Storage and Handling

of Audio and Magnetic Materials', in *Preservation of Library Materials, op. cit.*, Vol. 2, pp. 55-66, 67-73.

9   Pamela W. Darling and Duane E. Webster, *Preservation Planning Program: An Assisted Self-Study Manual for Libraries*, Expanded 1987 ed. (Washington, D.C.: Association of Research Libraries, Office of Management Studies, 1987), p. ix – A 1.

10   Council on Library Resources. Committee on Preservation and Access, *Brittle Books: Report of the Committee on Preservation and Access* (Washington, D.C.: Council on Library Resources, 1986), p. 9.

11   Alexander Wilson, *Library Policy for Preservation and Conservation in the European Community* (München: K.G. Saur, 1988), p. 58.

12   *Keeping Your Words* (London: British Library, 1984); *Slow Fires: On the Preservation of the Human Record* (Santa Monica, Calif.: American Film Foundation, 1987).

13   Patricia Chapman, 'The Balloon Goes Up!' *Library Conservation News* 16 (1987): 1-2.

14   Rolf Dahlø, 'Preventing Future Needs for Conservation', *Library Conservation News* 25 (1989): 1-2.

15   Darling and Webster, *op. cit.*, p. ix – A 14-15.

16   'Preservation Education in ARL Libraries', *SPEC Kit* 113 (1985); *Preservation Planning Program Resource Notebook, op. cit.*

17   'Preservation Education in ARL Libraries', *SPEC Kit* 113 (1985), pp. 78-80.

18   *Users' Guide to the Conservation of Library Materials* (Stanford University Libraries, 1980), in *Preservation Planning Program Resource Notebook, op. cit.*, pp. 175-184.

19   'Care and Handling of Library Materials: A User's Guide to Preserving the Yale University Library's Research Collections', in *SPEC Kit* 113 (April 1985), p. 77.

20   Jocelyn Foster, 'Are You a Book Batterer?' *College and Research Library News* 44, 4 (1983): 117.

21   'Librarian Superhero Debuts in Preservation Comics', *Library Journal* (1 October 1988): 21.

22   'Menu-Riven Library Fights Back', *American Libraries* (April 1987): 306.

23   'Buy a Bit of Brittle Book: Librarian Packages the Problem', *Library Journal* (15 June 1988): 16.

24   'Preservation Education in ARL Libraries', *SPEC Kit* 113 (1985), p. 75.

25   Alexander Turnbull Library, *Rules for Use of the Library and Reading Rooms* (1989).

26   Hocken Library, *Reader Information* (1989).

27   Robert DeCandido, 'Out of the Question', *Conservation Administration News* 38 (1989), p. 24.

28   See Note 12 above.

29   As indicated in John Feather and Anne Lusher, *The Teaching of Conservation in LIS Schools in Great Britain* (Loughborough: Department of Library and Information Studies, Loughborough Institute of Technology, 1988).

30   See *Preservation Education Directory*, 6th ed., compiled by Christopher D.G. Coleman (Chicago, Ill.: Association for Library Collections and Technical Services, ALA, 1990).

31   The Columbia courses, despite their closure, have served as a significant model for the education of preservation administrators. They are described in Carolyn Harris, 'Education for Preservation Administration: The Role of the Conservation Education Program of Columbia University's School of Library Science', *Conservation Administration News* 42 (July 1990): 8-9, 24; 43 (October 1990): 4-5, 29.

32   As reported in Jeanne-Marie Dureau, 'Approaches to Training in Preservation and Conservation' in *Preservation of Library Materials, op. cit.*, Vol. 2, p. 16.

33   Melvyn Barnes, 'In-House Conservation Education', in *Conservation in Crisis: Proceedings of a Seminar...1986* (London: British Library, 1987), p. 39.

34   Peter Havard-Williams, 'Conservation in Library and Information Science Education', *Library Conservation News* 10 (1986): 5, 9; Y.P. Kathpalia, *A Model Curriculum for the Training of Specialists in Document Preservation and Restoration* (Paris: Unesco, 1986).

Chapter 6

Disaster Preparedness

Introduction

'Disaster planning' is perhaps a misleading term for what is now an accepted part of every library's preservation program. It is also known by several other names, among them disaster control planning, disaster containment, contingency planning and risk management. Disaster planning is in essence a set of rehearsed actions which will minimize the effect of a disaster, whatever its magnitude, on the library and will assist in restoring the library and its collections to a usable condition in as short a time as possible.

The term 'disaster' covers a wide range of events. One useful definition is that of Anderson and McIntyre:

> The use of the word disaster has gained currency among archivists and librarians to describe an unexpected event with destructive consequences to their holdings. It may be a small-scale incident or a full-blown emergency, but in either case it requires prompt action to limit damage.[1]

If we use this definition, then disasters in libraries are frequent. Every library building (in fact every building, regardless of its use) will, simply because it is a building, have a disaster at some stage; every librarian will take part in at least one during his or her professional career. Flood (or at least water damage) and fire are the most likely to be experienced. Other disasters are cyclones (or tornados and hurricanes), earthquakes, terrorist action, wars and explosions, although in all of these it is likely that fire and/or water damage will add to the physical dislocation of the library's collections. Fire and water damage will be noted here. Some writers include mutilation, theft and vandalism of library collections in their definition of 'disasters'; they are noted briefly in the section on security in Chapter 4.

A disaster plan is an essential element of preventive preservation. The best protection against disasters is to make every attempt to minimize the likelihood of them happening. Disaster plans require that library housekeeping is regularly carried out, that library buildings are appropriately constructed and fitted out and that they are regularly maintained, and that the library's staff is well trained. A disaster plan, in other words, is simply one aspect of good library administration practice. It is a relatively straightforward preservation measure to plan and implement in a library, and indeed has many benefits – such as increased staff awareness of and participation in preservation – if it is carried out as one of the first parts of a program which aims at integrating preservation into all aspects of the library's procedures.

In the words of Sally A. Buchanan, a writer on disaster planning:

A written plan is the single most important step in preparing for disasters. First, such a written document acknowledges that disasters are possible, and that there is a commitment on the part of the organization to accept responsibility in a sensible and logical way. Second, preparation and a written plan eliminate panic, assure proper decisions, reduce the damage to collections, and limit the cost of recovery. Third, a plan consolidates ideas and provides step-by-step instructions which are clear and easy to follow for anyone who is called upon to use them.[2]

Not all libraries have a disaster plan yet, although there is no doubt that all, whatever their size and type, should have one. It is also true that more and more libraries throughout the world are planning and implementing disaster contingency procedures. To give just one illustration of this, in 1986 a survey of about 175 Canadian college and university libraries indicated that only 14 per cent had disaster plans in place.[3]

Some Library Disasters

It is, unfortunately, all too easy to locate published descriptions of library disasters, in every country and of widely varying magnitude. Disasters are likely to strike at night or at the weekend or during a public holiday, at any time, that is, when the library is unattended or has only minimal staffing or security personnel. Examples of this are: 2 a.m. on a Monday morning at the Library of Parliament, Ottawa, Canada, 1952; Christmas Day in Darwin, Australia, 1975; on a Saturday at Concordia University Archives, 1982; 7 p.m. on a Sunday for the National Library of Australia fire, 1985; 8 p.m. on a Sunday at the Library of the Academy of Sciences of the USSR, Leningrad, 1988.[4]

Spectacular library disasters overseas have been frequent, from the destruction of the library at Alexandria, perhaps in the second century BC, to the present. Most recently, the 1966 floods in Florence, Italy, were a major impetus for the development of disaster planning, including the refinement of what have since become standard salvage techniques for water-damaged books and paper materials.[5] To move two decades on, a fire started by an arsonist in 1986 destroyed about 400,000 books and caused considerable other damage in the Los Angeles Public Library system's Central Library. Another 700,000 volumes were salvaged by commercial drying processes, mainly freeze-drying.[6]

In 1988 the Library of the USSR Academy of Sciences Library was the site of a fire which burned for nineteen hours before being extinguished. The fire was caused by defective electric wiring. Among the items destroyed were 400,000 volumes consumed by the fire, and one-quarter of the newspaper collection, many titles of which were unique. Water caused considerable damage, and subsequent mould and fungi growth was prolific. A total of seven-and-a-half million volumes were reportedly affected.[7] Radio and television news coverage of civil unrest in Rumania resulting in the overthrow of the Ceaucescu government reported the destruction of the Romanian State Central Library in December 1989.

While not all library disasters are so devastating, the lesser disasters described in the literature can also provide useful lessons. A more or less random sample of recent smaller disasters in North American libraries follows. A high school in the Bronx, New York, was destroyed by fire (probably arson) in 1983.[8] In 1985 a fire caused by lightning at the library of the Dalhousie Law School, Nova Scotia, destroyed 60,000 volumes and much of the library's furnishings and fittings, including its card catalogue.[9] An accidental electrical fire and its consequences at the Portsmouth Public Library, Virginia, in 1988, are described in 'The Library Has Blown Up!'[10] More recently the San Francisco earthquakes in 1989 deposited many books on the floors of libraries, including 300,000 at the Los Angeles Public Library and about 75 per cent of Stanford University Library's stock.[11] Similar lists could readily be constructed for other countries.

Not all is gloom and doom in library disasters: one positive aspect, especially of large-scale disasters, is that new and better techniques for recovering damaged library items evolve. This can readily be noted from the experience of the 1966 Florence floods, to which we owe many of our present techniques of retrieving, storing and drying wet materials. More recently the Los Angeles Public Library fire, after which several hundreds of thousands of books were frozen to await drying, promises to result in the establishment of new standards for freeze-drying books, and the 1988 fire at the Library of the USSR Academy of Sciences has resulted in international cooperation in dealing with major disasters on an unprecedented scale and in the use of the concept of phased conservation processing.[12]

While the history of disasters in libraries is long, the history of disaster planning is not. As already noted, the 1966 Florence flood was the catalyst for developing techniques of salvaging water-damaged paper-based materials. It also provided the impetus for libraries to plan for the likelihood that disasters would occur and for quick recovery from them if they did. Several American library disasters in the decade following were also influential in establishing the need for disaster plans. Vacuum freeze-drying of frozen books (described later in this chapter) was developed after 1966 and is now accepted as a standard technique.

It was not, however, until the late 1970s that it could be said that disaster planning was widely recognized as an essential part of good library management. The publication in 1978 of Bohem's disaster plan for libraries

of the University of California was important because it provided a
framework on which disaster plans in other institutions could be based.[13]
Another milestone was the publication in 1985 of Anderson and McIntyre's
disaster plan for Scottish libraries and record offices, an influential work
which has been adopted as the basis of many disaster plans throughout the
world.[14]

Objectives of a Disaster Plan

Before noting what a disaster plan *is,* we should be clear about what it *is not.*
A disaster plan is not concerned with the general emergency procedures for
handling situations which threaten the safety of people in libraries. These
procedures are usually developed in conjunction with other organizations, for
example the local fire brigade or a campus emergency services office, and
may be published in a separate document from the disaster plan. The disaster
plan recognizes that these emergency safety procedures for people exist and
follows on from them; it is in fact a plan for the steps which come after safety
of people has been assured, and relates to the safety of the collections. A
disaster plan, in other words, assumes that the safety of the library's staff and
users is paramount and has been attained.

The key ingredients of disaster planning are preventive – preventing
disasters by planning, reducing hazards, establishing procedures – and
reactive – coping with a disaster by putting into practice already established
and rehearsed procedures. Swartzburg provides a detailed list of objectives.
She notes the aims of a disaster plan:

1. To lessen the potential for loss by anticipating the possibilities
   and appropriately reducing them whenever possible.
2. To assure that agencies, both public and private, who will be
   called in during an emergency understand the nature of the
   library's collections and its priorities.
3. To establish normal conditions after a disaster promptly and
   efficiently.
4. To lessen the chances of recurrence by taking advantage of
   experience gained.
5. To assure that adequate orientation and training have been given
   to the staff and that this training is updated on a regular basis.
6. To assure frequent inspection by appropriate agencies to prevent
   changed conditions from having a deleterious effect upon the
   safety of the building.[15]

Another helpful list is provided by Sally A. Buchanan, who notes six general
guidelines for developing a response to disasters in libraries:

1. Accept responsibility for planning.
2. Plan in advance.

3. Use common sense.
4. Educate yourself and others about disaster planning.
5. Adapt advice to local situations when the ideal is not possible.
6. React to a disaster quickly and in accordance with a plan.[16]

Developing a Disaster Plan

Exactly how a disaster plan is developed depends on a number of factors such as the size of the library, the number of staff and whether any special funding is available, for example to hire a consultant to assist in the process. Computer software is available to assist with preparation.[17] If possible, the plan should be developed cooperatively by library staff. There are many positive benefits of such cooperative activity, including an increase in the general preservation awareness of all library staff and a greater knowledge of the aims of the institution. All personnel involved will need to cultivate 'a deliberately fatalistic mentality',[18] perhaps difficult but necessary to ensure that all probable eventualities are foreseen.

One approach to develop a disaster plan is given in the Association of Research Libraries' *Preservation Planning Program: An Assisted Self-Study Manual for Libraries*.[19] This is intended for larger libraries, but the approach could be readily modified for use by smaller libraries. A small study team (four to seven people is recommended) is established, made up of people with a broad knowledge of the library's complete range of activities. The team, using checklists in the self-study manual, assesses the library's current vulnerability to disasters, outlines a disaster plan, and determines future needs to allow the plan to be completed and implemented. The next step, implementing the plan, is up to the library's manager, whose job is to consider it with other priorities, ideally as one part of an integrated preservation program.

Contents of a Disaster Plan

What should be in a disaster plan? The core ingredients are knowledge of the building, the collections, disaster prevention, recovery techniques, the availability of outside help and the existence of a decision-making structure. Most plans have four parts: prevention, response, reaction, recovery.[20]

Prevention is by far the most important aspect of any disaster plan and its associated activities, as it is indeed of all parts of a library preservation program. In a disaster plan prevention covers: actions taken to minimize the risks posed by unauthorized access, fire and flood; actions taken to minimize the damage a disaster will cause by using appropriate storage equipment and library fittings which protect the items in the collections; provision of security copies of important materials and tools, such as the library's catalogue; and special arrangements to ensure the safety of the library and its collections during unusual periods of increased risk such as building operations or when materials are being exhibited. Insurance should also be considered here.

Response includes the activities which need to take place to make a disaster plan usable. It covers preliminary planning stages as well as the essential updating needed to keep the plan current. Topics included are: establishing and training the disaster response personnel; identifying and marking irreplaceable material for priority salvage in a disaster; assembling and maintaining equipment which will be required in a disaster; listing key personnel, services and sources of equipment and keeping these lists up-to-date; instituting procedures which notify members of the disaster response team and allow them to be assembled rapidly; establishing contact with conservation personnel and facilities in the region who are able to offer support in a disaster; and updating procedures regularly.

Reaction deals with the procedures to be followed when a disaster has occurred. Here are noted: raising the alarm; assembling personnel; making the disaster site safe for personnel; preparing a preliminary assessment of the damage; briefing salvage teams; entering the disaster site; and removing, cleaning, packing and transporting damaged materials.

The final section of a disaster plan covers the recovery of damaged material back into usable condition. Here are noted: establishing a conservation program to recover damaged material; cleaning and rehabilitating the disaster site; replacing treated material in the refurbished site; and analysis of the disaster and improvement of the disaster plan.

The exact form a disaster plan takes will vary according to the institution's specific needs. The following are typically present:

> a clear summary of emergency procedures (for both human life and the collections) to be followed for each likely type of disaster: fire, water damage, bomb threats, etc.;
> a list of personnel to be contacted if an emergency occurs;
> a list of regional and national consultants and services;
> lists of equipment and supplies on hand, and of sources for equipment not on-site;
> procedures for getting emergency funds from the parent organization;
> floor plans of the library with locations of priority materials and equipment for salvage clearly marked;
> summary of insurance coverage and insurors;
> list of arrangements made for regular building inspections, covering building maintenance, plumbing, electrical facilities, roofs, drainage, water pipes, etc.;
> list of arrangements made for regular inspection of security equipment such as alarm systems, and fire detection and fire extinguishing equipment.[21]

Anyone who is contemplating establishing a disaster plan (and this should mean all libraries who do not already have one) would do well to examine a range of plans from other institutions and adopt from them the features and layout best suited to their library.

Prevention: The First Phase

The old adage that prevention is better than cure is as true for disaster planning as it is for other aspects of preservation. As noted above, the prevention stage aims at identifying causes of disasters and at minimizing the risks posed by the library building itself, storage equipment and fittings. The three major causes to be prevented are unauthorized access, fire and flood.

An essential first step is to carry out a building inspection. Such an inspection may already have been done as part of the environment survey described in Chapter 3, which evaluates the suitability of the building for storage of library materials and, particularly relevant to disaster planning, examines characteristics of the building and building security. Swartzburg provides a list of features of the building which should be examined for disaster planning and, if necessary, altered if they are a potential hazard. She poses questions under twelve headings, some of which are listed here to indicate the kind of matters which need to be addressed.

History. How old is the building? Has it ever had fire or water damage? If so, were the causes eliminated or only patched up?

Heating plant ...Are all openings connecting the building to the heating plant properly protected with fire doors?... Is fuel storage safe?

Electricity ...Has insulation on wiring become worn or deteriorated?

The roof. When was it constructed? Are there signs of old or new leaks?

Windows. Are they tight? Are they ever left open for ventilation...?

Fire protection equipment. Are automatic sprinklers or fire detection devices installed and are they maintained...?[22]

Similar lists are given in several other sources, for example, in the Toronto Area Archivists Group's *An Ounce of Prevention*. Building survey forms from the University of Michigan Library will assist in framing questions about the 'architecture' (that is, the building), heating and cooling systems, 'water' (plumbing, leakage, pipes), security and fire hazards.[23]

Much can be done during the planning stages of a new library building to prevent disasters occurring throughout the life of the building. More information will be found in the 'Building Design' section of Chapter 4.

It should not be forgotten that the collections themselves and their storage equipment may be hazards, although this is relatively unlikely.

Examples of this include the presence of volatile nitrate film in a collection, and of combustible furnishings.

The importance of routine housekeeping and building maintenance in preventing library disasters needs to be stressed again. To use an obvious example, regular instruction of the staff in fire prevention procedures combined with regular examination and maintenance of fire extinguishing equipment lessens the possibility that a fire, should it start, will spread. Perhaps less obviously, frequent rubbish collections will also reduce that possibility. Routine housekeeping and maintenance measures have already been noted in previous chapters. More about them will be found in the sources about disaster planning already mentioned, *An Ounce of Prevention* in particular containing helpful checklists.

Another category of preventive actions relates to making backup or duplicate copies of significant material and storing it at a site other than the library. Two categories of material are relevant here: administrative materials, for example inventories of the collection such as catalogues; and significant material in the collections.

Computerized catalogues have dramatically increased the ease with which backup copies of catalogues can be made. Most libraries now either have access to a national database listing their holdings or have tape backups of their catalogue stored off-site and regularly updated as a routine matter, or microfiche copies of their catalogue; and CD-ROM copies are starting to appear. Libraries still with a manual catalogue may wish to duplicate it and keep a copy away from the library, although the problems of doing this for a large card catalogue are immense. Important material in the library's collections can also be considered for security copying, and the copy housed elsewhere than in the library. Some libraries carry out this activity as a routine matter, for example, with newspapers or university theses.

Because many library disasters have occurred during building renovations special care needs to be taken when these activities are being carried out. Measures such as liaising with building contractors and impressing on them the need for extra safety precautions, or covering stacks with polythene sheeting when work on roofs is being carried out, are examples.

Preventive measures against disasters affecting computer data and hardware are noted in an excellent article by Bruce R. Miller.[24] In addition to the usual requirements such as building security, some special requirements are helpful. An uninterrupted power supply prevents power surges and resulting data loss. Fire alarm sensors and sprinklers of recent design are suggested, as Miller considers that water damage is preferable to smoke damage for computers. Moisture detectors could be installed underfloor.

The matter of insurance is not covered here, but note that reduced premiums will result from an ability to demonstrate that a disaster plan exists and that disaster prevention measures have been taken.[25]

Response: The Second Phase

The response stage of disaster planning is that which is concerned with producing and documenting the disaster plan and with keeping that plan up-to-date. It is, like the first stage described above, part of preventive preservation because it is concerned with putting into place mechanisms which, if (or more likely when) implemented, will prevent more deterioration occurring than that which is directly a result of fire or flood damage.

The main activities to be undertaken here are: to form a disaster response team whose members are trained and who are likely to be available at the time of an emergency; to put together documentation, for example building floor plans, a list of personnel and their addresses and telephone numbers, a list of equipment, lists of suppliers of items needed during an emergency such as crates, newsprint or generators; to arrange for access to freezer capacity; to arrange a mechanism for paying for emergency needs; to adopt measures which ensure that damage is minimized if a disaster happens, for example, raising materials in the collections off the floor, ensuring that shelving has canopies on top to lessen water damage; and to test and keep current the disaster plan.

The first step is to establish a disaster response team chosen from the library's staff. The team should consist of members who together have a good overall knowledge of the library's collections and activities; some should also be senior enough to feel comfortable about making major decisions during a disaster. If possible – and this is probably very difficult to determine in advance – they should be cool, calm and collected during high-pressure emergency situations, for the decisions they may have to make then will sometimes have to be taken rapidly and will have a major impact on the salvage operation. If possible, the ability to improvise solutions from resources to hand should be sought. Common sense is probably the most essential qualification.

This team will be trained in disaster response techniques, and, in particular, in methods of entering a disaster site, identifying which actions are appropriate, removing material and making decisions about recovery techniques. One commonly used method of training is to participate in disaster workshops, where a disaster site can be simulated and techniques can be practised. The training will need to be regularly updated.

One early task for the team is to identify material which is irreplaceable and which should therefore be salvaged first in a disaster. This material should ideally be marked, for example its location noted on a floor plan or the enclosure it is kept in clearly labelled. Determining priorities is often a major and ongoing task, requiring clear definitions of the library's objectives, its collection development policy and the place of its holdings in the national collection. (What is hinted at here is, of course, the Research Libraries Group Conspectus approach, which is discussed in Chapter 9.) The disaster plan is concerned with only one aspect of this, the clear identification and marking of irreplaceable and important material.

An essential step is to gather together and maintain equipment which will be needed in recovery from a disaster. This equipment can usefully be separated into two categories: smaller items which can be assembled and placed in 'disaster boxes' at several sites throughout the library; and larger, usually more expensive items which can be stored at a central location, possibly away from the library but still close to it.

The contents of a disaster box vary from library to library, but will probably consist of items with which to clear up liquid spills or other hazardous materials (bucket and mop, perforated paper towels, sponges, dustpan and brush), material to cover parts of the collections in order to prevent further damage (polythene sheeting, scissors, polythene bags) and material used to organize activities during a disaster (whistle, pencils or chalk and writing paper, protective clothing such as gloves). These items are often housed in containers which can be easily moved around, for example, a disaster box in common use in libraries in Australia uses a large lightweight container on wheels with a handle designed for domestic rubbish disposal.[26]

Higher value and bulky items can be housed in a central store. Such items may include equipment and supplies such as plastic crates, wet-dry vacuum cleaners, pumps, dehumidifiers or fans, and further supplies of items in the disaster boxes likely to be used up rapidly such as polythene sheeting and paper towels.

A typical list of disaster control supplies and equipment is given in Table 5. Note that the quantities of any item purchased and kept in stock will depend on the size of the library.[27]

Making lists, the keystone of all library service, is also a central part of disaster planning. Lists of key personnel, services, and sources of equipment must be established and – very important – kept up-to-date. These lists must be available at locations both inside and outside the library. Personnel to be listed must obviously start with members of the disaster response team and should also include senior library staff, staff of services of the parent organization (for example, campus security or city council engineers department) and conservators in the region who have agreed to be available if a disaster should happen. Not only should lists be made, but procedures will need to be devised which notify personnel of the disaster and enable them to assemble rapidly. Lists of the location of important features of the building such as electrical switchboards, gas mains taps or water mains stopcocks will also be useful.

Services and sources of equipment to be listed include freezing and cold-store facilities, local transport hire businesses, local equipment hire businesses, plumbers, electricians, locksmiths. It will be necessary to contact these services and arrange for the use of their facilities after a disaster: for example, an agreement with a local commercial freezing firm could be negotiated whereby for a retainer a certain proportion of their freezer space is guaranteed to be available on demand. Lists of people in the area with training or experience in disaster response who have indicated that they are willing to assist can be compiled.

Table 5. Disaster Supplies and Equipment

Protective Clothing
Waterproof coats and trousers
Gumboots
Plastic safety helmets
Plastic aprons
Gloves (cotton or disposable plastic)

Cleaning and Packing Equipment
Mops and buckets
Buckets with lids
Squeegees
Slurpex
Water spray bottles
Chux
Wettex cloths
Sponges
Paper towels
Gladwrap
Scissors
White blotting paper
Clean newsprint
Polythene bags (various sizes)
Polythene sheets
Adhesive tape and dispensers
Plastic dustbin liners or rubbish bags

Disaster Site Entry Equipment
Polythene sheets (heavy duty)
Lamps
Torches and batteries
First-aid equipment

Supplementary Equipment
Plastic crates
Trolleys

Damage Recording Equipment
Clipboards
Pens and pencils
Notepads
Labels (tie-on)
Whistles
Chalk

Finally in this section, the plan and its lists need to be kept current. To do this a timetable for regular checking of the plan needs to be established, and a staff member (most likely to be a member of the disaster response team) appointed to carry out the checking.

Reaction: The Third Phase

The third phase of disaster planning is, unlike the first two, reactive rather than proactive. It is concerned with the procedures which should be followed when a disaster occurs.

Steps one and two are to raise the alarm and to assemble personnel. The procedures to do this should already be in place and well rehearsed. Fire alarm procedures and evacuation procedures should ensure that any immediate danger to people is minimized and that fire-fighting activities begin. What may need to be added to the presumably already existing emergency procedures for raising the alarm and evacuating personnel are procedures which also contact the leader of the disaster response team. The leader can then decide whether the team should be assembled; if this is required, then, the procedures already established in phase two should ensure that this is carried out rapidly.

The next step is to ensure that the disaster site is safe to enter. In major disasters the site will be declared safe by a senior officer of the fire brigade or police, while in smaller emergencies the disaster response team leader may be responsible. It is essential to ensure that the site is safe. This may involve such actions as turning off the mains power supply, turning off the gas, opening (or closing) windows and so on.

Once the disaster site is safe to enter, a preliminary assessment of the damage needs to be made by the leader of the disaster response team. The aim here is to make an estimate of the extent of damage and what equipment and supplies will be required. With this assessment made, the assessor can brief salvage personnel and make a preliminary allocation of tasks. Full care is needed when entering a disaster site, even when it has been declared safe. There could be, for example, water on the floors or obstructions caused by collapsed shelving.

Once the site can be entered and the extent of the damage has been ascertained, the next step is to remove damaged material. Several actions are involved. First, damaged material needs to be packed for transporting to a safer place, usually in plastic crates (milk or bread crates) or cardboard archives boxes. It needs to be recorded (brief details only, for example call number or brief title) so that it can be located later and for insurance assessment purposes. Photographic documentation may also be useful for insurance claim reasons. A treatment area needs to be set up, close to the disaster site if possible, to carry out minor treatment such as air-drying slightly wet material. An area for packing material which is to be frozen may also need to be established.

These actions require prior training, and preferably also some experience. The weather is often a critical factor in determining what action is required. If the temperature is low, then more time may be available to salvage wet books than if the temperature is high, when the possibility of mould growth is greatly increased. A first step is often to reduce the moisture content of the air (the air will be humid if a fire has been put out using water, for example) so that mould growth is hindered. There are many dos and don'ts, far too many to be noted in this chapter, and it is important that the best procedures are known and followed. Speed in assessing the damage to each item is essential, but mistakes can sometimes lead to items being made unusable by the application of inappropriate treatments.

To give some examples, shelving should normally be emptied from the top down to minimize the possibility of its collapse; dirty items must not be rubbed or brushed, as this only causes the dirt to penetrate further into the item, but may be gently washed down with clean water; wet open books should not be closed. Non-paper materials usually require different handling from paper materials, and these requirements must be known. These and many other actions and techniques need to be learnt by the members of the disaster response team. Some of them are noted in the 'Salvage Techniques' section following, and further information will be found in the bibliography. One essential book is Peter Waters' *Procedures for Salvage of Water-Damaged Library Materials*.[28]

Recovery: The Final Phase

The final phase is that of establishing and carrying out a program to restore both the disaster site and the damaged materials to a stable and usable condition. It is assumed here that damaged material has been removed from the site and immediate danger to it has been averted, by its treatment near the disaster site (for example, damp books have been air-dried).

At this stage there is more time available for careful planning. The immediate threat to the material has been removed, and what is now required are decisions as to which material needs to be restored to usable condition first, and what the best methods of restoring it are. Advice from a conservator will be needed. An assessment of available conservation options and an estimate of costs will need to be made. (Some options are noted in the following section.) Note that a less expensive option for some materials is to discard a damaged item and purchase a replacement, always assuming that it is still available. It is at this stage that the value of recording each item as it was removed from the site and sent to one of several destinations will be fully realized, as this record will allow decisions to be made, such as whether an item is to be unfrozen, discarded, replaced or rebound. Insurers will need to be contacted. In a disaster which has affected a large number of items it is likely that a phased conservation program will be needed to cope with the quantity and with the cost of restoring it to a usable condition.

The disaster site itself needs attention. It must be made habitable again. Steps such as clearing debris and drying carpets or floors should be taken, but other less obvious steps may also be necessary. The need to lower humidity levels was noted above; effective methods are the use of dehumidifiers and fans to keep air circulating. Good ventilation is important. Mould growth may need to be inhibited by washing walls, ceilings, floors and shelving with a fungicide: a conservator should advise on the best treatment. The temperature and relative humidity should be checked regularly to make sure that they have stabilized. Only when they have been stabilized at acceptable levels (noted in Chapter 4) should material be moved back in.

Refurbishing the disaster site and replacing damaged material in it may well provide an opportune time to assess and address problems. For example, shelves could be relocated so that they are no longer under water-pipes, the lowest shelf in each bay could be raised, or canopies could be fitted on the top of shelving. For the material itself, evaluation could be made of the kinds of enclosures used: did the boxes or containers afford any protection, or should open-topped pamphlet boxes be replaced by storage units with an enclosed top which might give more protection from water coming from above?

The final step in the recovery process is to assess the actions taken in order to improve the disaster plan. All staff involved with the disaster should be included in the assessment and their suggestions noted and, where appropriate, included in the disaster plan.

Salvage Techniques

Noted here are some of the more important techniques of treating damaged material and disaster sites in order to make them usable. Methods for drying wet and frozen materials and for controlling mould are described. As techniques are constantly improved, it is essential to keep informed of current practice, for example by attending workshops regularly and by reading the preservation literature.

Drying Techniques

Air-drying is the simplest technique to dry wet material. It works best on items which are damp rather than wet, and which are not too thick. The aim is to expose damp surfaces to an air flow which has a lower moisture content, thus drying out the damp item as moisture is transferred to the air flowing over it. A damp book can be stood up on its end and its pages fanned out, or its pages can be interleaved with absorbent paper. Although this is an effective technique which does not require expensive equipment or materials (fans and interleaving paper are the main requirements), it is tedious, labour-intensive and time-consuming.

Freeze-drying has been used since 1972 as a method of drying water-damaged paper-based materials. Wet items are first prepared for freezing. Wet books are put in polythene bags and then placed spine down in a plastic crate or a box made of strong cardboard. They are then frozen, usually in a commercial blast freezer at a temperature of -21°C or lower; the faster the freezing process the better, because the ice crystals formed will be smaller and less damaging to the items. They can be kept frozen for a long period, until such time as resources are available for drying them. The frozen items are then placed in a vacuum chamber in which a vacuum lowers the boiling point of water and causes the ice to evaporate without going through the liquid state. The water vapour is drawn off as it is produced. It is a slow process, with drying runs taking from one and a half to three weeks, but it can be hastened by heating the walls or shelves of the chamber up to about 37°C.[29]

A.E. Parker has described the freeze-drying process and its effects on various kinds of material.[30] Although water stains and cockling of paper can result, and some bindings will become slightly distorted, the end result produces items which can be put back for use in a library collection. The process does not kill mould spores and care must be taken to prevent mould growth. The equipment is expensive and the process time-consuming, but the technique is widely available commercially and is effective.

Other methods of drying are available. The use of microwave ovens has been described several times in the library literature, but is still an untested technique and is best avoided until more is known about its effect on paper, glue and binding material. Dry air purging is a technique for large-scale treatment. The whole building or site is sealed by wrapping it in plastic sheeting, and dry air at about 26°C and 15 per cent relative humidity is pumped through. This technique is most effective on thin loose items such as paper-based records. It has the advantages of working rapidly and of being applied to materials in situ, but is a high-tech solution and can only be used where the site can be effectively sealed off.

It has already been noted above that library materials other than paper-based materials may require different salvage techniques to make them usable. The salvaging of water-damaged computer floppy discs is one example, described in a 1986 article.[31] Slightly wet disks were air-dried using a hairdryer to provide a cool air flow. Soaked disks were removed from their plastic sleeves, carefully wiped dry, then hung up to air-dry. When dry they were put into a new sleeve and copied. All data were recovered.

Mould Control

Most disasters involve water, either because water was the cause or because water was used to extinguish the source. With excess water comes increased humidity and the possibility of mould growth. Mould control techniques are for this reason often required in the aftermath of a disaster. They can be classified into two groups: those which do not use chemicals, and those which do.

Controlling mould growth by altering environmental conditions has already been noted, both in a section earlier in this chapter ('Reaction: The Third Phase'), where the reduction of moisture content was noted, and in Chapter 4. If mould is already present, it can be cleaned off, but precautions are necessary. The affected items must only be cleaned in an area separate from other materials, so that mould is not spread. It can be done outside, for instance, or in a fume-cover or beneath a fume-hood. A vacuum cleaner can be used. Masks and gloves should be worn. Some people may be affected with respiratory problems caused by the mould, and attention should be paid to this.

Control without using chemicals is also possible during the freeze-drying process. The vacuum chamber can be flooded with CO_2 (carbon dioxide) gas which removes the oxygen necessary for mould to grow.

Mould control using fungicides is an area where considerable specialist knowledge is needed. A conservator or a specialist in the use of fungicides should always be consulted. The major fungicides in use at present are thymol, ortho-phenyl phenol and ethylene oxide. None is without its problems. Thymol is toxic and its use is banned in some jurisdictions. Ortho-phenyl phenol, while of lower toxicity, can cause health problems such as eye irritations. Ethylene oxide has been identified as a carcinogenic. It is highly toxic and thus effective as a fungicide, but is very harmful to humans as well. It can only be used under controlled conditions, and any material treated with it needs careful airing before it can be handled. Chapter 7 notes chemical techniques for controlling mould.

Gamma irradiation is also sometimes used to kill mould. It is an effective non-chemical method, but has possible harmful effects on cellulose and protein and has not yet been widely adopted. Research is being carried out into other techniques for controlling mould, such as those using low pressure and nitrogen.[32]

Conclusion

If a disaster plan is being considered, then an important step is to note the contents of disaster plans of other libraries or similar organizations such as archives. Local libraries should be approached first to see if they have plans; local precedent is important because there will have already been listed sources of equipment, materials and expertise nearby, and because there may be the possibility of regional cooperation. One published disaster plan, for the Nebraska State Historical Society, is found in the Society of American Archivists' Problems in Archives Kit X, *Disaster Prevention and Preparedness*.[33] Another useful manual to assist in disaster planning is the excellent *Planning Manual for Disaster Control in Scottish Libraries and Record Offices* already referred to.

A chapter as brief as this cannot offer more than an introduction to disaster planning in general and can only describe some basic principles and a few salvage and recovery procedures. It is no more than a guide to producing a disaster plan. It is limited in its emphasis to paper-based materials, and while most library collections still consist largely of material in this category, there is an increasing amount of other media which need different handling and treatment in a disaster. With these caveats in mind it is imperative that all libraries prepare a documented, rehearsed and up-to-date disaster plan. Steps towards this are: 1) read widely; 2) learn and practise techniques by attending a disaster planning workshop (perhaps you will need first to initiate one in your area); 3) make sure your library starts planning for disaster; and 4) ensure that the staff of your library are trained in disaster response techniques.

Notes

1   Hazel Anderson and John E. McIntyre, *Planning Manual for Disaster Control in Scottish Libraries and Record Offices* (Edinburgh: National Library of Scotland, 1985), p. 9. I am indebted to Alan Howell for many of the ideas expressed in this chapter.

2   Sally A. Buchanan, *Disaster Planning: Preparedness and Recovery for Libraries and Archives; A RAMP Study with Guidelines* (Paris: Unesco, 1988), p. 7.

3   Claire England and Karen Evans, *Disaster Management for Libraries: Planning and Process* (Ottawa, Canadian Library Association, 1988), pp. 128-129.

4   I am indebted to Bruce Smith for supplying some of this information.

5   One excellent account of the Florence floods is Anna Lenzuni, 'Coping with Disaster', in *Preservation of Library Materials: Conference Held at the National Library of Austria, Vienna, April 7-10, 1986*, ed. Merrily A. Smith (München: K.G. Saur, 1987), Vol. 2, pp. 98-102.

6   Tom Watson, 'Out of the Ashes: The Los Angeles Public Library', *Wilson Library Bulletin* (December 1989): 34-38, 41, describes the fire and its aftermath.

7   'Leningrad Library Fire', *Abbey Newsletter* 12, 4 (1988): 59-61; 'Special Report: Fire at the USSR Academy of Sciences Library', *Library Journal* (15 June 1988): 10, 12; 'Soviet Library Fire', *Conservation Administration News* 34 (1988): 16.

8   *American Libraries* 15 (April 1984): 201.

9   *Library Journal* 110, 19 (1985): 14.

10 Dean Burgess, 'The Library Has Blown Up!', *Library Journal* (1 October 1989): 59-61.

11 *Library Journal* (15 November 1989): 15; *Library Journal* (December 1989): 20.

12 Peter Waters, 'Phased Preservation: A Philosophical Concept and Practical Approach to Preservation', *Special Libraries* 81, 1 (1990): 35-43.

13 Hilda Bohem, *Disaster Prevention and Disaster Preparedness* (Berkeley, Calif.: University of California, 1978).

14 Anderson and McIntyre, *op. cit.*

15 *Conservation in the Library*, ed. Susan Garretson Swartzburg (Westport, Conn.: Greenwood Press, 1983), pp. 22-23.

16 Buchanan, *op. cit.*, p. 105.

17 James W. Morentz, 'Computerizing Libraries for Emergency Planning', *Special Libraries* 78, 2 (1987): 100-104.

18 *Keeping Archives*, ed. Anne Pederson (Sydney: Australian Society of Archivists, 1987), p. 228.

19 Pamela W. Darling and Duane E. Webster, *Preservation Planning Program: An Assisted Self-Study Manual for Libraries.* Expanded 1987 ed. (Washington, D.C.: Association of Research Libraries, Office of Management Studies, 1987).

20 This and following sections rely heavily on *Disaster in Libraries: Prevention and Control,* ed. Max W. Borchardt (Camberwell, Vic.: CAVAL, 1988), which is based on Anderson and McIntyre, *op. cit.*

21   This list is based on one in *RLG Preservation Manual*. 2nd ed. (Stanford, Calif.: Research Libraries Group, 1986), pp. 132-133.

22   *Conservation in the Library* (1983), *op. cit.*, pp. 20-21.

23   John P. Barton and Johanna G. Wellheiser, *An Ounce of Prevention: A Handbook on Disaster Contingency Planning for Archives, Libraries and Record Centres* (Toronto: Toronto Area Archivists Group Education Foundation, 1985), pp. 10-15; *Preservation Planning Program Resource Notebook*, comp. Pamela W. Darling; rev. ed. Wesley L. Boomgaarden (Washington, D.C.: Association of Research Libraries, Office of Management Studies, 1987), pp. 309-318.

24   R. Bruce Miller, 'Libraries and Computers: Disaster Prevention and Recovery', *Information Technology and Libraries* 7, 4 (1988): 349-358.

25   For more on insurance see Donald L. Ungarelli, 'Insurance and Prevention: Why and How?', *Library Trends* 33 (1984): 57-67, and sections in John Morris, *The Library Disaster Preparedness Handbook* (Chicago, Ill.: American Library Association, 1986).

26   Another mobile version, a salvage trolley, is described in Robert Hill, 'Salvage on the Move', *Library Conservation News* 16 (1987): 3, 8.

27   Based on *Disaster in Libraries* (1988), *op. cit.*, p. 26.

28   Peter Waters, *Procedures for Salvage of Water-Damaged Library Materials*. 2nd ed. (Washington, D.C.: Library of Congress, 1979).

29   A comprehensive study is John M. McCleary, *Vacuum Freeze-Drying, a Method Used to Salvage Water-Damaged Archival and Library Materials: A RAMP Study with Guidelines* (Paris: Unesco, 1987).

30   A.E. Parker, 'The Freeze-Drying Process: Some Conclusions', *Library Conservation News* 23 (1989): 4-6.

31   Nancy B. Olson, 'Hanging Your Software up to Dry', *College and Research Libraries News* 47, 10 (1986): 634-636. See also Larry N. Osborne, 'Those (In) destructible Disks; or, Another Myth Exploded', *Library Hi-Tech* 7, 3 (1989): 7-10, 28.

32   Summarized in 'Fumigation', *Conservation of Library Materials: The Newsletter of the Special Interest Group of the Australian Library and Information Association* 5 (1989): 1-4.

33   Judith Fortson-Jones, *Disaster Prevention and Recovery Plan Nebraska State Historical Society* (1980), in *Disaster Prevention and Preparedness*, Problems in Archives Kit X (1982).

Chapter 7

Preserving the Artefact: Book Maintenance and Repair Procedures, and Binding

Introduction

This chapter describes conservation procedures which are commonly applied to objects in library collections to keep them in good repair and to prevent future deterioration. It is concerned, as Morrow and Dyall put it, with 'those aspects of in-house physical maintenance and repair that prevent needless deterioration and return damaged items to usable condition.'[1] The primary emphasis here is on paper-based material, especially books. Library materials other than those on paper are not noted here, although some general guidance about such formats is to be found in Chapter 2 and in other sources.[2] Only those procedures which are relatively simple are noted here.

The intention in this chapter is not so much to describe how to carry out the repair and maintenance procedures, but rather to put each procedure into the context of an overall library preservation program: where each procedure fits into the program, when it is appropriate and when it should not be applied, and who might carry out each procedure. The repair and maintenance operation is only one part of an integrated preservation program, along with other components such as commercial library binding (noted below in this chapter), staff and user education, reformatting (microfilming or photocopying, for example) and environmental control. Careful coordination between the repair and maintenance operation and other parts of the preservation program is essential if the preservation dollar is to be spent to produce the best, most economical result.

Three texts have been used as the basis of this chapter, and should be referred to for further information, particularly for more detailed descriptions and illustrations, of how to carry out maintenance and repair procedures. They are Carolyn Horton's *Cleaning and Preserving Bindings and Related Materials*, 2nd ed. (as this was published in 1969, some of the techniques she describes may have been superseded); Carolyn Clark Morrow and Carole Dyall's *Conservation Treatment Procedures*, 2nd ed.; and Helen Price's *Stopping the Rot*, 2nd ed.[3] Some procedures are also described in Cunha and Cunha's *Library and Archives Conservation* (1983) and in Ritzenthaler's *Archives and Manuscripts: Conservation* (1983).[4]

The chapter concludes with sections about binding which examine the significance of binding as a preservation technique and note some factors to be considered in binding library materials.

The Importance of Professional Advice

In an ideal world there would be enough trained and experienced conservators and conservation technicians employed in libraries to carry out all repair and maintenance procedures, and all other conservation procedures as well. The reality is that only a small handful of libraries have such staff, and only a few of those will have enough of such staff. It is far more likely (after the most likely case, where no repairing and maintenance of the stock are carried out) that a librarian or other staff member will be in charge of untrained personnel and will have the responsibilities of training staff, supervising their work on an ongoing basis and keeping up-to-date with the latest conservation procedures.

George and Dorothy Cunha note that perhaps as much as 80 per cent of conservation treatments in the library can be carried out by non-specialist staff – students or volunteers, for example. They strongly emphasize the need for employees who are careful, have clear instructions to follow, and are well supervised.[5] The supervisor, perhaps a conservator but in reality much more likely to be a librarian, must make it his or her top priority to become informed and stay informed about the procedures available and about new techniques being developed and introduced. There is more danger in applying an inappropriate treatment to a deteriorated item than in doing nothing at all; this point is developed below. Keeping up-to-date can be done by keeping abreast of the conservation literature and by seeking regular advice from a conservator, perhaps on a regular consultancy basis. A conservator should also be hired at the initial stages to set up the repair and maintenance program.

It is essential that those who are responsible for deciding which conservation procedures to apply know what they are doing. If there is any doubt at all, the advice of a conservator should be sought.

Selection for Treatment: Choosing the Best Procedure

Selection is a key element in the repair and maintenance program. The question: 'Which items are selected for treatment?' must be addressed first. This is one of the major decisions to be made in any preservation program, and must be made in terms of an item's physical condition, value and use, and with regard to the collection development policy of the library. The questions involved in selection of items to be conserved will be examined in more detail in Chapter 8.

The second question to pose is: 'Who chooses the treatment?' The answer depends on the nature of the library and its collections. For special items, for example valuable books with special value to the collection, liaison between subject specialist and conservator or preservation librarian is necessary to determine the value of an item in relation to the cost and nature of its treatment. An early printed book may warrant full-scale treatment (disbinding, deacidification, paper repair, rebinding) on the grounds of its importance to the collection, while another early printed book which is more peripheral to the collection may warrant nothing more than the construction of a protective box. For books in a circulating collection, it is more likely that the choice of treatment is made by staff at the circulation desk, applying guidelines to decide on commonly occurring problems such as loose hinges on a binding, paper tears or the need for a new spine.

'Which treatment to apply?' is the third question. Answers need to be based on a knowledge of what is feasible for the library in technological, financial and practical terms. As already noted, the value of an item to a collection, both at present and in the future, must also be considered. For routine items, guidelines can be developed to allow decisions to be made quickly and efficiently. For example, the decision could be made to put all thin pamphlets in acid-free envelopes. Costs are also important here too. Comparative costs of replacement, microfilming, of standard repairs and of binding costs should be known and regularly updated and used as part of the decision-making process. The selection of which treatment to apply to special items needs to be considered more fully.[6]

Importance of Using Archival-Quality Materials

It is essential to use only high quality materials in the repair of library items. Nothing should be used which is, or could be, harmful to the item. For example, paper or board used in repairs should be acid-free and preferably alkaline-buffered so that acid is not introduced into the item or added to what is already present; adhesive should not be made from chemicals which are harmful, and its action should be reversible. The IFLA *Principles for the Preservation and Conservation of Library Materials* clearly state that 'materials used in bindings, covers, boxes, etc., should all be of archival quality to ensure the materials themselves do not result in chemical damage to library materials. Paper and board, etc., should be acid-free with an initial pH of 7 or higher.'[7]

Care is required when selecting and purchasing materials. As one example, not all plastic film sold under the name Mylar is acceptable. Some grades of Mylar used for food packaging are coated with polyvinylidene chloride; polyvinylidene chloride is not archival, as it can break down to hydrochloric acid.[8] The three manuals noted above (Horton, 1969; Morrow and Dyall, 1986; Price, 1989) all include directions on which kinds of materials to use, and advice can be sought from a conservator about local sources for such materials.

Ethical Aspects

The ethical aspects of conservation procedures have already been referred to in Chapter 1, where Roger Ellis' repair rules were noted. These rules should guide all personnel who choose and apply conservation treatments. To refresh the reader's memory, they direct the conservator to ensure that all procedures are reversible, that procedures must not alter the evidential value of the item being conserved, that procedures must not weaken or damage the item, and that the minimum amount of action necessary to repair the item should be applied. Some of these points are expanded here.

Reversibility of treatments is required because the state of the conservator's art is still such that there can sometimes be doubt about the long-term effects of some conservation treatments, despite the best intentions of all concerned. The rule of reversibility, that an item can be taken back to the condition it was in before treatment was applied, has been developed as an insurance policy in case the longer-term evidence indicates that damage is being caused by that treatment.[9] Lamination and silk backing of paper are examples of treatments which were at one time widely applied but are now recognized as damaging to some materials.

Compatibility of problem and solution is required: that is, the treatment applied should be of approximately equal strength to the material being repaired. The consequences of not observing this tenet are that deterioration of the item being repaired is more rapid than it was before the treatment was applied; in other words the treatment has caused more harm than good. For example, if an unsuitably strong repair material is used on weak paper, it will actually exacerbate the damage because it puts more stress on weak parts near the stronger repair material. The converse is also true.

Another principle to be observed sometimes is that of benign neglect. It may on occasion be that the best treatment is to do nothing. This may arise when, for example, there is no acceptable solution yet developed; in such cases careful handling and storage, and reducing use while awaiting an acceptable solution (or doing the research to develop a suitable technique oneself) is best.

Documentation of treatments applied may be necessary for some items in a library collection, especially for special or valuable items. Examples of documentation forms are given in the literature.[10] Such documentation is not necessary for the routine maintenance and repair of items in the collection.

REFURBISHING AND COLLECTION MAINTENANCE

Refurbishing the Collection

Many library collections are in extremely poor condition overall, and it may be possible to institute a refurbishing project if resources can be found. Such a project aims at collection maintenance, through cleaning all items in the collection and its physical surroundings, applying protective measures to items which need them, such as boxes around damaged or fragile items, carrying out minor binding repairs, identifying items which require more advanced conservation work, and reshelving the refurbished items.

Carolyn Horton describes the procedures involved in refurbishing a collection in *Cleaning and Preserving Bindings and Related Materials*, in which she gives a work flow diagram which forms the basis of the following section.[11] Her directions are intended for collections which contain a wide range of bindings, for example vellum and leather bindings, but can be adapted for other collections. A preliminary step is to alter any features which have caused the deterioration, for example, to change any unsuitable lighting and heating conditions in the stack areas (see Chapter 4). The steps to follow are:

1   Set up a work area and obtain equipment and supplies.
2   Establish documentation procedures.
3   Remove the books from the shelves.
4   Dust the books.
5   Sort the books into two categories:
    a)   those which require professional conservation treatment; in these cases, record titles, and either send to the conservation laboratory for treatment, or reshelve for later action.
    b)   those which can be treated in the library (for these, see next steps).
6   Sort books in category 5 (b) into two categories:
    a)   cloth, paper, vellum, alum-tawed bindings;
    b)   leather bindings other than alum-tawed.
7   For books in category 6 (a):
    a)   sort into treatment categories (clean, repair corners, enclosure, etc. – see later in this chapter);
    b)   apply the appropriate treatment or treatments;
    c)   reshelve.
8   For books in category 6 (b):
    a)   treat (see later in this chapter);
    b)   apply leather dressing;
    c)   carry out any other treatment required;
    d)   reshelve.

Horton's descriptions of establishing procedures and of cleaning will be helpful, as will her directions about the careful transport of items. However, some of the treatments she describes may have been superseded (for example, her advice on treating leather bindings). It is essential to seek the advice of an experienced conservator, at least during the planning stages of any refurbishing program.

Descriptions of several refurbishing projects have been published. The Long Room Project at Trinity College, Dublin, is described in *Preserving Our Printed Heritage*.[12] This description indicates the major activities involved:

removing books for treatment; vacuum cleaning the shelf surface; vacuum cleaning the binding; dry-cleaning the text block; documentation; cleaning tawed and vellum covers; consolidating 'red rot' on leather bindings; leather dressing; minor repairs to the binding; joint tackets (a method devised at Trinity College Library to reattach boards as a temporary measure); the book shoe; the phase box; new leather spines; and lining the shelves.

The second project described is that at the Parker Library at Corpus Christi College, Cambridge. Here a survey carried out by a conservator resulted in improvements to equipment used in the reading room and in a maintenance program, for which the library was closed for five months. Storage facilities and shelving were considerably upgraded, a regular cleaning program instituted, and a refurbishing program started. Special attention was paid to the many important manuscripts in the collection, and their rehousing and conservation are described.[13]

A third project was carried out on the Law Library collection at the Library of Congress.[14] Here the steps carried out were: dusting of books and shelves; documentation; cleaning and oiling of leather bindings; treatments such as wrapping in polyester jackets, boxing in phase boxes, placing in alkaline-buffered envelopes; lining the shelves.

The three projects described above relate to library collections which contain large quantities of special materials, especially old printed books and manuscripts. There is no reason why a refurbishing program cannot be carried out in any kind of library. One aspect of the Parker Library project was that a special Furbishing Team worked only on Saturday mornings. This concept could be readily applied in libraries where minimum disruption of the normal routine is essential.

Ongoing Collection Maintenance

One major aspect of ongoing collection maintenance is a regular cleaning program. The importance of this, and the requirements for and effects of such a program, have already been noted in Chapter 4. Another ongoing activity should be keeping the shelves tidy, to ensure that books are kept upright and well supported (see Chapter 5).

Ongoing collection maintenance involves the same activities as in the refurbishing project noted above, except that it is carried out as a continuing activity. How this is arranged depends on the library and its staffing arrangements. In larger libraries a staff member could be employed whose primary task is to move through the stacks cleaning, tidying and carrying out minor repairs. Smaller libraries could set a series of goals, such as that a particular part of the collection should be examined and maintenance carried out at specified times. The ideal is to have every item in a collection examined at least once every two years. Although this is an ideal which is probably rarely achieved, it is worth aiming at. The results, in terms of making more items as usable as possible for as long a time as possible, will repay the effort.

REPAIRS

'An active and well-organized book repair program is a vital maintenance activity' in the library, notes Carolyn Morrow, because of the sharp decline in the quality of book manufacturing and, more particularly, in paper quality and publishers' bindings.[15] This section considers the range and nature of simple repairs which can be readily carried out to maintain the collection in good and usable condition. Regularly carrying out repairs such as these will result in financial savings: it is obviously cheaper to spend five minutes tightening the hinges of a book and to keep it out of circulation for a day or two than to have the book rebound at a later stage at a much greater cost, with the book unavailable for several weeks or several months. Some fumigation procedures are also noted here.

The treatments noted here are not for special or rare materials. They are intended to be applied only to the *repair* of circulating materials – books and serials – and works in reference collections which receive heavy use. Special or rare materials have different requirements, where the evidence of use and the consequent physical state of the work may be important evidence for the scholar. The list of basic repairs noted here is not comprehensive. A good description of more advanced techniques is found in Morrow and Dyall's *Conservation Treatment Procedures*.[16] It should be emphasized again that considerable care in selecting and applying conservation procedures is necessary. If in doubt, ask the advice of a conservator; and use caution by testing the method on a sample initially.

Equipment

What equipment is needed, and where is it best located in the library? The answer to both of these questions is – it depends. The equipment required varies from the extremely simple and inexpensive – a bone folder, a cutting mat or board, scissors, a soft brush – to the more expensive and space-consuming – a standing press or board shears. Simple treatments do not usually require sophisticated equipment. The 'tool kit' suggested by Helen Price for the simple repairs she describes in *Stopping the Rot* contains nothing which is difficult to obtain or which, with two exceptions, a vacuum cleaner and a light-box, should cost more than a few dollars.[17] Her list is:

scissors	long steel rule	cutter
set square	cutting board	pencil
white plastic eraser	document cleaning pad	weights
soft dusting brush	vacuum cleaner	bone folder
lens cleaning tissue	methyl cellulose paste	satay stick
flat nosed tweezers	fine nosed tweezers	lightbox
white blotter	polyester film	clean duster
pure eucalyptus oil	distilled water	cotton wool
magnifying glass	fine spray bottle	PVA adhesive

A full-scale conservation laboratory is not necessary for running repairs of the kind noted here. A mobile workstation is a possibility, one which can be moved around the stacks as part of an ongoing repair program. Its top could provide a working surface, with storage for equipment and materials in cabinets beneath. A fixed workstation taking little space is described in the *Preservation Planning Program Resource Notebook*, together with lists of tools and materials.[18] This workstation can be located in a corner of a staff area. Setting up a conservation laboratory is a major task, and is noted in the literature by Walsh and by Ritzenthaler.[19]

Preliminary Examination

It is obvious that items must be examined in order to decide whether they need repairs carried out to them, and to decide what sort of repair is required. This examination should be the opportunity to note the presence, or not, of other factors and may provide the opportunity to remedy minor faults. For example, anything which is enclosed in the book should be located and probably discarded: paper (probably acidic) used as bookmarks, paperclips, pins, rubber bands – all will mark the book's paper. If such enclosures are relevant to the item, as, for example, newspaper clippings of reviews of that item, then they should be placed in an acid-free envelope and kept with the book to await further treatment. Acid migration may be apparent. This may have arisen from tissues placed over plates in older books, originally intended to protect the plate but in reality having exactly the opposite effect, or from acidic paper used in book-plates, or from inserted newspaper clippings. It may on occasion be possible simply to remove and discard the offending paper; or, if insertions are to be kept, they can be placed in a separate envelope.

Descriptions of the treatments noted below are found in the five texts cited in notes 3 and 4 at the end of this chapter. In the descriptions below these sources are cited briefly as: Cunha, 1983; Horton, 1969; Morrow and Dyall, 1986; Price, 1989; Ritzenthaler, 1983.

Timings of each procedure, where given, are taken from Morrow and Dyall, 1986. *It is essential that these sources be referred to for more detailed descriptions, in particular for illustrations, of the procedures, before any repairs are attempted.* In addition, if at all possible, an experienced practitioner should be observed carrying out the procedures. It is assumed here that the reader has some knowledge of the structure of a book. If this is not the case, the illustrations in Horton, 1969, especially that on page 15, and in Morrow and Dyall, 1986, will be helpful.

Dealing with Acid Migration

Acid migration is recognized by staining or browning and occurs when acid moves from paper to adjacent paper of lower acidity. Ideally the offending acidic paper should be removed and discarded. Sometimes this is not desirable because the acidic paper is printed on (captions for plates are one common example) and needs to be retained for its informational content. In these cases, sheets of archival paper should be placed on either side of the acidic paper, or after the flyleaf if the end-paper is acidic (Horton, 1969, pp. 26-27.)

Cleaning Paper

The surface of paper sheets, usually single sheets rather than those in bound volumes, will on occasion need to have dirt removed. The dirt is brushed off with a soft flat brush, a solid white soft plastic eraser used, or a document cleaning pad applied, according to the kind of paper and its condition (brittle papers, for example, will not be able to stand much or any abrasive action). Caution is recommended initially, to test the effect of the cleaning procedure on the surface being cleaned. Caution should also be displayed when cleaning paper with manuscript annotations, which may be archivally significant; they may, on the other hand, be more in the nature of graffiti. White cotton gloves should be worn to keep hands clean, and work surfaces should be kept clean to avoid further soiling of the paper being cleaned (Cunha, 1983, p. 144; Horton, 1969, p. 32; Price, 1969, pp. 20-21; Ritzenthaler, 1983, pp. 95-98).

Cleaning Bindings

Soiled cloth bindings can be cleaned by one of several methods, none of which is, though, reported as particularly effective. Proprietary cleaning preparations may be used; soap and water should be used only on waterproof bookcloth, but not on other bookcloth because it will remove the sizing and colour; or an eraser can be applied. The cleaning of leather bindings is noted below in the section 'Leather Cleaning and Dressing' (Horton, 1969, p. 34).

Relaxing Paper

Paper sheets which have been rolled up for a long period of time need careful unrolling or 'relaxing' to avoid the possibility that they will break into fragments if forced open. In the relaxing process moisture is reintroduced into the paper, whose fibres can then flex again, and the paper is unrolled by flattening it under weights and blotting paper. Moisture can be introduced by using one of several methods (it may first be necessary to test the ink or paint on the paper for solubility in water): spraying with distilled water, placing the paper between moistened blotters, or by using a humidification chamber. A humidification chamber can be easily improvised, for example from a plastic rubbish bin or from polythene sheeting (Price, 1989, pp. 22, 28; Ritzenthaler, 1983, p. 90).

Removing Adhesives

Most readers will be familiar with the damage caused to paper by pressure-sensitive adhesive tapes, such as Sellotape, which when they age become brittle and discolour the paper they are attached to. Pressure-sensitive adhesive tapes will normally need to be removed from paper. This is done by carefully applying small quantities of a solvent and, as the adhesive softens, pulling the tape off. This process is slow and calls for considerable patience and care. Given the difficulty of removing pressure-sensitive adhesive tape, it is obvious that the best solution is never to apply it in the first place (Horton, 1969, p. 27).

Mending Tears in Paper

The standard method of repairing tears in paper is by patching them with strong acid-free paper which is as near transparent as possible. Handmade Japanese papers of various sorts (Sekishu and Tengujo are frequently used), which are long-fibred and which can themselves be torn easily to fit the shape of the tear which is to be repaired, or lens cleaning tissue are usually used. A good archival-quality adhesive is also essential; starch-based paste (Cunha gives a recipe) or methyl cellulose paste are used. This method involves cutting or tearing two patches a little larger than the shape of the tear to be mended, applying the adhesive on both sides of the paper being repaired, sticking on the patches, and allowing the repaired tear to dry under weights. (Price suggests that two patches, one on each side, are needed when using lens tissue, whereas Ritzenthaler suggests that for repairs using Japanese paper only one side needs to be patched.) The time needed is about five minutes per mend (Cunha, 1983, pp. 145-148; Horton, 1969, p. 27; Morrow and Dyall, 1986, pp. 105, 113; Price, 1989, p. 24; Ritzenthaler, 1983, p. 102).

Heat-set tissue is also used to mend paper. This is thin tissue paper impregnated with resins which, when heated by a tacking iron with pressure applied, adheres to the paper. Again the tissue is torn or cut to fit the tear, laid on top of the tear and an iron applied. It is not suitable for applying to all kinds of paper, but is commonly used to repair tears in newspapers, for example, prior to microfilming them. About five minutes per mend is required (Cunha, 1983, pp. 148-149; Morrow and Dyall, 1986, pp. 113-116).

Tightening Hinges

Publishers' case bindings are structurally weak and, if roughly treated (in book return chutes or by careless handling), it is common for text blocks to sag or pull away from their covers. If not repaired at an early stage, rebinding will be necessary. The few minutes needed for this procedure and its small cost are obviously preferable to expensive and time-consuming rebinding. To tighten a book's hinges, a knitting needle or satay stick coated with PVA glue is used to apply adhesive to the end-papers where they have pulled away from their covers, on the sides nearest the covers; protective waxed paper is then inserted between the endpaper and the flyleaf to prevent glue spreading where it is not wanted; and the book is dried under weight. Each hinge-tightening procedure requires about five minutes (Horton, 1969, p. 29; Morrow and Dyall, 1986, p. 15).

Enclosures; Tipping In

It is occasionally necessary or helpful to keep together a book and items which are not an intrinsic part of that book, for example letters from the author of the book, or newspaper clippings. Some of these items can be enclosed in an acid-free envelope and kept near the book, correctly labelled (see Horton, 1969, p. 24). Others can be tipped in, that is, glued in with a thin strip of adhesive applied down one side of the page (see Price, 1989, p. 36), or hinged in, by gluing them to a hinge made from a thin strip of paper which is in turn glued to the book (see Horton, 1969, pp. 24-26). Tipping in is also used to reattach loose single pages to books.

Leather Cleaning and Dressing

Leather bindings need ongoing maintenance to ensure that they are in good condition and do not become dry and brittle. They need to be treated initially to provide a protective coating, then a leather dressing needs to be applied at regular intervals. Because suggested treatments vary from author to author, and because experience is necessary to identify the kinds of leather bindings to which treatments should be applied (these treatments are not appropriate for all leather bindings), it is essential to get expert advice. Both Horton and Ritzenthaler recommend the use of a potassium lactate solution for the initial treatment to introduce protective salts and to neutralize acids in the leather. The use at Trinity College Library Dublin of hydroxypropyl cellulose in alcohol to strengthen the leather before dressing it is noted in *Preserving Our Printed Heritage*.[20]

Regular leather dressing was recommended in past years, suggested frequencies varying from once per year (Price) to once every five years (Ritzenthaler). Recent studies of the effects of leather dressing suggest that it has no preservative effect and may in fact be positively harmful.[21] The dressing, made up according to different formulas which take account of the environmental conditions in which the collections are stored and which usually contain neat's-foot oil and lanolin, is rubbed into the leather, left to dry for about twenty-four hours, then polished (Horton, 1969, pp. 43-54; Price, 1989, p. 37; Ritzenthaler, 1983, pp. 109-113).

Refurbishing Bindings

Bindings will frequently need more extensive repair than the simple tightening of hinges. Torn endsheets may need to be replaced, spines renewed, the text block recased using the original case, a new cover put on, headpieces and tailpieces repaired, or corners rebuilt. These procedures, while not especially difficult to learn, require more technical knowledge and experience, and more equipment and materials, than the procedures noted above. They can usefully be included in a repair and maintenance program, but only if further commitments of time and money are made. Another essential requirement is that expert advice from a binder or conservator is available at several stages: establishing the program, teaching the staff who will be carrying out the repairs to bindings, and monitoring the program regularly. If there is an in-house bindery already established, there should be no difficulty in establishing routines to deal with binding refurbishment on an ongoing basis; but if no bindery is present, serious consideration should be given in a large library to establishing a repair program which has binding refurbishment as a major component. Morrow and Dyall, 1986, and Horton, 1969, describe and illustrate many of the procedures for refurbishing bindings.

Fumigation

Chapter 4 notes methods other than fumigation which are used to control insect and other biological pests in libraries. These are 'passive' methods, that is, they do not require the use of chemical pesticides. As already noted in Chapter 4, chemical methods are only a temporary solution and have little or no residual effect, and in fact much chemical fumigation carried out in libraries may be unwarranted. Recent legislation in several countries has banned the use of chemicals once commonly used for fumigation: as Mary Wood Lee has stated rather disarmingly, 'All biocides have some level of mammalian toxicity.'[22] Because the use of chemical fumigation methods requires considerable expertise and may pose considerable health risks to both the fumigator and anyone who handles chemically treated materials, it is essential that expert advice is sought before any fumigation or other chemical control measure is carried out; indeed the application of chemical fumigation by amateurs (all librarians, that is) should not even be contemplated. It is also especially important that up-to-date information is obtained about the chemicals before they are applied, as knowledge about the health hazards of chemicals changes rapidly.[23] This section notes some of the simpler methods of chemical fumigation in common use in the recent past: they are described here with the proviso that *expert advice must be sought before applying them.*

Thymol has been widely used in the past to fumigate infested library materials, although its use is now prohibited in the United Kingdom. It is applied by placing affected materials in an air-tight chamber with a dish of thymol crystals, which is then heated by being placed near a low wattage light bulb. The material being fumigated is exposed to thymol vapour for periods varying from three days to one week. The thymol vapour must not be inhaled and care must be taken to avoid this, especially when opening the thymol chamber at the completion of the treatment. Skin contact with the thymol crystals must also be avoided. Concerns about the toxicity of thymol are summarized in a 1989 article in *Conservation of Library Materials.*[24] Ritzenthaler describes in detail procedures for the use of thymol and also for ortho-phenyl phenol.[25]

Ortho-phenyl phenol has been widely used despite some doubts about its effectiveness as a fungicide. It can be applied in several ways, for example by mixing it with alcohol and applying it as a fog or spray, or by mixing it with alcohol and allowing it to evaporate in a sealed chamber or other enclosed space. As with thymol, care must be taken to avoid inhaling the vapour of ortho-phenyl phenol or allowing skin to come into contact with it.[26]

Tissue paper can be coated or soaked with a fungicide and placed inside books which need to be treated; the book with its tissues is then placed in a sealed plastic bag for several months. A description of how to make fungicidal tissue using a 5 per cent solution of sodium ortho-phenyl phenate is given by Baynes-Cope.[27] Care must be taken when handling this solution, as it is caustic.

It must be reiterated that untrained personnel – this includes all librarians – should not attempt to apply any chemical fumigation methods without first seeking expert advice.

PROTECTIVE ENCLOSURES

This section examines the use of enclosures other than bindings (such as boxes or encapsulation) to protect items in library collections. Binding is discussed in the next division of this chapter.

Protective enclosures have in recent years become an important tool for preventive preservation. The principle which underlies their use is that any wear and tear will cause deterioration of the enclosure rather than the item itself. Furthermore, the enclosure will provide the conditions for a micro-environment to exist; this will act as a buffer to slow down the rate of change in environmental conditions (Chapter 4 notes the harmful effect of rapid changes on items in library collections). Enclosures also provide protection from water, smoke, heat and other destructive agents, and thus are an important technique for disaster prevention in libraries. Enclosures in common use are many and varied: encapsulation for single sheet items, folders for unbound documents, boxes of various kinds for larger items and for bound items whose bindings have been damaged, slip cases for bound items, and shrink wrapping.

Encapsulation

Single sheet items can be encapsulated between sheets of a chemically inert transparent plastic such as Mylar. Encapsulation is usually used for very fragile items or where heavy use is expected. Items enclosed in this manner can be handled and can easily be removed from the encapsulation should this be required. Two Mylar sheets at least 2.5 centimetres larger than the item to be encapsulated are cut, the item is laid on one sheet and the other placed on top, and the edges of the Mylar are sealed together. Sealing can be done either by using double-sided adhesive tape (see the sources below for the recommended type), by sewing, or by a more expensive process, using an ultrasonic welder. About eight minutes per item is the time needed for this procedure (Cunha, 1983, pp. 152-156; Ritzenthaler, 1983, pp. 106-108; Morrow and Dyall, 1986, pp. 117-122; Price, 1989, pp. 26-27).

Phase (or Phased) Boxes

The term 'phase' comes from the fact that this procedure was developed as an early phase in a conservation program at the Library of Congress. The intention of phase (or phased) boxes was to provide protection for items and to keep together all parts of them (detached covers and the rest of a book, for example) until such time as further conservation treatment could be carried out. This procedure is now widely used throughout the world to provide a protective enclosure for damaged or fragile bound items. To make a phase box, acid-free card is cut and folded according to a predetermined pattern. The box is typically secured by velcro 'coins', or by cloth ties and washers. Each phase box takes about thirty minutes to make, at a low cost for materials (Cunha, 1983, pp. 163-168; Ritzenthaler, 1983, pp. 115-120; Morrow and Dyall, 1986, pp. 132-141; Price, 1989, pp. 34-35).[28]

Other Boxes

As well as phase boxes, many other kinds of boxes are used as protective enclosures for library materials, and descriptions of how to construct them are plentiful. They include double-tray boxes (Morrow and Dyall, 1986, pp. 142-

163), boxes made from corrugated card which are suitable for a wide range of materials (Price, 1989, pp. 30-31), a 'poorman's solander box' (Price, 1989, pp. 35-36) and a 'one-piece box with corner flaps' designed for small books.[29]

Document Folders

Documents, pamphlets and thin items generally can be stored in a document folder. This is made from acid-free card cut and folded to a standard pattern (Cunha, 1983, pp. 157-162; Price, 1989, pp. 32-33).

Slipcases

Slipcases can be constructed to protect bound volumes from abrasion, light and dust. Slipcases usually require the skills of a trained binder and take some time to construct. However, Price describes the construction of a simple slipcase made from card. Another design, which is simpler to construct than the traditional slipcase, has been used at the National Library of Australia since 1987 to protect books in the Australiana collection in the Ferguson Room (Price, 1989, p. 38).[30]

Shrink-wrapping

Shrink-wrapping is being used to enclose low-use items in library collections, such as less frequently used unbound newspapers and serials. The equipment used is the same as that employed in manufacturing industries to package material for shipping. Fragile materials may be placed between boards before the shrink-wrapping is applied to give them greater rigidity and strength. Shrink-wrapping has also been used to provide protection during a library move.[31]

BINDING

Binding is another form of protective enclosure, but was excluded from the section immediately above because it is a large and important topic which deserves a section of its own. Many items in library collections are received in the library already bound by the publisher, and are usually placed straight onto the shelves. The low strength of the usual trade binding, the case binding, has been noted in this chapter,[32] and some of the repairs necessary because of its weakness described. Trade bindings are often adhesive-based rather than sewn, with consequent lack of strength and difficulty of rebinding at a later date.

Libraries bind materials for several reasons. One is the need to strengthen items which were manufactured in a format unsuitable for the rough and tumble of library use; paperbacks are the usual example of this. Another is the need to rebind items whose bindings have become too worn to offer protection to the text block of the book. Yet another is to put together in a more conveniently shelved unit items which were issued serially, or which were issued separately, such as pamphlets; security is another part of this reason, as it is considered more difficult to steal a large bound volume than a small unbound item, and such an item is less susceptible to damage. Also relevant is binding for preservation reasons, that is, to offer protection to fragile items, thus extending their life as useful items in library collections.[33]

Binding repair has been noted above in this chapter. What follows is an examination of binding in relation to libraries and to preservation. It is primarily concerned with commercial or trade library binding, rather than specialist binding of items in library collections.

Binding as a Preservation Measure

Binding has traditionally been the major preservation activity in libraries, and in many cases the only preservation-related activity. This has led in many cases to the application of inappropriate binding styles to library books, without regard to factors such as how long the book might be retained in the collection, or the strength of the paper in relation to the binding. Newspapers are a good example of this latter point: many old newspapers on brittle paper have been bound together or rebound when the paper strength is simply insufficient to support it, and considerable damage has resulted.

It is important to note here the different reasons for binding volumes in libraries and the consequent requirements for bindings of various kinds. Binding in order to achieve the maximum number of issues in a circulating collection before a volume is discarded, as might be the case in a public library's fiction collection, has different requirements from binding a volume in a research collection, where the main criterion is more likely to be to achieve the maximum life possible for that item. Different again is the requirement for binding or rebinding of an item in a special collection, where the overriding requirement will be to retain the features of the item and its previous binding for evidential reasons. Still another reason is simply that of cost. If a volume needs to be retained, for whatever reason, it is, as Swartzburg notes, 'cheaper to rebind a volume when it can still be rebound commercially than to replace it.'[34]

Other decisions to be made when binding are concerned with the physical structure and physical condition of the volume to be bound, in relation to the kind of binding to be applied. The two basic requirements are that the leaves are fixed together in a way which causes the least possible damage (ideally this should be a reversible procedure) and that the text is given sufficient physical protection. A sample flow chart published in *New Library Scene* in 1984 indicates the possibilities which need to be considered. This flow chart assumes that some decisions have already been made: that the book is to be retained rather than discarded, that rebinding and not replacement is to occur, and that the paper of the item is sound and not brittle. The flow chart then proceeds:

> If the text block is already sewn and the sewing is intact and sound, then a new case should be added. If not:

> if the text block is made up of issues of periodicals which were published in single-section format, then sewing through the fold should be carried out. If not:

> if the text block is thin enough and the paper can absorb the adhesive, then double-fan adhesive binding should be used. If not:

> if the text has inner margins of half an inch [1.5 centimetres] or more, then oversew. If not:

> then box the item.[35]

Other factors may also need to be considered. One example is binding of material which is likely to be photocopied, of which periodicals are a good example. Damage from photocopying can be reduced by binding them in blocks of not more than 5 centimetres, with double fan adhesive binding being preferable to oversewing (depending on the paper quality). This is especially the case for paper with a small inner margin, as it can be opened out further with less damage if double-fan adhesive binding is used.[36]

Essential further readings about library binding are the eighth edition of the *Library Binding Institute Standard for Library Binding* and Merrill-Oldham and Parisi's *Guide to the Library Binding Institute Standard for Library Binding*.[37]

Kinds of Bindings

The sample flow chart noted above indicates several different kinds of bindings in common use. A full description of these is beyond the scope of this book; however, excellent descriptions of them are plentiful in the literature, and these are essential reading for anyone who is involved with binding library materials.[38] A brief description of the four main methods is given here; other methods are also used on occasion.

Recasing
For a volume with a damaged or detached case, whose sewing is intact and strong, a new case can be attached. What is left of the old case and, if necessary, the old endsheets is removed, new endsheets are attached, and a

new case constructed and attached. Advantages of recasing include the fact that less damage is done to fragile materials, it is less expensive than resewing through the fold, and no trimming is needed. Providing a new case can mean that a book is usable for many years at a smaller total cost than the combined cost of carrying out repairs such as tightening hinges and repairing corners and spines; the time a book is out of circulation for repair is also a factor to be considered.[39]

Sewing through the Fold
This method can only be used to bind materials that have been issued in gatherings. Each gathering is sewn through its folds and attached to two or more linen tapes. These are pasted to a cloth mull which is in turn attached to the cover boards. The resulting binding is strong and easily opened out, and will withstand the pressures of photocopying. Volumes bound in this way can be readily rebound if necessary.

Double-Fan Adhesive Binding
In this process a small amount of paper needs to be cut off the spine to produce a clean edge. An adhesive is then applied while the book is fanned out first one way, then in the other direction. Some small loss of margin occurs. The resulting volume can be opened nearly flat and is relatively strong.

Oversewing
Oversewing is the strongest of these methods but a book bound by this method has the undesirable characteristics of not being able to be opened fully, of being difficult to rebind, and, if the paper becomes brittle, of pages breaking off at the sewing edge. Books sewn in this manner require a wide inner margin (at least 1.5 centimetres). To oversew, the book is divided into sections, then holes are punched obliquely through each section about 3 millimetres in from the edges, and each section is sewn through the holes and the sections linked together by lock stitching.

Other Binding Methods
Pamphlets and other items which do not have the protection of a case or other enclosure are often bound, or the paper cover is strengthened in some way. Simple covers can be quickly and economically constructed from boards and a buckram spine (Morrow and Dyall, 1986, pp. 81-92). Paperback books are often reinforced before they are circulated, for example, by adding cloth hinges to the inner joints and adding thin board to the inside of paper covers, or by adding board covers and a buckram spine (Morrow and Dyall, 1986, pp. 93-104). Music scores are one example of library materials which, because of the flimsy form in which they are usually published, require special reinforcement or binding to withstand the heavy use they will receive when issued.[40]

Strengthening Paperbacks

It has traditionally been considered that paperbacks are not sufficiently strong to withstand life on a library's shelves and that they require some form of strengthening before being added to a collection. This view had led to policies such as that all paperbacks must be bound or reinforced before being made available to library users. Economic stringencies have caused such policies to be reconsidered, and research into other possibilities – including not binding or strengthening at all – has indicated that some traditional assumptions about the need for reinforcement are not valid. Presley and Landram, for example, concluded that in the academic library context blanket binding of all paperback books was unnecessary and significant cost savings could be achieved by binding paperbacks only if their use warranted it.[41] For popular reading collections evidence gathered by John O. Christensen suggests that prebinding of paperbacks is an unwarranted expense which adds little to increasing their circulating life and that the much less expensive process of covering with contact paper increases durability to a similar extent.[42] Note, however, that a British experiment concluded the opposite: that for paperbacks in circulating collections reinforcement by adding a hard case binding was the only viable method.[43]

For those librarians who have read and assessed the published evidence and wish to reinforce paperbacks for their collections, Morrow and Dyall (1986, pp. 93-104) provide descriptions of two methods.

Commercial Library Binderies

Until recently large libraries usually ran their own binderies as a normal part of their operation, but this is seldom the case today. Most binding is now carried out by commercial library binderies. Commercial library binderies have received adverse criticism in preservation circles because they have been perceived to apply unthinkingly one style of binding to all material, regardless of how appropriate the binding might be: oversewing, for example, was often used for almost all volumes regardless of the amount of inner margin, the fragility of the paper or the need to open out the volume. While there is no doubt that commercial library binders were guilty on this count, it is equally certain that the guilt must be shared by librarians, who did not acquaint themselves with the possibilities of more appropriate binding methods, and who did not insist that these methods were made available and were used when necessary.

In using the services of a commercial library bindery it is essential to specify clearly the library's requirements. Several examples of guidelines for library binders, and of specifications and contracts, are available in the *Preservation Planning Program Resource Notebook*.[44] Some general principles should be observed: trimming of volumes should ideally not be carried out; original sewing should be retained if possible; all materials used should be as durable and stable as possible, and acid-free; books with brittle paper should not be rebound commercially.[45]

Notes

1   Carolyn Clark Morrow and Carole Dyall, *Conservation Treatment Procedures: A Manual of Step-by-Step Procedures for the Maintenance and Repair of Library Materials.* 2nd ed. (Littleton, Colo: Libraries Unlimited, 1986), p. 2.

2   Useful sources include Richard Fothergill and Ian Butchart, *Non-Book Materials in Libraries: A Practical Guide.* 3rd ed. (London: Bingley, 1990); Helen P. Harrison, 'Conservation and Audiovisual Materials', *Audiovisual Librarian* 13, 3 (1987): 154-162; Klaus B. Hendriks, *The Preservation and Restoration of Photographic Materials in Archives and Libraries: A RAMP Study with Guidelines* (Paris: Unesco, 1984); Siegfried Rempel, *The Care of Photographs* (New York: Nick Lyons Books, 1987); Alan Ward, *A Manual of Sound Archive Administration* (Aldershot: Gower, 1990), Chapter 6.

3   Carolyn Horton, *Cleaning and Preserving Bindings and Related Materials.* 2nd ed. (Chicago, Ill.: American Library Association, 1969); Morrow and Dyall, *op. cit.;* Helen Price, *Stopping the Rot: A Handbook of Preventive Conservation for Local Studies Collections.* 2nd ed. (Sydney: Australian Library and Information Association, New South Wales Branch, 1989).

4   George Martin Cunha and Dorothy Grant Cunha, *Library and Archives Conservation: 1980s and Beyond* (Metuchen, N.J.: Scarecrow Press, 1983), Appendix E, F; Mary Lynn Ritzenthaler, *Archives and Manuscripts: Conservation; A Manual on Physical Care and Management* (Chicago, Ill.: Society of American Archivists, 1983), pp. 73-81, Appendix B.

5   Cunha and Cunha, *op. cit.,* pp. 97-99.

6   These matters are discussed in Carolyn Clark Morrow, *The Preservation Challenge: A Guide to Conserving Library Materials* (White Plains, N.Y.: Knowledge Industry Publications, 1983), pp. 82-85.

7   J.M. Dureau and D.W.G. Clements, *Principles for the Preservation and Conservation of Library Materials* (The Hague: IFLA, 1986), no. 55, p. 16.

8   Thomas O. Taylor, 'Not All Mylar Is Archival', *Abbey Newsletter* 13, 5 (1989): 81.

9   The principle of reversibility has been questioned: see Richard D. Smith, 'Reversibility: A Questionable Philosophy', *Restaurator* 9, 4 (1988): 199-207.

10   Ritzenthaler, *op. cit.,* pp. 12-14.

11   Horton, *op. cit.*

12   Anthony Cains and Katherine Swift, *Preserving Our Printed Heritage: The Long Room Project at Trinity College Dublin* (Dublin: Trinity College Library, 1988).

13   Nicholas Hadgraft, 'The Parker Library Conservation Project, 1983-
      1989', *Library Conservation News* 24 (1989): 4-7.
14   Merrily A. Smith, 'Care and Handling of Bound Materials', in
      Preservation of Library Materials, ed. Merrily A. Smith (München:
      K.G. Saur, 1987), Vol. 2, pp. 49-50.
15   Morrow, *op. cit.*, p. 80.
16   Morrow and Dyall, *op. cit.*
17   Price, *op. cit.*, p. 20.
18   *Preservation Planning Program Resource Notebook*, comp. Pamela W.
      Darling; rev. ed. Wesley L. Boomgaarden (Washington, D.C.:
      Association of Research Libraries, Office of Management Studies,
      1987), pp. 549-558.
19   Timothy Walsh, 'A Typical Archival Conservation Laboratory',
      Archives and Manuscripts 7, 5 (1979): 268-275; Ritzenthaler, op. cit.,
      pp. 81-86.
20   Cains and Swift, *op. cit.*, p. 10.
21   Ellen McCrady, 'How Leather Dressing May Have Originated', *Abbey
      Newsletter* 14, 1 (February 1990): 19-20.
22   Mary Wood Lee, *Preservation and Treatment of Mold in Library
      Collections, With an Emphasis on Tropical Climates: A RAMP Study*
      (Paris: Unesco, 1988).
23   See Mary Davis, 'Preservation Using Pesticides: Some Words of
      Caution', *Wilson Library Bulletin* 59 (February 1985): 386-388, 431.
24   'Fumigation', *Conservation of Library Materials: The Newsletter of the
      Special Interest Group of the Australian Library and Information
      Association* 5 (1989): 1-4.
25   Ritzenthaler, *op. cit.*, pp. 121-124.
26   Sandra Nyberg, 'Out of the Question', *Conservation Administration
      News* 33 (1988): 14-15, 23.
27   A.D. Baynes-Cope, *Caring for Books and Documents*. 2nd ed.
      (London: British Library, 1989), pp. 44-45.
28   A revised version of the Library of Congress's design is noted in Terry
      Mroz, 'The Phased Box at the CCA: A Revised Model', *Conservation
      Administration News* 32 (1988): 6-7. Phase boxes and other enclosures
      are noted in Frank Yezer, 'Housing, When and Why', *Library
      Chronicle of the University of Texas at Austin*, n.s. 44/45 (1989): 149-
      155.
29   Richard W. Horton, 'A One-Piece Box with Corner Flaps for Small
      Books', *Conservation Administration News* 39 (1989): 8-9.
30   'The Ferguson Slipcase Project', *NLA News* 5 (1989): 3; Wendy
      Smith, 'The Ferguson Slipcase', *Abbey Newsletter* 13, 5 (1989): 95-
      96.
31   Charles Hansen and Ted Honea, 'Shrink-Wrapping for Moving',
      Abbey Newsletter 14, 1 (February 1990): 17-18; 'New Use for Shrink-
      Wrapping', *NLA News* 4 (1989): 8.
32   See also John Trevitt, 'Permanence in Publishers' Edition Binding', in
      *Preserving the Word: The Library Association Conference
      Proceedings...1986*, ed. R. Palmer (London: Library Association,
      1987), pp. 90-94.

33   A good summary of this aspect, and an examination of costs, is P.
     Dobrovits, 'Is Binding a Luxury?', *Australian Academic and Research
     Libraries* 10, 2 (1979): 81-86.

34   Susan G. Swartzburg, *Preserving Library Materials: A Manual*
     (Metuchen, N.J.: Scarecrow Press, 1980), p. 65.

35   *New Library Scene* (August 1984): 22; a revised version is in *New
     Library Scene* (August 1985): 16.

36   Amrita J. Burdick, 'Library Photocopying: The Margin for Caring',
     New Library Scene 5, 3 (1986): 17-18.

37   *Library Binding Institute Standards for Library Binding*, 8th ed.
     (Rochester, N.Y.: Library Binding Institute, 1986); Jan Merrill-Oldham
     and Paul Parisi, *Guide to the Library Binding Institute Standard for
     Library Binding* (Chicago, Ill.: American Library Association, 1990).

38   Examples are Jan Merrill-Oldham, 'Binding for Research Libraries',
     New Library Scene 3, 4 (1984): 1, 4-6; Paul A. Parisi, 'Methods of
     Affixing Leaves: Options and Implications', *New Library Scene* 3
     (1984): 9-12. A glossary of terms, with illustrations, is given by Parisi
     and Merrill-Oldham, 'The LBI Standard for Library Binding: The
     Glossary', *School Library Journal* 33, 2 (1986): 96-98.

39   Sally Grauer, 'Recasing: A Discussion between Librarians and
     Binders', *New Library Scene* 8, 4 (1989): 1, 5-8.

40   Methods are described in Deborah R. Miller, 'The Challenge of Binding
     Music', *Conservation Administration News* 32 (1988): 8-9.

41   Roger L. Presley and Christina Landram, 'The Life Expectancy of
     Paperback Books in Academic Libraries', *Technical Services Quarterly*
     4, 3 (1987): 21-29.

42   John O. Christensen, 'Extending Life for Popular Paperbacks', *Library
     Journal* (1 October 1989): 65-66.

43   John Turner, 'Binding Arbitration: A Comparison of the Durability of
     Various Hardback and Paperback Bindings', *Library Association
     Record* 88, 5 (May 1986): 233-235.

44   *Preservation Planning Program Resource Notebook* (1987), *op. cit.*,
     pp. 585-601.

45   Helpful guidelines are noted in the *RLG Preservation Manual*. 2nd ed.
     (Stanford, Calif.: Research Libraries Group, 1986), pp. 150-156.

Chapter 8

Preserving the Intellectual Content: Reformatting

Introduction

The preceding chapter described some techniques for preserving the physical object, that is the artefact. Preservation of the artefact is warranted when the item has some special value as a physical object; preservation of only the intellectual content is justified when this condition does not apply. While any artefact can be repaired and conserved to keep it near to its original physical condition, the reality of limited budgets and responsible use of resources means that preservation of the artefact is not always possible.

For most items in library collections preservation of the intellectual content, by putting it into another, more durable physical format, is all that is feasible and may be all that is required. Microfilming is currently the major type of reformatting (also called substitution) undertaken in libraries, although its paramount position is under threat from optical storage devices and conversion to digital data. The fact is that 'if the bulk of materials are to remain available for the future, microfilming is currently our best preservation solution.'[1]

Reformatting is an essential component of an integrated library preservation program. It should have equal status with the other major elements of the program: environmental control, careful handling and storage, education and training, disaster preparedness planning, maintenance and repair techniques. Reformatting can be applied to different categories of items in a library collection. For example, some items in the library collection will merit both reformatting, to save the artefact from further wear, and conservation of the artefact, although such cases are restricted to items of special significance to the library. Possibly only a sample of the artefacts will be conserved, to give some indication of the physical nature of the items for future bibliographers and historians. More usual is the case where the original item, probably already heavily deteriorated, is discarded after reformatting; alternatively, the original may be retained but stored in low-cost (perhaps off-site) storage in the knowledge that it will still deteriorate rapidly to a condition where it is no longer usable.

In addition to the decisions which must be made at the local level when reformatting is carried out – can another copy of the item be obtained, does the item have merit as an artefact, and so on – the wider picture must be always kept in mind. Resources for preservation, insufficient at the local level, are similarly insufficient at the regional, national and even international level. These limited resources can best be used by maintaining and contributing to keeping of records about what has been reformatted (especially microfilming) to ensure that reformatting is carried out once, and once only, for any one item. This will be further noted below in the section 'The Importance of Bibliographic Control'.

Another essential is for the master surrogate copies to be correctly stored so that copies for use can be made as long into the future as possible. As the aim of reformatting is, after all, to make usable the intellectual content of an item for as long as possible, it follows that correct storage of the master copies is a vital part of any reformatting program.

The main decisions to be made in the reformatting process are: does the item need preservation attention; is it possible to replace the item; and does it need to be retained in its original form? If the answer to the third question is 'no', which format is best? These questions are addressed below.

Selection for Preservation

Three questions concerning selection for preservation must be asked in the preservation program: the first, whether or not an item (or a collection of items) should be treated; the second, what kind of treatment is required and is it appropriate to the item (or items); and the third, what can be afforded in relation to the library's broader goals? Here it is assumed that the third question has been answered and resources are available for reformatting. It is also assumed that the library's collection development policy is clearly defined and understood, and that it contains guidance about the relative strengths and research value of subject areas within the total collection. This section examines the factors which need to be considered when answering the first question.

Much has been written about selection of items for preservation, which is one of the key decisions to be made in any preservation program. A succinct statement of the decision process is Wesley L. Boomgaarden's 'Preservation Decision Flow Chart' noted in Gwinn's *Preservation Microfilming* and reproduced here.[2] The first major decision noted on this chart, 'is this damaged, deteriorated, unstable, or brittle paper-based item important to retain in some format?', is to be made taking into consideration 'the institution's collection development guidelines', that is, its collection development policy. If the answer to this first major question is 'no', the options then available range from the totally passive 'reshelve without action' to the more active 'deaccession'.

Preservation Decision Flow Chart

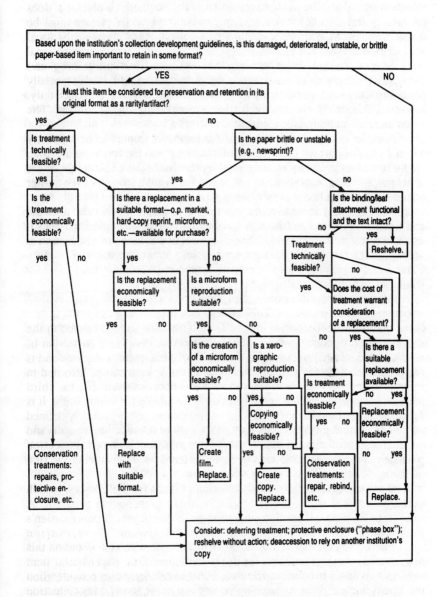

Reproduced with permission of the American Library Association, *Preservation Microfilming: A Guide for Librarians and Archivists*, edited by Nancy E. Gwinn, p. 39; © 1987 ALA.

The four main aspects of each item to be considered in a preservation selection policy are: the physical condition of the item; how heavily it is used; its rarity; and its economic, aesthetic, historical or other value. These considerations can also be applied to whole collections or groups of items, as well as to individual items.

Several attempts have been made recently by librarians to establish a theoretical framework to assist in this decision-making, but these are not yet as sophisticated as those developed by archivists in drawing up disposal and retention schedules: the archivist's long-established concept of 'intrinsic value' in archival materials, for instance, offers a framework which may well be of considerable use to librarians.[3] Atkinson, for example, has developed a useful typology which offers a helpful starting point. He considers that there are three classes of library materials to be preserved: Class 1 preservation has as its purpose 'to preserve materials or groups of materials that have a high economic value'; Class 2 preservation 'to preserve materials currently being used, or very likely to be used on the basis of what is currently being used'; and Class 3 preservation (the most problematical) 'to maintain for posterity low-use research materials'.[4] The difficulties of defining this third class are great. Child's response to Atkinson's typology examines more closely his Class 3 and argues for a greater emphasis on non-paper material, so that the whole range of human endeavour is preserved.[5]

More recently the concept of the 'great collections' approach for selection has been promoted. This strategy begins with an assessment of how comprehensive a collection is in specific subjects (the Conspectus approach) and identifies collections which could be preserved (usually by microfilming) in their entirety.[6] A specific example of this approach is the Core Agriculture Literature Project based at Cornell University, which uses techniques such as citation analysis to identify important works.[7]

Physical Condition
The current physical condition of an item or a collection, in particular the degree of brittleness of paper, needs to be assessed. However, the current physical state is not the only criterion which should be considered. The extent of likely deterioration may also need consideration: for example, an item printed on newsprint may be in acceptable condition now but will deteriorate quickly.

Use
Factors to consider in this category include the item or collection's past history of use, and its potential for use in the future. Decisions about aspects such as how it supports the curriculum being taught by the institution which the library serves, or its research value and use in the future, may need to be made.

Rarity

Some items are readily definable as unique: manuscripts, books with important annotations or decoration, some rare books. Other items may be rare because of their conditions of issue, for example, in a limited edition. Rarity usually indicates clearcut cases of preservation of the artefact in original format.

Value

Value can be determined in many ways, of which the main ones are monetary, aesthetic, historical and bibliographical. Monetary value is probably the easiest to identify, by referring to the benchmark prices set at auction or by booksellers. These can be relatively easily ascertained from publications which list current prices for out-of-print books. Aesthetic value is, again, probably relatively easy to judge in most instances, for many styles of bindings, illustrations and printing have been recognized as having aesthetic merit. Historical value encompasses such aspects as significance for a particular institution, for example the founder's own signed copy, and research value, for example first editions of novels significant for their importance in textual studies. Bibliographical value relates to the physical elements of a book or other item, that is, to its printing, physical structure and binding, and its significance as evidence of technological development.[8] Other value may be defined by the nature of the subject field, for example, textual studies call for investigation of all variant editions, and some bibliographical studies require that as many copies of what appear to be the same item are examined; by the place of publication, for example Californian imprints in California; by association, for example, an item was the property of a famous person or was signed by that person; and by other factors. Another point which might need to be considered is whether the library has assumed primary collecting responsibility in a particular field on a regional or nationwide basis.

Identifying Items for Preservation

Once the exact criteria and their relative weighting have been established, the next question to be answered is: how are items in the collections which meet these criteria to be identified? This question may apply to whole collections as well as individual items: a collection may, for example, 'represent the breadth of thought or the publishing record of a specific subject or a time period' and thus be identified as a priority for preservation.[9] Use is relatively easy to ascertain for items in a circulating collection, as the most heavily used will become obvious as they pass through the hands of circulation staff. As already noted above, an attempt may need to be made to ascertain future use for research purposes.

Physical condition can be identified as part of other library operations: the circulation staff will notice brittle items or the reference staff heavily used items which are deteriorating. Stack maintenance staff, and indeed all library staff, can be trained to recognize problems and to bring them to the attention of staff responsible for the preservation program. Acquisitions staff may routinely identify new material which is fragile and which has priority within the library's collection development policy. Serials staff may make the decision to microfilm in lieu of binding.

Another method of identifying material for preservation treatment is to examine systematically the collections for items which meet the defined criteria; here poor physical condition should be obvious with some training and practice. Surveys, of the whole collection or of selected parts, are another method (see Chapter 3). Random sampling of collections may indicate areas where a high percentage has deteriorated, thus suggesting strongly that the whole of that collection needs attention. Review of collections by imprint date is another possibility, for example where it is known that the paper was especially brittle during a particular period – newspapers published between 1905 and 1920, say. Selection for preservation may also take place as part of a larger cooperative project, as is the case in several countries for microfilming of newspapers.

Useful checklists which list criteria for selection decision-making are found in *SPEC Kit* 138.[10]

Yet another question is: who should make the decision about whether an item should be preserved? Here the answer is that it should probably be a cooperative effort, taking note of the opinions of the conservator or preservation librarian and also the subject librarian, if there is one, or the librarian who has the most direct contact with that part of the collection. The final decision must be made by those who have the closest involvement with the collection – curators, subject specialists and other staff involved with collection development and collection management. It must be made, though, in the light of advice given by the preservation librarian or conservator, which in turn is based on up-to-date knowledge about the range of conservation options available, their current costs and their advantages and drawbacks. In some instances users of collections, who may have a more detailed knowledge of a part of a collection, may take part in deciding whether an item or collection should be preserved.

Preservation of Artefact, or Intellectual Content?

Once the decision has been made to preserve an item, the next question is whether to retain the item in original format or whether it is sufficient to preserve only the item's intellectual content in another, more durable, format. This question was addressed in Chapter 1. To summarize the points made there, preservation of the artefact is warranted when the item has special value as a physical object, for example because it is old, it has beauty, it is rare, it has some historical or bibliographical significance, or it has a high monetary value. It may in some cases also be warranted when there would be a significant loss of quality, for instance if colour reproduction or legibility would be reduced. Preservation of the intellectual content is applicable when none of these conditions applies. The *RLG Preservation Manual* contains a full listing of 'Considerations in the Retention of Items in Original Format', which has as its main headings: evidential value, aesthetic value, importance in the printing history of significant titles, age, scarcity, value (financial), physical format/features of interest, exhibit value.[11]

While any artefact can be repaired and conserved so that it can be kept near to its original physical condition, the processes and time involved can make this an expensive activity, and the technical solutions may not be particularly effective. For example, deacidification of paper will arrest further deterioration but will not strengthen the paper, which will still remain brittle and will be difficult to handle. The reality of limited budgets and responsible use of resources is that preservation of the artefact is impossible in every case. For most items in library collections preservation of the intellectual content, by putting it into another, more durable physical format, is all that is economically feasible and is in fact all that is required.

Boomgaarden's Preservation Decision Flow Chart, reproduced above, notes the next steps to be taken if an item is deemed to be worthy of preservation in its original format. First, it must be decided whether conservation treatment is technically feasible; if so, whether it is economically feasible, and then which treatment or combination of treatments is required. These decisions will need to be made in conjunction with a conservator. The conservation treatments most likely to be applied are: minor repairs to bindings and tears in paper; commercial rebinding; a full conservation treatment consisting of aqueous deacidification, encapsulation or conservation binding; adding a protective enclosure, such as a phase box; or polyester encapsulation for single sheets.[12] One point to note is that there remains the option of taking no action at all. This might arise if no technically or economically acceptable treatment was available at the time, leaving no alternative but to retain the item until money was available or an appropriate treatment could be developed. It may also be possible to replace the item with another copy, but this will only apply to items whose artefactual value does not stem from some unique characteristic, such as a special binding or manuscript annotations. The section that follows notes the procedures available for locating replacement copies.

Copyright laws may be relevant to the preservation selection decision. Those who make such decisions need to be aware of the appropriate legal provisions which govern the ownership of copyright and the right to reproduce copyright materials in their country.[13] Indeed, copyright is increasingly being recognized as one of the major issues requiring resolution before large-scale preservation programs can be fully implemented.[14]

Searching for Replacements

Once the decision has been made to preserve an item, the next step is to ascertain whether a replacement copy is available in a format acceptable to the library. This could be a reprint, a microform version or another copy of the book purchased in the second-hand market. Such a search may take the following path. First, a search of the library's catalogue is made to ascertain whether there is another copy of the item held by the library and, if so, whether it is in a better condition than the item to be preserved and can serve instead as the copy to be retained. Second, a search is made of the standard trade bibliographies to see if reprints or microform copies are available or if the item is still in print. These tools include general works such as *Books in Print* and *British Books in Print*, and more specialized works like *Books on Demand, Guide to Reprints, Guide to Microforms in Print* and the *National Register of Microform Masters*.[15] Helpful information about search procedures, and sample forms, are provided in Chapter 2 of *Preservation Microfilming* (1987).

The Importance of Bibliographic Control

The preceding section points out the importance of maintaining effective bibliographic control of preservation copies, in whatever format. The availability of information about what has been preserved in microfilm or in another format is crucial to any institution actively operating a preservation program, because it allows the financial and human resources available to be better used by avoiding duplication of effort. Can we afford, for example, to microfilm one periodical twice when another of equal significance remains untreated? Avoiding duplication of effort and expense is obviously highly desirable.

That an effective bibliographic structure is essential to any large-scale preservation effort, and that present systems are inadequate, is noted in many places in the preservation literature.[16] Examples of some which have been established are the British Library's register of microfilm masters in MARC format, and the records of newspapers microfilmed during the United States Newspaper Program.[17] The Research Libraries Group's automated bibliographic system, RLIN, now accommodates preservation information, particularly of locations of microfilm masters and intention to microfilm; this information was in 1991 issued on a CD-ROM entitled *RLIN Preservation MasterFile*.[18] RLIN has exchanged records of microfilming data with OCLC, another major bibliographic utility in the United States, and has also exchanged microfilming data with the British Library and with the Bibliothèque Nationale, Paris.[19]

Recent changes to the MARC record format (a standard which allows bibliographic data in computerized format to be exchanged between libraries and countries) now allow it to accommodate preservation data in field 583. Eight groups of preservation data elements can be recorded:

1   physical characteristics of the item, including alkaline, acidic and brittle paper; original binding; not original binding; binding not intact; and content lost or obscured;

2   preservation action, including reformatting, conservation and mass deacidification;

3   dates, including review, queue and completion;

4   priority information, expressed in levels from one to ten;

5   primary collecting responsibility indicator;

6   microform characteristics information, including generation, emulsion and polarity;

7   item availability;

8   copyright.[20]

As the MARC format is widely accepted internationally as the basis of large computerized library systems, it is clear that the potential for adding preservation information to computerized library systems is already present and should be encouraged in the future.[21]

One important form of bibliographic control for preservation is registration of microfilm masters. One example will suffice. The British Library has established a Register of Microform Masters which lists the titles microfilmed in its in-house microfilming project. It will eventually be developed into a union list of microform masters in Britain.[22]

Which Format?

The final decision to be made is which format to choose for the preservation of the intellectual content of deteriorated items. The formats most likely to be chosen at present are preservation photocopying and microfilming, with conversion to digital data coming a close third. Preservation photography may be used for original black-and-white photographic prints. Less likely choices are the use of facsimile publishing or transcription.

Michael Roper poses a series of questions to be answered when the choice of format is being made.[23] The first group of questions relates to the purpose of the conversion to another format: is it for substitution of a deteriorating original which will be discarded after reformatting, or is it to provide a backup copy of an especially valuable item to be stored at another location for security purposes, or will it be used for reference purposes while the original is still retained? Next, questions relating to the needs of the user should be put. Does the new format allow ready access? How rapidly can the information be located? How heavily will the item be used? Technical questions need to be considered. What is the life expectancy of the new format? What are the optimum conditions of the new format for storage and access? Will further format conversion be needed, for example if hardware needed to access it becomes obsolete? Can the conversion be carried out locally, to the appropriate standards? Cost factors also need to be taken into account: the costs of conversion, obviously, and also costs associated with storage, maintenance and cataloguing of the new format. Other factors, too, may be relevant, as Roper notes.

The recent development of techniques for handling, storing and manipulating digital data has considerably altered the preservationist's perspective of the supremacy of microfilming as the most feasible format in which to preserve the intellectual content of deteriorated items. Many studies have addressed the issues raised by these developments. One of them, written by Michael Lesk and published by the Commission on Preservation and Access in 1990, analyzes eight media: magnetic disk, optical WORM (write once read many) disk, digital videotape, digital audiotape, conventional magnetic tape, CD-ROM, magneto-optical erasable disk and digital paper. It concludes:

> if we assume that the expertise and the capital investment are available, digital image storage is not more expensive than microfilm. Like microfilm, it saves space compared to paper, and digital technology is improving rapidly. This digital storage is an appropriate experiment today for the larger libraries, or for groups of libraries.[24]

Lesk's overall conclusion notes that microfilm still has an important role; it is

> in a similar price range as digital imagery, but is today more accessible to the conventional research library. Because microfilm to digital image conversion is going to be relatively straightforward...librarians should use either method as they can manage, expecting to convert to digital form over the next decade.[25]

Other writers predict for microfilm a role complementary to digital data storage.[26]

The rest of this chapter notes specific formats, their advantages and disadvantages, and some of the factors which should be considered when they are being used.

PRESERVATION PHOTOCOPYING

Photocopies can be made, either in-house or by an outside contractor, of items where only the intellectual content is to be preserved. The process is essentially the same as the normal photocopying process, the major difference being that alkaline paper of appropriate archival quality should be used. The copy made, either single- or double-sided, can be bound if required. No special skills are required to carry out this process, and most libraries will own a photocopying machine. The costs of the process are made up of paper and machine running costs, and labour costs of copying, collating and binding.[27]

Photocopying is best used to copy smaller items. Books which are too long, say over 100 pages, will probably cost less to microfilm.[28] It is an especially suitable format for heavily used items, where microfilm with its difficulties of use and user resistance may be less appropriate. It is not appropriate for works with coloured or high quality black-and-white illustrations, although these could be encapsulated and bound into the photocopy.

Preservation photocopying has some advantages over other formats. It can, if required, produce a copy which is in the same or very similar format as the original, for example, a photocopy of a book can be trimmed to the same size as the original, then bound and handled in the same way. The result is relatively permanent if appropriate alkaline paper is used. The image should be stable and durable; a spokesman for the Xerox Corporation is quoted by Morrow as expecting the fused thermoplastic polymer image to last longer than the paper.[29] Preservation photocopying is a practical format for smaller and medium-sized libraries which already own or have access to appropriate equipment.

This process has, however, some less positive aspects. One is the harshness of the process which may cause damage to fragile items. While this may not be a problem in some cases, for example when the original is to be discarded after photocopying, in other cases where the original is to be retained it may be a significant deterrent. Careful handling while copying and the use of appropriate machines will assist, and these are noted in Chapter 5. Another negative feature is that the photocopying process does not produce a master copy. This has been called by Ellen McCrady 'preserving without increasing access',[30] that is, no master is usually made from which other copies could be taken. It is, of course, possible to make a master copy to be stored in secure conditions and used only to make further copies for use, but this practice is not yet widespread. Another negative aspect, when this process is compared with microfilming, is the higher cost for items with a large number of pages, especially when the cost of binding or providing a protective enclosure is also taken into account.

Preservation photocopying offers a useful alternative to microfilming, but there are still some issues to be resolved. These include the need for standards to be developed and adhered to, the production and storage of master copies when appropriate, and the bibliographic control of these masters. A possible future development of significance is the use of colour photocopying.

MICROFILMING

There is no doubt that microfilming is currently the most widely used format for preservation copying, and present indications are that this will remain the case in the near future, despite the strong challenge of optical discs and magnetic digital data storage. Major libraries throughout the world are strongly committed to microfilming, as shown, for example, by the granting of US$1.5 million to the British Library by the Andrew W. Mellon Foundation in 1988 to fund a five-year preservation microfilming program.[31] Microfilming already has a long history of use in libraries,[32] and a considerable amount is known about it, including its longevity if stored under appropriate conditions.

Formats and Film Types

Microforms are produced in several formats. Of these, microfilm and microfiche are the most likely to be encountered in libraries, although other formats, for example aperture cards, will also be found. Libraries have traditionally produced or purchased 35 millimetre microfilm, this being the size for which archival standards have been developed because it allows for a larger image which, being less reduced, is of higher quality. Some commercial microfilm publishers have used 16 millimetre microfilm, and this will also be found in library collections. Microfiche, considered by many users as preferable to the film format, is also heavily represented and is perhaps now the major format in which microforms are commercially published.[33] Although film has been the traditional format in which preservation microfilming has been produced (and the following section assumes 35 millimetre film is the standard), microfiche has been gaining attention recently.[34]

    Three types of microfilms are available: silver-gelatin, diazo, vesicular. Only silver-gelatin film which has been carefully processed to the appropriate standards should be used for archival master negatives which will be retained for long periods of time. However, it is important that it be carefully stored and handled, as it is susceptible to damage from fungi, water and mechanical abrasion. Working copies can be silver-gelatin, but diazo and vesicular have advantages where durability in day-to-day use is more important than archival life. Both diazo and vesicular film are less expensive and more scratch-resistant than silver-gelatin.[35]

Steps in Microfilm Production

The major steps to be taken in producing microforms are selection, preparation of the original, filming, processing and inspection of the film. Selection is noted above in this chapter. The preparation stage is an important one. Here the processes involved are two: physical preparation, and bibliographic preparation. Physical preparation includes such actions as collation or checking that the item to be microfilmed is complete, removal of the binding (although this is not always carried out, especially on items where the binding has some artefactual importance), cleaning pages and repairing tears in the paper. Bibliographic preparation involves making a bibliographic record for the item and preparing targets which will be placed in the appropriate section of the item (such as a target for title, details of magnification and producer of the microform, change of title of a periodical) and filmed with it. These processes are described in detail and illustrated in *Preservation Microfilming* (1987).[36]

The filming process itself is straightforward, and anyone familiar with basic photographic procedures would find little of surprise when observing it. Experienced camera operators are important, for they will take the care to produce a high quality result. Again, a good description of the filming process is found in *Preservation Microfilming* (1987).[37]

The processing of the film is of utmost importance in determining the archival life of the negative master. The developing process is, as with other photographic processes, one where the metallic silver image is fixed with a solution containing thiosulphate. If the fixing solution is not thoroughly washed off during the developing process, then the residual thiosulphate may result in staining and fading of the image. Tests to determine whether levels of residual chemicals are acceptable have been developed and should be applied; they are noted further in the 'Standards' section below.

Inspection of the developed film is also an essential part of producing preservation microfilms. In addition to carrying out the tests for chemical stability already mentioned, physical examination of the film should be carried out to determine whether any mechanical problems, such as scratches and abrasions, are present, whether the density reading is acceptable, and whether the film is bibliographically complete, that is, whether any pages have been missed. These processes are described in *Preservation Microfilming* (1987).[38]

Standards

A wide range of standards covering all aspects of microform production and storage has been published. They cover four areas: vocabulary, quality, compatibility, specific applications. Standards relating to vocabulary are concerned with promoting the use of standard symbols and terms to indicate such things as the start and end of a reel. They also describe standard ways in which the images are positioned on the reel of film or fiche. Standards relating to quality cover such aspects of microfilming as methods of processing and storage. Compatibility standards are aimed at ensuring that all microforms are manufactured to the same sizes, using reels of the same dimensions, so that they can be used throughout the world. The fourth group, standards relating to specific applications, describe what should be done when newspapers, press cuttings, technical drawings and other similar kinds of materials are filmed.

Standards have been issued by the standards organizations in many countries as well as by the ISO (International Standards Organization). A list of the appropriate ISO standards is given in *Preservation of Library Materials*

(1987), and others are described in *Preservation Microfilming* (1987).[39] Standards are constantly revised and updated, and it is necessary to ensure that the latest version is used. The local branch of the Standards Association or other relevant organization should be contacted for up-to-date information.

Costs of Microfilming

It is fair to say that microfilming has cost advantages over other reformatting processes in current use and over restoration treatments, especially for items with many pages. The higher cost of preservation photocopying over microfilming for items over about 100 pages has already been noted. Comparison of costs of microfilming and other conservation treatments indicates that microfilming costs about 50 cents per page (actually per exposure, but we will assume here that there is one page per exposure) compared with about US$1 per page for encapsulation, and similarly high or higher costs for complete restoration (these are 1987 costs).[40] The cost of full restoration (cleaning, deacidifying, buffering, mending, and rebinding or repairing the original bindings) of fourteen eighteenth- and nineteenth-century record books and diaries was, in the mid-1980s, US$5305, compared with US$780 for microfilming the same items.[41] Figures from the British Library for 1986, based on a 300-page book, were:

Furbishing/repair	£0.88
Box (made to measure archival quality)	£18.72
First binding	£8.68
Conserve and rebind in buckram	£67.08
Microfilm (35mm)	£19.50
Microfilm, record in Register of Microform Masters	£21.68
Microfilm, record in Register, box original	£40.40
Microform, record in Register, conserve original	£88.76[42]

Although these comparisons may not be the most appropriate, because the choice may be between different formats into which to convert an item's intellectual content, rather than (as suggested here) between whether to preserve the artefact or the intellectual content, they do serve to suggest one reason why microfilming has become a valuable preservation procedure.

Figures for the costs of microfilming are readily available. A rough working figure of about US$50 per monograph is generally used, although this can vary from about US$25 to US$75 per monograph, the main variables being the size of the item microfilmed and local labour costs.[43]

More precise figures were established in a study carried out by the Research Libraries Group in 1984. The seven participants established that the average cost per monograph varied between US$25.81 and US$75.80, with a median cost of US$48.20. This study included in its costings not only the cost, in cents per exposure, of the microfilming step, but also the labour costs of identifying and retrieving items, preparing circulation records, searching for already available microforms, curatorial review, indicating intent to microfilm to RLIN, physical preparation, preparing targets, filming, inspecting the films, cataloguing, storage of the master, and the materials costs of the filming and storage processes. Some administrative costs were excluded.[44]

Chapter 6 of *Preservation Microfilming* (1987) is a full examination of the costs involved in microfilming library materials. It provides a framework which will enable costs of a microfilming program to be estimated, and it suggests ways in which costs might be controlled or reduced. It is essential reading for anyone interested in cost factors of the microfilming process.

Microforms: Pros and Cons

Cost advantages are not the only positive factors of microfilming. Another major advantage is the long-term stability of microforms, if appropriate processing standards, storage conditions and handling procedures are observed: lifetimes of more than 1000 years have been expressed in the literature.[45] The space-saving factor, especially for serials, may be significant. Microforms are able to be cheaply and easily copied once a master has been produced. Paper copies of part or all of them can be readily produced if microfilm or microfiche reader-printers are provided. The equipment needed to access microforms is a simple optical device. It is not 'high-tech', with a high probability of becoming obsolescent in a short time, as is the case with the technology needed for optical disc formats and for materials which are converted to computer data.

There are, of course, less desirable features of microform. The most often cited as an argument against microfilming is that they are difficult to use. Take the attitude of a fictional character:

> But those dreadful microfilm readers! I had expected to enjoy a pleasant day with the fragile crackle of old newspapers in my hands. Instead I had the devil of a time pressing buttons, twirling knobs, and peering into an obscurely lit screen. What a disappointment it was! And what a crashing ache in the temples and the back of the neck I developed before the whole unnatural experience was over.[46]

While there is undeniably some substance to many users' complaints about using microfilm, few libraries have considered it a high priority to provide equipment, both readers and reader-printers, which is more than barely adequate. Top quality equipment can increase considerably user comfort. It is admittedly expensive, but it is unfortunately rarely found in libraries.

The production, storage and handling of microforms require strict adherence to standards, which can sometimes be expensive and difficult to maintain. They can be easily damaged by careless handling and storage. An example was the 'redox blemish' scare of the 1960s. Because these occurred only on silver-gelatin microfilm, which was the standard for long-term storage, there was great concern about the viability of microfilm for preserving library materials. Research blamed the blemishes on a combination of chemical factors, such as the release of gases from the materials of which the storage cartons were made. The solution was to develop new standards for processing and storing the film.[47]

Not all formats in which library materials are produced are suitable for microfilming. Experience has shown that the best candidates for conversion to microform, on the basis of the poor physical quality of their paper and of heavy use, are: brittle books and pamphlets, newspapers, long runs of serials on low quality paper, statistical materials, scrapbooks, vertical file material, government reports and some manuscript materials. Less suitable for converting to preservation microform are: some illustrated materials (especially those with coloured illustrations), materials having artefactual value (as noted in earlier sections in this chapter), materials with poor contrast between image and background, such as heavily discoloured materials, and materials which are being or have been microfilmed by commercial publishers.[48]

A final point to note is that, despite the advantages and disadvantages expressed here, for many items there is simply no economically or technologically viable alternative to microfilming currently available if preservation of an item is required.

Establishing a Microfilming Program

One early example from the large body of literature about preservation microfilming is Pamela Darling's 'Developing a Preservation Microfilming Program'. It is full of common sense and is still well worth reading for the general points it makes about establishing a microfilming program.[49] There is a major decision to be made at the start: whether to establish an in-house microfilming unit, or whether to use the services of a commercial microfilming business. For all but the largest libraries this is probably not a difficult decision, made along the same lines as the decision about whether to establish a bindery in-house or to send books out to a commercial library bindery.

If a microfilming unit is established in-house, the advantages of being able to supervise the work closely and to maintain a high level of security over the material being filmed will probably be outweighed by the expensive capital outlay (on cameras, equipment for processing film, splicing equipment, microfilm readers and testing equipment; premises are also needed), the difficulty of recruiting skilled personnel, and the ongoing expenditure on equipment, maintenance and supplies. Although contracting out to a commercial microfilming business provides access to specialized equipment and skilled personnel without the need to provide in-house space, facilities, equipment and staff, a lower degree of security is usually available, the transporting of items to the firm's premises is likely to result in damage (especially to fragile items) and possible loss, and close supervision is more difficult.

Assuming that the services of a contractor will be used, then advice is again available in the literature to assist in setting up a workable program. Sherry Byrne has described the steps to be taken.[50] It is important first to establish clearly the physical nature of the material which is to be microfilmed, so that the contractor can ascertain such factors as how much physical preparation is needed, and whether especially careful handling is required. A project manager, either someone already familiar with the technical and other requirements of microfilming or someone who is able and willing to learn, should be designated. Technical specifications (including standards) and microfilming instructions should be prepared, as should sample materials. The contractor should be visited and requirements discussed; a willingness on the part of the contractor to work closely with the library is an important ingredient, as are technical ability, appropriate equipment and skilled personnel. The results obtained from microfilming the sample materials should be reviewed as part of the process of deciding which contractor to use. A contract should be prepared and maintained, and Byrne provides a sample contract.

Other publications are helpful. The experience of the Library of Congress is described in two contributions to the literature, which both usefully describe the procedures which need to be established.[51] *Preservation Microfilming* (1987) is also invaluable.

Although this section has been concerned entirely with microfilming programs run by only one library, the possibility of cooperative programs should be considered. Many cooperative programs have been established, and some are noted below.

Storage of Microform Masters

The importance of correct storage of microform master negatives has been noted several times already in this chapter. To ensure as long a life as possible for the masters, it is essential that the current standards be followed. One recently published example of the many now available is the Australian standard (AS 3674-1989) which prescribes for archival storage of master negatives a separate room or vault and defines the fire resistance required. The room or vault should be maintained at a temperature not exceeding 21°C (although lower temperatures are desirable), the relative humidity kept at a non-fluctuating level set between 20 and 40 per cent, and a slightly positive air pressure should be maintained. Dust should be filtered out by the use of mechanical filters, and any gaseous impurities removed. Light levels, particularly of ultraviolet light, should be as low as possible. Packaging and housing of the master microfilm also needs attention: reels and containers need to be of archival quality, and the shelves or cabinets where they are stored should be non-combustible. More information is given in Chapter 4 of *Preservation Microfilming* (1987).

Appropriate storage facilities may be too expensive for the individual library to provide, but they are sometimes able to be rented from a commercial storage business. The standards maintained in facilities such as these will ensure that master negatives are retained for as long as possible, the time certainly measured in decades and probably in centuries.

Many microfilming programs make a second copy of the master negative (an interim master) for duplicating purposes. Unlike the master, this need not be stored in quite such stringent storage conditions, and will be available when a copy of the negative is required, without causing damage to the master. If the interim master becomes damaged, for example because of frequent copying in the case of a popular item, then the master can be used to make another interim master negative.

Some Microfilming Programs

Cooperative microfilming programs have for many years been recognized as an effective way of preserving national heritage collections, and consequently several major cooperative programs at the national level have been established in Europe, the United Kingdom and the United States. The best known of these is probably the Research Libraries Group's series of cooperative preservation microfilming projects which is based on the collection strengths of the members of the RLG. Their initial aim has been to microfilm monographs published in the United States between 1870 and 1920. The guidelines used in the program are published in the *RLG Preservation Manual*, 2nd ed. (1986).[52]

The preservation of newspapers has been a major concern in several countries, because of the importance of their contents and the fragility of the newspaper as artefact. The Newsplan program in the United Kingdom is one example of a major newspaper preservation program, which aims at bibliographic control of the newspapers and at their preservation through microfilming. A pilot project undertaken in 1983 and 1984 established the viability of methods of collecting information about surviving newspapers and their physical condition, and of determining priorities for microfilming them. The plan is being carried out on a regional basis using funds provided by both the British Library and regional sources.[53]

The United States Newspaper Program is funded by the National Endowment for the Humanities, which provides money at three sequential levels. The first enables states and territories to plan comprehensive newspaper projects; the second funds the surveys required to ascertain bibliographic and holdings information in each region. A requirement at this second level is that the bibliographic records be made available nationally by contributing them to a nationwide computerized database, OCLC. The third step provides finance for microfilming newspapers which are considered most useful to retain for research purposes.[54] Many other countries have developed newspaper microfilming programs. One example is New Zealand, whose National Library has actively microfilmed newspapers for many years and has allocated increased resources to this project since 1983.[55]

An example of a different kind of program is the microfilming of low-use materials at the British Library. A large quantity of this material is microfilmed 'for purely conservation purposes', the microfilm issued to readers, and the originals stored.[56] An example of a program limited to one institution is the University of Michigan's Brittle Book Microfilming Project. Its procedures, costings and other concerns are described in two articles published in *Microform Review*.[57] The Pacific Manuscripts Bureau was established in 1968 to preserve unpublished works relevant to the Pacific islands. The Bureau carries out this task by locating manuscripts of value and microfilming them. It is sponsored by libraries in Australia, New Zealand and Hawaii.[58]

PRESERVATION PHOTOGRAPHY

Preservation photography is normally applied only to original black-and-white photographic prints. The aim is to produce a master negative plus another negative (the interim master negative) from which prints can be taken as required. The master negative should be stored in the best possible conditions, for example in low temperature storage with the appropriate relative humidity, light and other levels, and should only need to be accessed on the rare occasions when the interim master is worn out and another interim master is needed. Prints can be taken from the interim master negative whenever required, for example to make a reference copy, or for exhibition purposes. Needless to say, high quality equipment and materials should be used, and the services of professional photographers should ideally be contracted.

DIGITAL DATA

Considerable attention is now being paid to the possibility of converting the intellectual content of items in library collections into digital data by electronic means and storing it on magnetic tapes or discs. Both textual and pictorial information can be converted, for example by using optical character recognition (OCR) devices which convert texts into their digital code equivalent, or by using scanners to convert text or, more usually, pictures into an analogue form. Text can also be input by keyboarding. In addition to information already in another format being converted to digital format, much information is now originated in digital form and may appear only in that form in the library (for example as computer magnetic tapes and discs). Once the text or pictorial image is converted to digital data it is possible to enhance the image using a computer, in order to improve the legibility of poor quality originals.

The British Library has developed an image digitizer (noted in Chapter 5) to allow copying of items in its collection. The image on the page is converted to a digital electronic signal which may be stored, displayed on a screen, sent to another destination or printed out. In 1991 the British Library funded a research project to investigate some of the factors involved in converting library material to digital data. This project will investigate the digitization of both microfilm and printed library material.

Digital data have considerable advantages. They can be rapidly duplicated and speedily transmitted without deterioration through electronic communications networks to wherever the user is working. They allow a high degree of storage space compression. They can be stored on a variety of media and can be transferred from one type of storage medium to another. They can offer rapid retrieval of and access to the information they represent. Their ability to be transmitted through electronic communications networks has been recognized as especially significant and is being investigated in several projects. When fully developed, such techniques allow access from sites anywhere in the world to electronic copies of original items. The implications for the preservation of items, by reducing handling of the original copies and by obviating the need to conserve several copies at different sites, are immense.[59]

When considering digital data for preservation, one must also be aware of the many challenges and questions which need to be faced.[60] One of the most important is the longevity of the physical media used to store the data. Current estimates of the life of optical discs, for instance, are about ten years, clearly not sufficient for library and archival purposes and considerably less than the life of the paper the information was transferred from. Although aging tests on optical discs are being carried out, by the British Library for example, the results are not yet available.

A second issue is that of the obsolescence of equipment. One rule of thumb suggests that sophisticated equipment, such as computer hardware and the recording and playback hardware needed for optical discs, becomes obsolete about every ten years and must be replaced, and the data converted to the new format. The enormous costs and effort involved are at present too great to contemplate, at least in library preservation terms. However, the possibility of converting high quality microfilm to optical disc at a later date, when the problems associated with the newer medium have been solved, is being successfully addressed.

Storage of digital data on magnetic tape, magnetic disk or other magnetic media raises similar questions. Their archival longevity is not yet known, so there is a need to rewrite the data every five to ten years to minimize the possibility of data loss through deterioration of the magnetic field. If digital data stored on magnetic media are used for reformatting, then the library is committed to a high standard of storage, periodic rewinding of tapes (as frequently as every six months is recommended by some authorities) and reconversion to other formats as they are developed in the future. The cost, especially in staff time, is high, and the implications for library management are considerable.[61] In addition to paying careful and sustained attention to the magnetic tapes and discs, it is necessary to preserve the hardware in working condition, and to maintain accurate documentation.

Other potential problems include the security of the data, for example data loss by accidental or malicious actions, and copyright concerns (noted earlier in this chapter). Much has been written about concerns relating to the archiving of digital data, particularly about the need for standards,[62] and about the effects that loss of data could have on keeping society's memory – the phrase 'the amnesiac society' has been coined to describe this.[63] Another issue relates to the current costs of conversion to digital data relative to other methods such as microfilming. The implications of greater access to digital information for all aspects of library operations are considerable – librarians are indeed re-evaluating their role as a result – but they are outside the scope of this book.

DIGITAL DATA STORAGE MEDIA

Media for storing digital data are constantly being developed, improved or superseded, and any discussion of them here can only be taken as a description of the current situation. Noted briefly here are the major formats in use at the time of writing.

Optical Discs

The use of optical discs as a format for storing large quantities of information is now well established in libraries. Although the potential of this format for preservation purposes has been eagerly explored, there are at present some major disadvantages which militate against its use as a preservation medium, especially where archival qualities such as longevity are required. As Bernard J.S. Williams put it in 1986, 'the technology is far from mature, standards are lacking and continuity and technological obsolescence pose major problems.'[64]

Optical discs, both analogue and digital, have data impressed in a series of pits onto a thin sheet of metal using laser technology. The metal sheet is sandwiched between two transparent layers and the information on them is read by a laser, which does not come into physical contact with the metal sheet. There is thus no direct contact and no mechanical wear on the metal sheet. They are capable of storing very large quantities of data, both textual and graphic, in a compact format. The most common examples of optical discs to be found in libraries are compact discs and CD-ROMs (compact discs – read only memory), and the larger videodiscs are sometimes present.

Many features of optical discs seem to be ideal for storing digital data. Their compactness is a definite plus, as ·is the enormous quantity of information they can store. Techniques have been developed which allow rapid access to the information stored on optical discs. However, conservators, and librarians and archivists concerned with preservation have approached this format with caution, despite its many positive features, because its permanence has not been clearly established (as already noted above).[65]

Optical disc use in library preservation is at present largely confined to providing a working copy of original items in high use collections where the fragile originals are still retained, rather than for items where the original artefacts are discarded after reformatting. One well-documented example of optical disc use of this nature is the Library of Congress's Optical Disk Pilot Program, which has produced discs containing both text and pictures.[66] Other examples are described by Alexander Wilson.[67]

There is little doubt that the use of optical discs for preservation will increase when the outstanding problems of this format are solved. In Alexander Wilson's words, 'the potential of optical disc technology for library preservation purposes is so great that this volatile field must be kept under continuous scrutiny.'[68]

Magnetic Media

Digital data have conventionally been stored on half-inch tape. Other magnetic media in use at present are magnetic discs ('hard' or Winchester disks, or floppy disks) and magneto-optical erasable disks which combine features of both magnetic and optical technology. In Chapter 2 some of the problems of using magnetic media for archival storage are noted. It is worth reiterating here the vulnerability of magnetic media to the actions of heat, light, humidity (or its absence), magnetism, dirt and erasure. Magnetic tape provides one example. The care of magnetic tape in archival situations needs to be of a high standard if the integrity of the data is to be retained. High levels of environmental control are required. Data will need to be refreshed by rewinding tapes on a regular basis, as often as every six months being recommended in British Standard BS4783 Part 2, 1988. Equipment must be scrupulously maintained. The data will probably need to be transferred to another more current medium at several stages during their life in order to ensure accessibility.

Other Media for Digital Data Storage

As already noted, new media are constantly being developed. Some which are still in the experimental stages or have been only very recently introduced are digital videotape, digital audiotape and digital paper. Lesk's 1990 report to the Commission on Preservation and Access should be referred to for further details.[69]

The possibility of using semiconductor memory for large-scale storage of digital data for preservation purposes was noted in a 1986 report on storage at the National Archives of the United States. The conclusions at that time were that the costs of the hardware and electricity, combined with the possibility of complete loss of data if the power supply was interrupted, were too great.[70] This may possibly become an acceptable method in the future as the costs of semiconductor memory decrease and as new technological developments occur.

OTHER REFORMATTING METHODS

Two further reformatting methods, publishing and transcription, are used, although neither of them is particularly common. Publishing may be either of a facsimile of the item or of the text, usually edited. Facsimile publishing is usually reserved for manuscripts or other works which have extensive manuscript additions or additional illustrations. Because publishing is an expensive process, this method of reformatting is normally used only when there is the likelihood that sufficient copies will be sold to recoup the financial outlay.

Transcription of the text by typing or wordprocessing has been frequently used in the past, for example for heavily used genealogical records and other manuscripts. Because it is very labour-intensive, and because the possibility of transcription errors is high, this method is not a serious contender as a technique for addressing the preservation problems of libraries.

Notes

1   *Preservation Microfilming: A Guide for Librarians and Archivists*, ed. Nancy E. Gwinn (Chicago, Ill.: American Library Association, 1987), p. 4. I am heavily indebted to this excellent book for the section on microfilming in this chapter. The reader should also consult the *Manual of Archival Reprography*, ed. Lajos Körmendy (München: K.G. Saur, 1989).

2   *Ibid.*, p. 39.

3   See 'Intrinsic Value in Archival Materials' in *A Modern Archives Reader: Basic Readings on Archival Theory and Practice*, ed. Maygene F. Daniels and Timothy Walch (Washington, D.C.: National Archives and Records Service, 1984), pp. 91-99.

4   Ross W. Atkinson, 'Selection for Preservation: A Materialistic Approach', *Library Resources and Technical Services* 30, 4 (1986): 344-347.

5   Margaret S. Child, 'Further Thoughts on "Selection for Preservation: A Materialistic Approach"', *Library Resources and Technical Services* 30, 4 (1986): 354-362.

6   *Selection for Preservation of Research Library Materials* (Washington, D.C.: Commission on Preservation and Access, 1989).

7   Peter McDonald, 'The Core Agriculture Literature Project: Setting Priorities for Preservation', *Abbey Newsletter* 15, 2 (April 1991): 17-18.

8   Noted in more detail by David F. Foxon, 'Priorities: A Bibliographer's View', in *Conservation of Library and Archival Materials and the Graphic Arts*, ed. Guy Petherbridge (London: Butterworths, 1987), pp. 221-225; and by Lisa B. Williams, 'Selecting Rare Books for Physical Conservation: Guidelines for Decision Making', *College and Research Libraries* 46, 2 (1985): 153-159.

9   *Preservation Microfilming, op. cit.*, p. 13.

10   'Preservation Guidelines in ARL Libraries', *SPEC Kit* 138 (1987).

11   *RLG Preservation Manual*. 2nd ed. (Stanford, Calif.: Research Libraries Group, 1986), pp. 82-84.

12   The advantages and disadvantages of each are noted in *Preservation Microfilming, op. cit.*, pp. 27-28.

13   Henry Olsson, 'Copyright Aspects of Reproduction', in *Preservation of Library Materials*, ed. Merrily A. Smith (München: K.G. Saur, 1987), Vol. 2, pp. 32-44.

14   Robert L. Oakley, *Copyright and Preservation: A Serious Problem in Need of a Thoughtful Solution* (Washington, D.C.: Commission on Preservation and Access, 1990).

15   These and other tools are noted in more detail in Carolyn Clark Morrow, *The Preservation Challenge: A Guide to Conserving Library Materials* (White Plains, N.Y.: Knowledge Industry Publications, 1983), pp. 93-113; and in *Preservation Microfilming, op. cit.*, pp. 40-53.

16   For example, Margaret Child, 'Is the Infrastructure in Place?', *National Preservation News* (May 1987), p. 19; William J. Welsh, 'Elements of a Worldwide Preservation Policy', in *Preservation of Library Materials* (1987), Vol. 1, pp. 12-13.

17   Valerie Ferris, 'Don't Film It If You're Not Recording It!', *Library Conservation News* 22 (1989): 3, 8; *The United States Newspaper Program: Cataloging Aspects*, ed. Ruth C. Carter (New York: Haworth Press, 1986).

18   'RLG and Chadwyck-Healey to Publish RLIN Preservation MasterFile', *Microform Review* 20, 1 (1991): 4, 6.

19   'OCLC and RLG Exchange Records', *Wilson Library Bulletin* (May 1986): 9; 'OCLC and RLG Announce Exchange of Preservation and Microform Set Records', *Research Libraries in OCLC* 18 (1986): 5; Betsy Kruger, 'Automating Preservation Information in RLIN', *Library Resources and Technical Services* 32, 2 (1988): 116-126.

20   *Conservation Administration News* 28 (1987): 11.

21   These issues and procedures are further examined in *Preservation Microfilming, op. cit.*, Chapter 5.

22   Diana Grimwood-Jones, 'Preservation', in *British Librarianship and Information Work 1981-1985: Volume Two, Special Libraries, Materials and Processes*, ed. David W. Bromley and Angela M. Allott (London: Library Association, 1988), p. 278; Ferris, *op. cit.*

23   Michael Roper, 'Policy for Format Conversion: Choosing a Format', in *Preservation of Library Materials* (1987), Vol. 1, pp. 59-67.

24   Michael Lesk, *Image Formats for Preservation and Access: A Report of the Technology Assessment Advisory Committee to the Commission on Preservation and Access* (Washington, D.C.: The Commission, 1990), p. 7.

25   *Ibid.*, p. 10. Other writers who address these points include Jerry Dupont, 'De-Romancing the Book: The Pyrrhic Victory of Microforms', *Microform Review* 19, 4 (1990): 192-197; Mark R. Yerburgh, 'Studying All Those "Tiny Tea Leaves": The Future of Microforms in a Complex Technological Environment', *Microform Review* 16, 1 (1987): 14-20.

26   One is Susan A. Cady, 'The Electronic Revolution in Libraries: Microfilm Déjà Vu?', *College and Research Libraries* 51, 4 (1990): 374-386; see also Donald J. Waters, *From Microfilm to Digital Imagery* (Washington, D.C.: Commission on Preservation and Access, 1991).

27   Preservation photocopying is discussed in Ellen McCrady, 'Reformatting Discussed at ALA', *Abbey Newsletter* 12, 6 (1988): 103; *Preservation Microfilming, op. cit.*, p. 28.

28   One hundred pages is suggested by the University of Michigan Library: see *SPEC Kit* 138 (1987), p. 58.

29   Morrow, *op. cit.*, p. 104.

30   McCrady, *op. cit.*, p. 103.

31   'Gift of $1.5m for Microfilming', *Library Association Record* 90, 12 (1988): 694.

32   The history of microfilming for library use is briefly noted in Thomas A. Bourke, 'The Microfilming of Newspapers: An Overview', *Microform Review* 15, 3 (1986): 154-157.

33   *Preservation Microfilming, op. cit.*, pp. 98-100, describes the characteristics of common formats.

34   Myron B. Chace, 'Preservation Microfiche: A Matter of Standards', *Library Resources and Technical Services* 35, 2 (1991): 186-190.

35   *Preservation Microfilming, op. cit.*, pp. 119-120, describes the film types. Another useful source is Helga Borck, 'Microforms', in *Conservation in the Library*, ed. Susan Garretson Swartzburg (Westport, Conn.: Greenwood Press, 1983), Chapter 6, pp. 129-138. See also Jeffrey H. Turner, 'The Suitability of Diazo Film for Long Term Storage', *Microform Review* 17, 3 (1988): 142-145.

36   *Preservation Microfilming, op. cit.*, pp. 70-95. See also Madeleine Perez, Andrew Raymond and Ann Swartzell, 'The Selection and Preparation of Archives and Manuscripts for Microreproduction', *Library Resources and Technical Services* 27, 4 (1983): 357-365.

37   *Preservation Microfilming, op. cit.*, pp. 96-108.

38   *Ibid.*, pp. 108-114.

39   Don M. Avedon, 'International Standards for Microforms', in *Preservation of Library Materials, op. cit.*, Vol. 1, pp. 68-77; *Preservation Microfilming, op. cit.*, pp. 114-116 and Appendix 1.

40   *Preservation Microfilming, op. cit.*, p. 23; see also p. 164.

41   *Ibid.*, p. 149.

42   Alexander Wilson, *Library Policy for Preservation and Conservation in the European Community* (München: K.G. Saur, 1988), p. 20.

43   *Preservation Microfilming, op. cit.*, p. 23.
44   Patricia A. McClung, 'Costs Associated with Preservation Microfilming: Results of the Research Libraries Group Study', *Library Resources and Technical Services* 30, 4 (1986): 363-374.
45   Alan Calmes, 'New Confidence in Microfilm', *Library Journal* (15 September 1986): 38-42; *Preservation of Historical Records* [report of the] Committee on Preservation of Historical Records (Washington, D.C.: National Academy Press, 1986), Chapter 5.
46   Nigel Krauth, *Matilda, My Darling* (Sydney: Allen and Unwin, 1983), p. 44. See also A.J. Anderson, 'Faculty to Library Director: We Hate Microfilm', *Library Journal* (15 October 1988): 50-52.
47   Ellen McCrady, 'The History of Microfilm Blemishes', *Restaurator* 6 (1984): 191-204.
48   *Preservation Microfilming, op. cit.*, p. 34.
49   Pamela W. Darling, 'Developing a Preservation Microfilming Program', in *Microforms in Libraries: A Reader*, ed. James A. Diaz (Weston, Conn.: Microform Review, 1975). Another helpful brief general guide is Ann Swartzell, 'Preservation Microfilming: In-House Initiated Microfilms', *Conservation Administration News* 34 (1988): 6-7.
50   Sherry Byrne, 'Guidelines for Contracting Microfilming Services', *Microform Review* 15, 4 (1986): 253-264.
51   Lawrence S. Robinson, 'Establishing a Preservation Microfilming Program: The Library of Congress Experience', *Microform Review* 13 (1984): 239-244; Mya Thanda Poe, 'Organizing and Implementing a Preservation Microfilming Program', in *Preservation of Library Materials, op. cit.*, Vol. 2, pp. 20-21.
52   Other cooperative projects and some of the issues that need to be addressed in such activities are noted in Carolyn Harris, 'Cooperative Approaches to Preservation Microfilming', in *Preservation Microfilming: Planning and Production: Papers from the RTSD Preservation Microfilming Institute ... 1988* (Chicago, Ill.: Association for Library Collections and Technical Services, ALA, 1989), pp. 55-65.
53   Eve Johansson, 'Newsplan: An Update', *Library Conservation News* 25 (1989): 25-26.
54   Pearce S. Grove, 'A Revolution in Newspaper Access', *Resource Sharing and Information Networks* 3, 1 (1985/1986): 101-114; *The United States Newspaper Program, op. cit.* (1986).
55   Penny Griffith, 'National Approaches to Newspaper Preservation: New Zealand', in *Newspaper Preservation and Access* (München: K.G. Saur, 1988) Vol. 2, pp. 316-325.
56   'Microfilm Projects in Progress', *Library Conservation News* 5 (1984): [2].
57   Janet Gertz, 'The University of Michigan Brittle Book Microfilming Program: A Cost Study', *Microform Review* 16, 1 (1987): 32-36; Margaret M. Byrnes and Nancy E. Elkington, 'Containing Preservation Microfilming Costs at the University of Michigan Library', *Microform Review* 16, 1 (1987): 37-39.

58 Bess Flores, 'The Pacific Manuscripts Bureau: An Agent for the Preservation and Distribution of Pacific Island Research Materials', *Microform Review* 18, 2 (1989): 103-108.

59 Some projects are noted in 'Maintaining a Good Image: Preservation on High', *Wilson Library Bulletin* (March 1991): 12; 'Commission Receives First Report on Digital Preservation Demonstration Project', *Commission on Preservation and Access Newsletter* 32 (March 1991): 3; Char Whitaker, 'Instant Images', *American Libraries* (October 1990): 854, 856.

60 A concise overview of advantages and challenges is in M. Stuart Lynn, 'Preservation and Access Technology: The Relationship between Digital and Other Media Conversion Processes', *Information Technology and Libraries* 9, 4 (1990): 309-336.

61 Further information is given in Colin Smith, 'Our Problems with Machine-Readable Records', *Archives and Manuscripts* 11, 2 (1983): 160-161; Roper, *op. cit.*, Vol. 1, pp. 59-67; Bernard J.S. Williams, 'Implications for Preservation of the Newer Information Media', in *Conservation in Crisis: Proceedings of a Seminar...1986* (London: British Library, 1987), pp. 57-64.

62 Victoria Irons Walch, 'The Role of Standards in the Archival Management of Electronic Records', *American Archivist* 53 (1990): 30-43.

63 Paul Sturges, 'Access to Information from the Past: The Birth of the Amnesiac Society', in Australian Library and Information Association 1st Biennial Conference, Perth, 1990 *Proceedings* (Canberra: ALIA, 1990), pp. 295-307. See also Paul Sturges, 'Policies and Criteria for the Archiving of Electronic Publishing', *Journal of Librarianship* 19, 3 (1987): 152-172; Monica Blake, 'Archiving of Electronic Publications', *Electronic Library* 7, 6 (1989): 376-386.

64 Williams, *op. cit.* p. 60.

65 A good summary of issues is given by Lindsay Howe, 'The Use of Optical Disc for Archival Image Storage', *Archives and Manuscripts* 18, 1 (1990): 89-118.

66 Joseph W. Price, 'Optical Disk Pilot Program at the Library of Congress' in *Preservation of Library Materials, op. cit.*, Vol. 1, pp. 156-159; Robin Alston, 'The Smithsonian Project: Image Capture and Retrieval', *Library Conservation News* 9 (1985): 6-7.

67 Wilson, *op. cit.*, Chapter 9, pp. 41-48.

68 *Ibid.*, p. 48.

69 Lesk, *op. cit.*

70 *Preservation of Historical Records* (1986), Appendix A, p. 93.

Chapter 9

Technological and Cooperative Strategies

Introduction

This chapter describes two sets of strategies which have been adopted to address the preservation problem in libraries. The first set is the development and application of technology, especially the use of technology which allows bulk treatment of deteriorated material. Examples of this are mass deacidification of paper, and the development and promotion of 'permanent' paper. The second set of strategies relies on cooperation among libraries and other institutions, usually over a long period, for their effect. Here are noted the development of regional cooperative conservation centres, measures to ensure bibliographic control of microfilm masters negatives, and the Conspectus approach and its application to the preservation of library materials.

Technological Strategies

Carolyn Clark Morrow has written that the success of efforts made in the field of preservation depends on the further development and application of scientific and technical processes to the problems.[1] While this may be an overstatement, it undoubtedly contains much more than a kernel of truth. Considerable success has already been achieved through applying new technology to the problems posed by deteriorating library materials. In some cases technology originally developed for other purposes has been recognized as applicable to library preservation and has been applied or adapted for library use. The use of vacuum packaging, more usually applied to the packaging of foodstuffs, is an example. In other cases a new technology has been developed specifically to address a problem or range of problems, for example the development of mass deacidification.

Technological developments do not come cheaply. There must be a willingness to invest time and money to accompany the desire to make such developments and apply them. Sparks notes:

No major technological development of civilization was accomplished overnight. Regardless of the era, every major advance required years of work to perfect. Then, as now, considerable funds and a willingness to learn from many failures were required before the project was a success. It was a long path from the Wright Brothers at Kittyhawk to the flight of the Concorde.[2]

He also suggests that the initiative and the funding for major technological developments, as well as the risk-taking, must come from national libraries throughout the world. This has indeed been the case: Sparks' own institution, the Library of Congress (although nominally not a national library), has funded considerable research into a mass deacidification process, and the British Library has to its credit such developments as an image digitizer and a process of strengthening paper.

Another important element of technological strategies is the recognition of the value of basic research. Research such as that into the physical and chemical makeup of materials used in the manufacture of library items is essential for the better understanding of the processes of deterioration, and thereby for the development of more effective ways to counteract these effects. It is also crucial to some preservation programs to have access to facilities where routine testing of materials and processes, such as testing microfilms for residual thiosulphate, can be carried out.

Examples are plentiful. They include – and this is by no means a comprehensive list – the development of the leafcasting machine which fills in holes and other missing parts of a sheet of paper (but of course not the image on it), the development of many techniques and standards used in microfilming, aqueous deacidification processes for paper, large-scale mass deacidification treatments, developments in and applications of optical technology, freeze-drying techniques using vacuum chambers, and the cold storage of materials. Some of these are noted in detail below.

Cooperative Strategies

The significance of strategies requiring cooperation among libraries has been recognized for several decades. They are now well established in the repertoire of techniques to address the preservation problem. The IFLA *Principles for the Preservation and Conservation of Library Materials* note this and are worth quoting in some detail:

Links with other libraries.
16.   In view of the necessity to preserve library collections for future generations of users it is essential that libraries work together on preservation policies at both national and international levels. It is necessary to emphasise that such national and international policies need to be applied not only to older library materials but also to those being produced today.
17.   National library associations and national libraries have a responsibility for formulating national policies and promoting their acceptance. IFLA has a responsibility to encourage the acceptance and

diffusion of professional principles of preservation and conservation administration through its channels.[3]

Cooperative projects have been set up in the United States and have provided models for similar programs in other parts of the world. Well-established programs in the United States are effective in areas such as cooperative agreements on collection building and retention policies, bibliographic control of microfilm masters and regional conservation centres.[4] Cooperation is recognized as the key in several major reports on preservation. The Ratcliffe report for the United Kingdom, published in 1984, recommended ten cooperative activities.[5] The Brittle Books report for the United States (published in 1986) makes it clear that cooperation is the key to programs to address the preservation problem in libraries in the United States, through such statements as 'Systematic and purposeful collaboration is essential.'[6] Their powerful argument is quoted in full:

> The brittle books problem will not be solved by accident. The scale is too great, the cost too large, and the setting too complex. A joining of forces...is needed. More than anything else, the projected cost of preservation demands program efficiency and credibility. Targets must be realistic, results visible, and benefits unquestioned. Even though the work will be done cooperatively, success in preservation will be dependent on the performance of each institution. Ideally, the program to preserve brittle books should improve the methods and enhance the principles of effective collaboration among libraries and research institutions, for while they are individually distinctive, they have a common cause.[7]

The last part of this quote indicates a trend in cooperative programs in recent years, away from the establishment of facilities which actually carry out conservation treatments (regional conservation laboratories, for example) towards putting in place mechanisms which encourage cooperative activities, such as resource-sharing agreements with associated retention and preservation policies. An example is the concept of a national bibliographic system for recording preservation actions, such as OCLC (the Online Computer Library Center) and RLIN (the Research Libraries Information Network) in the United States, which store on computer, and provide access to, bibliographic records about microform master negatives.

Carolyn Clark Morrow attempts a basic typology of cooperative preservation programs.[8] She considers that five different types of preservation cooperative services are feasible: information, consultation and surveying, cost-sharing, coordination, treatment. Information cooperative activities include newsletters and online directories. Consultation and surveying activities provide the services of experienced surveyors to assess the preservation requirements of a library (see Chapter 3). Cost-sharing activities include cooperative purchase schemes for expensive equipment, or indenting of conservation materials to provide discounts available to bulk purchasers. Coordination activities include preservation microfilming programs to eliminate duplication, providing centralized training courses, or coordinating library staff who have salvage experience to respond to disasters. Treatment cooperatives, although going out of fashion in the form of regional treatment centres, still have a place in activities such as providing specialized treatments for especially valuable artefacts.

Examples of some cooperative programs are given in detail later in this chapter.

TECHNOLOGICAL STRATEGIES

The following sections describe some of the most important examples of the application of advanced technology to preservation concerns. Two of the most significant, the development of permanent paper and mass deacidification processes, are described, as are a number of smaller projects.

Permanent Paper

So-called 'permanent' paper is not permanent. All paper is made from organic materials and will, in time, deteriorate. What we can aim at is to produce and use in our libraries paper which is as durable and permanent as possible, thus ensuring that the books and other paper-based items we are responsible for can be used for as long as needed. Chapter 2 notes the requirements for paper to be long-lived enough and strong enough to withstand the wear and tear imposed on it in library collections, and also describes the process of making paper. The significant facts are recounted here.

Modern methods of paper manufacture are able to produce paper which is both permanent and durable. Such paper is made of long cellulose fibres, and all chemical residues from the pulping and bleaching processes have been removed from it. It contains sizing material that is not harmful, and no lignin is left in it. This paper is usually made from chemical wood pulp. It has, as a minimum requirement, a pH of 7.0 or higher, but ideally an alkaline reserve is introduced to act as a buffer from acids which may come into contact with it from the air or from adjacent acidic materials. The pH of alkaline reserve paper is about 8.5 to 10.

Although much paper is not intended to be retained for any length of time, newsprint and wrapping paper being the most obvious examples, paper for purposes such as book manufacturing should be permanent. This is starting to happen, but it is a slow process and considerable effort must be made to ensure that more books are printed on long-lasting paper. In 1960 permanent paper was first produced commercially to specifications developed by Barrow. Standards based on Barrow's specifications have been developed and are being widely promoted at present.[9]

Standards for Permanent Paper

Barrow's 'Tentative Specifications for Durable, Non-Coated, Chemical Wood Book Papers' were published in 1960.[10] They included the requirements that there must be no groundwood and unbleached fibres present, that the pH must be not less than 6.5 at the time of manufacture, and that the paper must not show any 'sharp decline' after specified aging tests had been applied. Barrow's specifications eventually led, after further testing and development, to the publication in 1984 of the *American National Standard for Information Science D Permanence of Paper for Printed Library Materials*, ANSI Z39.48-1984.[11] Main features of this standard are that pH should be a minimum of 7.5, that no groundwood or unbleached pulp should be present in the paper, that specified levels of fold endurance and tear resistance should be met or exceeded, and that an alkaline reserve at a minimum prescribed level should be present. Standard testing methods are also described.[12]

This ANSI standard has been adopted by publishers in the United States, although not yet to such an extent that a majority of recently published books added to library collections are on paper that meets the standard. The number which are is, however, increasing, and on the verso of the title pages of many books can now be found statements such as 'The paper used in this publication meets the minimum requirements of American National Standard for Information Sciences – Permanence of Paper for Printed Library Materials, ANSI Z39.48-1984' or, an example of adherence to an earlier standard, 'This book is printed on acid free paper. The paper in this book meets the guidelines for permanence and durability of the Committee on Production Guidelines for Book Longevity of the Council on Library Resources.' A revised draft of the 1984 ANSI standard was circulated in 1989. This revision has expanded its scope, as its title, 'Permanence of Paper for Publications and Documents in Libraries and Archives', indicates.[13] No permanent paper standard has yet been published in the United Kingdom.[14] An International Standards Organization (ISO) working group is formulating an international standard for permanent paper.[15]

The Manufacture of Permanent Paper

If permanent paper is so clearly a 'good thing', why is it not commonly produced and more widely available? In Chapter 2 is found a short description of the process of manufacturing alkaline paper, and it is noted there that the differences between the sulphite process, which results in paper which is acidic, and the sulphate process, resulting in alkaline paper, are relatively minor. Why, then, have paper manufacturers not made the changes necessary to produce the more desirable paper? One reason is that paper for book manufacturing is an insubstantial part of total paper production, only about 1 per cent,[16] and this does not provide sufficient leverage to force the change on paper manufacturers.

The answer is largely an economic one. Briefly and in simple terms, the chemicals required may be more expensive, and more money may need to be spent on treating waste products.[17] Despite this, the trend has been towards more paper-mills converting to the production of alkaline paper. This apparent contradiction is explained by reductions in costs resulting from a combination of factors. Among these cost-saving factors are: alkaline paper is stronger and savings can be made by eliminating some chemicals added to maintain paper strength in the sulphite process; waste water and by-products of the alkaline process can be recycled, thus reducing the costs of effluent control; the paper-making machinery lasts longer because the alkaline process is less corrosive than the acidic process; energy savings can be made; and no major capital expenditure is needed to convert the machinery from an acid to an alkaline process.[18] It may be that the problems for libraries caused by acidic paper manufacture will be solved by default.

An indication of the changes which are taking place can be gained from the news items published in the newsletter, *Alkaline Paper Advocate*. 'Finland Is Nearly 100% Alkaline' declares one headline in that newsletter in 1988, and another item in the same newsletter notes the conversion of paper-mills in Canada and the United States.[19] A third notes that at the start of 1988 about 25 per cent of all coated and uncoated printing and writing paper produced in North America was alkaline.[20] By 1989 it was estimated that 50 to 60 per cent of paper manufactured in Europe was made by alkaline processes.[21]

Promoting the Use of Permanent Paper

Despite the intimation in the previous section that the main factor in the conversion from acidic to alkaline paper manufacture is economic and that librarians have had little or no part to play in it, the change can be hastened by the library profession. To the forces of business have been added the cries of librarians, publishers and authors.

> For the first time in many years there is reason to believe that paper-makers will change their process and start to make lasting paper again. There are so many advantages to them in the new process that this must come about. To speed the change to alkaline paper, every paper consumer, every magazine subscriber, every librarian, and every purchasing agent must make their voices heard.[22]

This message has been promoted in many ways and at numerous forums, some of which are noted here.

The American Library Association published in 1988 a work entitled *Preparation of Archival Copies of Theses and Dissertations*. This specified that the paper used must be 'selected for its permanence and durability', be 'acid-free with a minimum of 2 percent alkaline reserve', and the paper used for copies 'should also be on an acid-free paper with a 2 percent alkaline reserve'.[23] The review journal, *Reference and Research Book News* (ISSN

0887-3763), now notes in some reviews whether a book reviewed is printed on alkaline paper.[24]

Resolutions have been passed over the last decade at forums of librarians. The American Library Association passed a resolution in 1980 which called for improved quality of book production, noting the need for 'volumes free from self-destructive substances for all texts of lasting usefulness'; a preceding section makes clear that 'permanent/durable paper' is one major component. The American Library Association again called for the use of permanent paper in 1988 in its 'Resolution on Use of Permanent Paper in Books and Other Publications';[25] it passed a third resolution in 1990 supporting a national policy on permanent paper and supporting state legislation that required the use of such paper.[26] IFLA (the International Federation of Library Associations and Institutions) approved three resolutions at its 1989 annual conference in Paris. These urged the use of permanent paper by governments and publishers, the rapid completion of an international standard for permanent paper, and that IFLA itself use permanent paper for all its publications and documentation.[27]

Authors and publishers have joined forces with librarians to promote the use of permanent paper. In 1989 authors and publishers in the United States signed a declaration of their 'commitment to use acid-free paper for all first printings of quality hardcover trade books in order to preserve the printed word and safeguard our cultural heritage for future generations.' The declaration was signed by authors of the prominence of Isaac Asimov, Susan Sontag, Barbara Goldsmith, Maurice Sendak and Kurt Vonnegut; publishers included Columbia University Press, Simon and Schuster, Doubleday, Harper and Row, and Macmillan.[28] Another move involving the book trade was the decision made by the United States Government Printing Office, the largest printer in the United States, to use permanent paper for selected documents.[29] In England the Publications Division of HMSO (Her Majesty's Stationery Office) was in 1990 producing about one-third of the 9000 titles it publishes each year on permanent paper.[30] Professional societies, concerned that their publications might not survive into the future, have begun to publish on permanent paper. One example is the American Psychological Association, which from 1986 printed seventeen of its journals on acid-free paper.[31] Some of the states in the US have passed laws which require the use of permanent or alkaline paper for some categories of government publications, and the federal government has also followed suit. In October 1990 President Bush signed a Congressional Joint Resolution which makes permanent paper use for some federal records a national policy.[32]

One potential problem for librarians will be the increasing use of recycled paper. If too high a percentage of recycled paper is used in the manufacture of permanent paper, weaker paper results from the shorter fibres which recycled paper contains by virtue of its having already been through the papermaking process. Regulations passed in several countries have made the use of paper which contains some recycled fibre mandatory for government departments, and the potential of these moves will be reflected in paper of lower strength in library collections.[33] Care will be needed to ensure that items whose life needs to be as long as possible are printed on paper which contains a low proportion of recycled fibre to virgin fibre.

Mass Deacidification Processes

The aim of mass deacidification processes is to neutralize the acid in paper in books and documents and add alkaline to the paper to leave it with a buffer to withstand future acid attack. Deacidification of individual sheets or documents was developed and refined by William Barrow in the 1940s and has been a standard technique of the conservator since that time. This type of technique involves the paper sheet being washed and soaked in an alkaline solution, and is known as aqueous deacidification. Mass deacidification, the subject of this section, is concerned with treating items (books and other paper-based material) en masse, ideally in batches of several thousand.

In mass deacidification processes gas or liquid is introduced into a sealed chamber into which the items to be deacidified have been stacked. A vacuum is introduced into the chamber which forces the gas or liquid to penetrate throughout the items. The gas or liquid used reacts with the paper to neutralize it and leave an alkaline residue to act as a buffer. Finally, waste products are withdrawn from the chamber.

Such processes require a high level of scientific, technical and engineering expertise and are expensive to establish and operate. Furthermore, only in very recent years have most of them been developed beyond the experimental stages, so there are still many unknowns about their use and costs. Several processes have now become available on a commercial basis, and better data should be published over the next few years, enabling more thorough evaluation of the advantages and costs of mass deacidification. The promise of these processes is, however, considerable.

Mass deacidification will not be the panacea for the acid paper problem. It does not return the paper in an already deteriorated book to its original condition: 'deacidifying a brittle book leaves you with a brittle book.'[34] With the growing realization that deacidification by itself is not enough, recent research has been directed towards finding a way to strengthen the paper in addition to neutralizing the acid and introducing an alkaline buffer. The best way of using mass deacidification will probably be preventive, to treat new acquisitions of paper-based items before they are added to the library's collection, rather than items already present in the collections. The decision about when to use mass deacidification is closely linked with other preservation processes and their effects. If, for example, permanent paper is more frequently used, fewer new acquisitions will require mass deacidification; if all or most new acquisitions are routinely treated in a mass deacidification process, there is still the need to cope with the deteriorating items already in the collection by using microfilming and other methods already noted in previous chapters.

Several mass deacidification processes are now available, each with its promoters and detractors. A major study of five schemes (DEZ, Bookkeeper, Booksaver, Wei T'o, and a process developed by the Lithium Corporation) was undertaken by the Committee on Institutional Cooperation, which represents the largest university libraries in the United States.[35] This, plus the interest shown in developing mass deacidification facilities to be operated on a commercial basis, indicates that the processes are at last becoming viable for the library community.

The two major processes are noted below, and George Cunha's assessment of them according to the criteria used in his 1987 study is given.[36] These examine: uniformity of neutralization throughout the item; alkaline reserve; harmful nature to paper or other parts of the book; flexibility of process, as regards size and type of items processed; cost; availability of raw materials; speed of the process; safety and toxicity for operators of the process and for users of the deacidified items; whether chemicals volatilize out after deacidification; and whether new problems are caused by the process. It should be noted that the descriptions which follow are based on the best evidence available at the time of writing, but because the world of mass deacidification changes very rapidly the reader may wish to update them, for example by referring to recent issues of the periodicals noted in this book's 'Select Bibliography'.

The Library of Congress and the DEZ Process

Work began at the Library of Congress on developing a mass deacidification process as early as 1971, and at an early stage DEZ (diethyl zinc) gas was chosen as the active ingredient. Large-scale trials were held in 1978, but these pointed out two major problems: unwelcome ring-shaped deposits formed on book covers; and the deacidified paper was unduly sensitive to ultraviolet light. Solutions were devised to these and other technical problems, but further difficulties arose, relating to the safety of the volatile diethyl zinc and in particular to its transport and handling. Again solutions were developed to these problems, and the next stage was more full-scale testing.[37]

Increasing concern about the DEZ process was expressed in an article in *Library Journal* in 1986, on the grounds of its safety (there had been fires and an explosion at the test facility), lack of progress and heavy expenditure. The Library of Congress defended its position in a response in the same periodical, and then agreed to an independent review,[38] which was published in May 1988.[39] The DEZ process has now been licensed to Akzo Chemicals Inc., who will build and operate mass deacidification facilities on a commercial basis. In May 1991 Johns Hopkins University signed a contract with Akzo to treat books for a one-year period at an estimated cost of nearly US$11 per item. The Library of Congress has, meanwhile, rejected all bids received on its tender to treat one million books per year.[40]

According to Cunha's 1987 and 1989 reports, the DEZ process uniformly neutralizes, resulting in a pH level of 7-7.5 and an alkaline deposit equivalent to 1.5-2 per cent calcium carbonate. Discolouration of plastic book covers may occur on rare occasions. There is no residual odour. The process is flexible and can accommodate a range of items of different sizes and types, although highly coated glossy papers (usually in serials) are best separated from other types of paper and processed in a batch by themselves. Cunha in 1987 estimated the cost to be US$2.50 to $3.00 per book, but Akzo expects to charge US$6 to $10. An estimated fifty to fifty-five hours will be needed to process 7500 books. Diethyl zinc reacts violently with water, but safety matters have been addressed and this process should be safe for operators; the zinc oxide which remains in the processed books as a buffer is probably safe. Chemicals will not volatilize out after deacidification. The process does not introduce any new problems, except for some plastic book covers, as already noted. Although the DEZ process is not primarily aimed at strengthening the paper which goes through the process, Cunha reports that the folding endurance of treated paper increased 'by a factor of 3-5'.[41]

The Wei T'o Process

Richard Smith has for many years been associated with mass deacidification research, and he holds the patents for a process he developed and named Wei T'o. The active ingredient in this process is methoxy magnesium methyl carbonate. In 1974 Smith was invited to develop a mass deacidification process for the Public Archives and National Library of Canada; tests of this were successful, and the facility has been operating satisfactorily since 1981.[42] It has been installed at the Bibliothèque Nationale's Centre de Conservation at Sablé, France.[43] The latest state of the Wei T'o process is that rights to it have been purchased by the Union Carbide Company. This may be especially significant because Union Carbide has experience with a method of paper strengthening using parylene. The combination of the two techniques could be a powerful one.[44]

Selection of the books to be deacidified is an important part of the Wei T'o process because some categories of materials are adversely affected: those containing ball-point pen ink and inks which are soluble in alcohol, and laminated plastic and some bindings. The books are air-dried for twenty-four hours to remove all moisture, which, if present during the process, reacts with the deacidification agent to form a solid. They are then placed in a vacuum chamber, the air is removed, and a deacidification solution containing methanol as a solvent is pumped in under pressure. When the books have been thoroughly wetted with this solution, the excess is drained off, the books are dried, and are then allowed to regain moisture and return to room temperature.

Up to the present the Wei T'o process has been operated only on a relatively small scale. However, it appears to be capable of handling considerably larger numbers of books by increasing the size of the vacuum chamber or installing more chambers, and by operating the facility continuously instead of for one shift only per day. The Wei T'o process is reported by Cunha as increasing the fold strength of paper by a factor between two and four.

Cunha's 1987 and 1989 reports assess the Wei T'o process. This process uniformly neutralizes, resulting in a pH level of 8.5 to 9.5 and an alkaline deposit equivalent to 0.7 to 0.8 per cent calcium carbonate. There is slight discolouration of groundwood pulp paper and some inks may be slightly soluble. There is no residual odour. The process can handle a wide range of sizes and materials and allows for adjustment of the level of alkaline reserve. The actual cost per volume in 1987 was US$3.00 to $3.50, with a lower projected cost of under US$2.00 if the process were run at greater capacity. One hour is required for thirty to sixty books; higher volumes are possible if required. The Wei T'o process is generally very safe. The process may introduce some new problems: some inks may be soluble, and discolouration of leather covers and coloured illustrations may occur.

The DEZ and Wei T'o processes still appear to be the main contenders among the available mass deacidification processes, although other processes are at advanced stages of development and will need careful evaluation when more is known about them, their costs and the results they produce. (Brief descriptions of the other processes are given below.) Cunha's 1987 and 1989 reports compare the two main processes. By increasing the size of the Wei T'o facility and operating it continuously 600,000 books per year could be treated; the DEZ process output is estimated at about one million per year. Wei T'o facilities can be installed almost anywhere in a library building, whereas the DEZ facility needs to be established in a separate building because of the potential hazards of diethyl zinc; in addition, staff to operate the DEZ process need to be more highly trained. Although accurate cost comparisons are not available, general indications suggest that the capital expenditure required to establish a Wei T'o facility is a little over half that required for a DEZ facility.

Wei T'o has also been used at Princeton University Library, but is there applied by spraying rather than in a vacuum chamber process. This installation and the results achieved by it from 1982 to 1989 are described by Susan Sayre Batton.[45]

Developments at the British Library

The British Library, recognizing that the existing mass deacidification processes do not address well the question of strengthening paper, began funding research in 1980. In the technique which has been developed, books are placed in a container from which air is removed by purging it with nitrogen. A gaseous acrylic monomer mixture (ethyl acrylate with methyl acrylate) is added to impregnate the books which are then irradiated with gamma rays, converting the monomers into polymers, and residual monomers are removed and the books aired. The resulting polymers add strength to the cellulose fibres, increasing the fold endurance by a factor of between five and ten.[46]

The British Library was in late 1989 seeking further funding to establish a pilot program and was also seeking commercial interest in developing the graft polymerization process.[47] No estimate of when this process might be commercially available has yet appeared in the literature, nor is there any indication of how many books it could potentially handle in one year, although the British Library was hoping to achieve costs comparable with the Wei T'o process for about 100,000 books per year.

Other Mass Deacidification Processes

Cunha's 1989 update to his 1987 assessment of mass deacidification processes lists at least ten processes in addition to the two already noted above. Some of these were already in operation at the start of 1989, although as yet full assessments of them are not available. The two processes operating in North America were the Wei T'o process in Canada (see above) and the Book Preservation Associates ammonia/ethylene oxide process in New Jersey. Several more in the United States were noted as approaching a stage where they could begin operation: the DEZ process (see above), the Bookkeeper process, and a process to be operated by Lithco (the Lithium Corporation of America). Other processes in operation which deacidify and strengthen paper, but do not operate on a large enough scale to be called mass processes, include one for newspapers developed at the National Library of Austria. Cunha noted that, with several processes already available and more to become available, the emphasis will be placed more and more on processes which strengthen as well as deacidify, and those which do not offer a significant increase in paper strength will be less attractive to libraries.

The BPA Process

Book Preservation Associates has developed a mass deacidification process based on the use of ammonia and ethylene gas which impregnates books in a large treatment chamber. It is reported by its developers to be a stable process which raises pH levels to 7.5 to 9 and adds an alkaline buffer. Cunha gives (in 1989) prices of US$3.00 to $5.00 per volume and suggests an annual throughput of seven million volumes. A small amount of preselection of items for treatment, to sort out old leather bindings, is required. The BPA process sterilizes books as well as deacidifying them. Cleveland Public Library has used its services for over 50,000 volumes, but no independent assessment of this test is yet available.[48]

Bookkeeper Process

The Koppers Company developed a deacidification process in the early 1980s which has since 1987 been further developed by a new company. This process does not involve dangerous chemicals or processes and is safe enough to locate in a library building. It uses fine particles of magnesium oxide dispersed in a fluorocarbon, which impregnate and adhere to the paper fibres. Surplus magnesium oxide particles provide an alkaline barrier. In 1988 the process was considered to have significant potential, but had not then been operated at a level above the prototype level, and its potential for large-scale use, although very promising, was still unproven.[49]

Lithco Process
Lithco (the Lithium Company of America) has patented compounds and processes which are proving effective in both deacidifying and strengthening paper. Tests indicate that paper is strengthened by a factor of ten to twelve, that pH levels after treatment are in the order of 7 to 9, and that an alkaline reserve in the range 1.5 to 2.3 per cent results.[50] A demonstration plant capable of handling 300,000 books per year was opened in May 1990, and a commercial facility able to treat one to three million books per year was scheduled to be operational in 1991.[51]

Viennese Process
The National Library of Austria has developed a process which is applicable only to newsprint and which deacidifies as well as strengthens. Volumes in a vacuum are impregnated with an aqueous solution, which includes calcium hydroxide as a deacidification agent and methyl cellulose as a strengthening agent, and are then freeze-dried. Fold strength is increased by up to six times. Fifty-six volumes of newspapers can be treated per week.[52]

The mass deacidification field is obviously in a stage of flux, and which processes become popular and which fall by the wayside cannot yet be foreseen. Cunha, in the 1989 update to his 1987 assessment, notes that one of the factors which will become of increasing importance is that those processes which use CFCs (chlorofluorocarbons) will need to be modified to meet increasingly stringent regulations governing the use of these ozone layer-destroying chemicals. It is possible that not all processes will be able to replace CFCs successfully and will therefore not remain viable.[53]

Further Technological Strategies

Although this section has concentrated on technological developments in the areas of permanent paper and mass deacidification processes, other areas have benefited and will continue to benefit from investigation into technologies which can be used to assist the preservation effort in libraries.

Research and development in many areas is needed. For example, research into the materials from which library items are constructed and into their methods of construction, with the aim of developing new materials and methods which are more durable and less susceptible to deterioration, is clearly useful. Research into preservation has included the development of aging tests to ascertain the longevity of newly introduced media such as optical discs, into disaster recovery techniques such as freeze-drying and its effects on various kinds of paper, and into the use of irradiation for the control of biological pests. In Britain research has included investigation of new methods of providing protection to bookbinding leather from atmospheric pollution, the use of gamma irradiation to control moulds on paper, and new techniques of copying materials carried out by the British Library and already noted in Chapter 5.[54]

COOPERATIVE STRATEGIES

Strategies requiring cooperation among libraries at regional, national and international levels are well established in the field of preservation. They have been recognized as the key to effective large-scale action in several recent major reports. Some examples are described below.

Cooperation in Preservation in the United States

The history of cooperative preservation programs in the United States has been noted by several writers.[55] There has been a long-standing commitment to cooperation, with bodies such as the Association of Research Libraries and later the Research Libraries Group, the Council on Library Resources and the Commission on Preservation and Access being instrumental in developing programs. The Research Libraries Group program has had most effect in addressing the preservation problem. One of its primary programs is preservation, and it has developed, for example, a preservation microfilming program and associated procedures for bibliographic control.[56] It has also developed the Conspectus approach to resource sharing, which has considerable significance for preservation and is considered in more detail below.

The Research Libraries Group has drawn up a statement of the preservation obligations of its members. It states that member libraries have an obligation to 'each other and to scholars nationwide to preserve their collections.' Member libraries are urged to establish local preservation programs to maintain their collections in good condition, and how to decide what is good condition is defined. If materials do not meet the criteria of being in good condition, then member libraries have an obligation to develop and apply as many options for preserving deteriorated materials as possible, including 'repair, rebinding, and restoration where appropriate', the purchase of replacement copies or reproduction in an archival quality format.[57]

The Association of Research Libraries adopted preservation as one of its principal objectives in 1983. It has developed the Preservation Planning Program to assist its members in ascertaining their preservation needs.[58] It has, like the Research Libraries Group, also developed a statement of 'Minimum Preservation Efforts in ARL Libraries'. This covers five areas. First, it states that every library should have a clearly defined statement of its preservation goals and objectives and a description of present and intended future preservation activities. Next, it emphasizes the importance of compiling basic statistics about preservation on a regular basis, to be used to monitor developments and progress. Third, the importance of a coordinated national effort in microfilming and preservation copying is emphasized, and the essential steps to achieve this are outlined. Fourth, the need to house collections which are unique or otherwise important to the national collection in appropriate environmental conditions is stated. Finally, the extent to which each member library should fund its preservation program is defined: at least 10 per cent of its expenditure on books, serials and other acquisitions, or at least 4 per cent of its total expenditure, should be allocated to preservation.[59]

International Cooperation for Preservation

In recent years the importance of international cooperation for preservation has been recognized, and to advance cooperation IFLA has adopted preservation as one of its core programs.[60] The IFLA Core Program on Preservation and Access was officially launched in 1986. Based at the Library of Congress, it also has regional centres in Tokyo, Canberra, Caracas, Leipzig and at Sablé.[61] Five primary areas are initially being concentrated on: the promotion and encouragement of preservation policies; research on methods and materials; coordination of the activities of IFLA and other organizations; education; and publications aimed at raising preservation awareness. The regional centres are also concerned with representing the preservation needs of their regions at the international level, as well as promoting preservation within their areas. It has, according to its Director,

> undertaken and contributed to activities that increase awareness, interest, and knowledge about preservation among individuals, institutions, and governments worldwide. All facets of the programme are oriented towards establishing an international milieu in which preservation activities can flourish and an international network of individuals and centres through which preservation information can flow.[62]

The 1990 report of the IFLA Core Program on Preservation and Access noted the activities of the Program.[63] These included the running of regional conferences, preparation of publications, among them the newsletter *International Preservation News*, developing an audiovisual program on the care and handling of audio materials, and administering the international program. The report notes also the activities of the regional centres in education and training, developing internship programs and technical research.

Regional Cooperation

One of the earliest cooperative preservation activities was the establishment and operation of regional conservation centres. These were established to make available the expensive facilities required for a fully equipped conservation laboratory. Initially the emphasis of these centres was on providing conservation facilities and on carrying out conservation treatments, that is, on restoration and conservation rather than on preventive preservation. More recently the emphasis of these centres has moved away from artefact conservation to preventive preservation, and they offer consultancy services to assist individual libraries in designing and implementing their own preservation programs.[64]

One of the most notable of the regional centres is the Northeast Document Conservation Center at Andover, Massachusetts.[65] It was established in 1973 and now offers all kinds of paper conservation treatment, conservation binding, a preservation microfilming service, educational programs and consultancy services in all aspects of preservation. It had thirty-five staff in 1988, fifteen of them conservators. Increasingly important is the Center's Field Service Program, which aims to bring preservation within the reach of smaller institutions by emphasizing preventive preservation rather than restoration. To this end the Field Service Program carries out surveys and offers advice. A disaster assistance service is available at all times. Education is an essential part of the Center's activities.

The Northeast Document Conservation Center model has not been widely adopted, largely because of the great expense involved in establishing such facilities and because of the shortage of fully qualified staff. Other cooperative activities have focused on providing advice and coordinating activities rather than providing facilities for conservation treatments on a regional basis. One example is the Illinois Cooperative Conservation Program.

Regional cooperation need not, of course, be restricted to the operation of conservation centres. Libraries in particular areas have cooperated in other preservation activities. In the US Midwest the Committee on Institutional Cooperation, established over three decades ago, has turned its attention to developing a regional preservation plan for its member libraries.[66] A state-based cooperative program, one of many examples of state-wide cooperative preservation activities, is being implemented in Massachusetts.[67]

National Preservation Programs

Several countries have established a national preservation program. Such programs have as their primary roles education and coordination. The National Preservation Office established in 1984 at the British Library is one example. Its aims were initially expressed as to 'promote awareness of pressing conservation problems, and the need for good practices; provide information and referral services on preservation issues; investigate and initiate debate on important national developments; encourage co-operative ventures.'[68]

The National Preservation Office has been active in promoting its aims. It has published much, especially significant being the papers presented at conferences it has organized, and has made and distributed videos on preservation matters. It is establishing an information service covering such fields as directories of conservators and equipment manufacturers and suppliers, and bibliographical information. It has assisted in conducting a survey into preservation teaching at library schools in the United Kingdom. These are only some of its activities. More recently its role has been extended to include library security. Activities in this area include promotion of the need for security, acting as an information and referral point, initiating debate about library security, and ascertaining the need for a United Kingdom register of missing books.[69]

While the US does not have a body specifically designated as a national preservation office, the Commission on Preservation and Access fulfils these functions. It is 'a private, nonprofit organization acting on behalf of the nation's libraries, archives and universities to develop and encourage collaborative strategies for preserving and making available the increasing portions of our deteriorating published and documentary record.' The Commission coordinates the nation-wide Brittle Books program, begun in 1988 cooperatively to reformat books at risk in US libraries. It has actively encouraged research into many aspects of preservation, among them the issue of selection for preservation and new technologies for reformatting such as digitizing (noted in Chapter 8). The Commission has established links with preservation activities internationally. Preservation education is another area in which it has been active.[70]

National preservation activities are also, of course, carried out in countries which have not yet established a national preservation office. They include the functions of national bibliographic control, the coordination of large-scale microfilming projects, and the Conspectus approach. These three activities are essential to any effective nationally coordinated preservation program.

National bibliographic control has already been examined in Chapter 8, and only the main features need to be summarized here. It is essential to avoid unnecessary duplication of effort, for example in microfilming projects. Already there exist bibliographic utilities whose services accommodate the requirements of recording preservation information, such as RLIN and OCLC in the United States. Considerable expertise is already available, and recent modifications in the MARC record format can allow further development to take place. One form of national bibliographic control is the registering of microfilm masters, of which the British Library's Register of Microform Masters is an example.

One US bibliographic utility has recently moved further into preservation activities. OCLC continues to offer and develop its bibliographic control activities in relation to preservation: it will, for example, convert records in the *National Register of Microform Masters* into machine-readable records. It has acquired a major preservation microfilming facility, MAPS (The Micrographic Preservation Service), and is conducting research into book deterioration and into digitization of microform materials. OCLC has established a Preservation Task Force to guide its preservation activities.[71]

National microfilming programs have already been noted in Chapter 8. Cooperative microfilming programs have long been recognized as effective preservation actions, and major projects have been established at the national level in many countries. Attention has been concentrated especially on the microfilming of newspapers, one example being the United States Newspaper Program.

Conspectus is a method of describing library resources and their strengths in specific areas, and of building up a composite picture of library resources on a large scale, say at the regional or national level. It was developed by the Research Libraries Group in the United States as a way of sharing responsibility for developing and preserving areas of subject strength, with the intention that the collections were, when considered as a single resource, maintained at a strong level in the face of declining acquisitions budgets. Institutions agree to take primary collecting responsibility for specified subject areas. The Conspectus data are mounted as a computerized database and are available for consultation.[72]

Recently the Conspectus approach has been applied to the whole of a nation's bibliographic resources. In Canada a Conspectus database has been established, and several European countries, Sweden and the Netherlands for instance, have also embraced the Conspectus concept. In the United Kingdom Conspectus has been promoted by the National Library of Scotland, the National Library of Wales and the British Library.[73]

Conspectus allows for the designation of institutions as having primary collecting responsibility: it is, clearly, only a short step from that to designating primary preservation responsibility. It seems likely that this will become part of the national preservation plans for some countries, among them Australia and New Zealand.

Notes

1   Carolyn Clark Morrow, *The Preservation Challenge: A Guide to Conserving Library Materials* (White Plains, N.Y.: Knowledge Industry Publications, 1983), p. 167.

2   Peter G. Sparks, 'Technology in Support of Preservation', in *Preservation of Library Materials*, ed. Merrily A. Smith (München: K.G. Saur, 1987), Vol. 1, p. 126.

3   J.M. Dureau and D.W.G. Clements, *Principles for the Preservation and Conservation of Library Materials* (The Hague: IFLA, 1986), p. 5.

4   Paul N. Banks, 'Books in Peril: Cooperative Approaches to Conservation', *Library Journal* (15 November 1976): 2348-2351.

5   F.W. Ratcliffe, *Preservation Policies and Conservation in British Libraries: Report of the Cambridge University Library Conservation Project* (Boston Spa: British Library, 1984), p. 69.

6   Council on Library Resources. Committee on Preservation and Access. *Brittle Books: Report of the Committee on Preservation and Access* (Washington, D.C.: Council on Library Resources, 1986), pp. 10-11.

7   *Ibid.*, p. 23.

8   Carolyn Clark Morrow, 'National Preservation Planning and Regional Cooperative Conservation Efforts', in *Conserving and Preserving Library Materials*, ed. Kathryn Luther Henderson and William T. Henderson (Urbana-Champaign, Ill.: Graduate School of Library and Information Science, University of Illinois, 1983), pp. 37-56.

9   Further references are given in 'A Basic Reading List on Permanence of Paper', *Alkaline Paper Advocate* 2, 1 (1989): 14. One item is specially recommended: Verner W. Clapp, 'The Story of Permanent/Durable Book-Paper, 1115-1970', *Restaurator* suppl. 3 (1972).

10   W.J. Barrow, *The Manufacture and Testing of Durable Book Papers* (Richmond, Va: Virginia State Library, 1960), p.31.

11   Described in Mark Roosa, 'U.S. Promotes the Manufacture and Use of Permanent Paper', *International Preservation News* 2 (1988): 1-3.

12   Further described in Roosa, *ibid.*; Walt Crawford, *Technical Standards: An Introduction for Librarians* (White Plains, N.Y.: Knowledge Industry Publications, 1986), pp. 169-170; 'Towards Permanent Paper: US Standard Reviewed', *Library Conservation News* 9 (1985): 8-9.

13   'Comments Are Invited on Paper Standard Revision', *Abbey Newsletter* 13, 7 (1989): 124-125.

14   *Alkaline Paper Advocate* 2, 2 (1989): 26.

15   'Standards Update', *Alkaline Paper Advocate* 3, 3 (August 1990): 31.

16   Gerald W. Lundeen, 'Preservation of Paper Based Materials: Present and Future Research and Developments in the Paper Industry', in *Conserving and Preserving Library Materials, op. cit.*, p. 82.

17   Robin Smeeton, 'Educating the Trade: The Development of a Standard for Acid-Free Paper', in *Conservation in Crisis: Proceedings of a Seminar...1986* (London: British Library, 1987), pp. 15-17.

18   Lundeen, *op. cit.*, pp. 73-85.

19   *Alkaline Paper Advocate* 1, 4 (1988): 27, 34.

20   Ron Westwood, 'Alkaline Paper-Making Conversion Rate Accelerates', *Alkaline Paper Advocate* 2, 1 (1989): 8.

21   Stephen A. Walkden, 'New Momentum for Alkaline Papermakers', *TAPPI Journal* 72, 11 (1989): 8.

22   John C. Williams, 'Review of Paper Quality and Paper Chemistry', *Library Trends* 30 (1981): 221.

23   Jane Boyd and Don Etherington, *Preparation of Archival Copies of Theses and Dissertations* (Chicago, Ill.: American Library Association, 1986), p. 1.

24   *Reference and Research Book News* 3, 3 (1988): 1.

25   'Good Resolutions', *Abbey Newsletter* 12, 2 (1988): 29-31.

26   'ALA's Third Resolution on Permanent Paper', *Abbey Newsletter* 14, 1 (February 1990): 2.

27   'IFLA Permanent Paper Resolutions', *Conservation Administration News* 40 (1990): 22.
28   'Landmark Declaration to Support Book Preservation Signed by Authors, Publishers', *Library Journal* (1 April 1989): 16; 'Authors and Publishers Pledge to Use Acid-Free Paper', *Abbey Newsletter* 13, 2 (1989): 31.
29   Roosa, *op. cit.*, p. 3.
30   Bob Barnard, 'The Way Ahead', *Library Conservation News* 26 (January 1990): 1, 7-8.
31   Susan Knapp, 'Putting the Fire Out: American Psychological Association Conversion to Acid-Free Paper', *Alkaline Paper Advocate* 1, 5 (December 1988): 57-58.
32   'State Laws Concerning Permanent Paper', *Abbey Newsletter* 14, 6 (October 1990): 108-109; Don W. Wilson, 'The National Archives and the Permanent Paper Law', *Alkaline Paper Advocate* 4, 1 (February 1991): 1-2.
33   'Recycled Paper', *Alkaline Paper Advocate* 1, 5 (December 1988): 52; 'Recycled Printing/Writing Paper', *Alkaline Paper Advocate* 3, 3 (August 1990): 34-35.
34   Carolyn Harris, 'Preservation of Paper Based Materials: Mass Deacidification Methods and Projects', in *Conserving and Preserving Library Materials, op. cit.*, p. 57.
35   'Deacidification Not Quite at Warp Speed', *Library Journal* (1 September 1989): 118, 120.
36   George Martin Cunha, 'Mass Deacidification for Libraries', *Library Technology Reports* 23, 3 (1987): 382; see also George Martin Cunha, 'Mass Deacidification for Libraries: 1989 Update', *Library Technology Reports* 25, 1 (1989).
37   Based on Harris, *op. cit.*, pp. 65-68. See also Peter G. Sparks, 'Mass Deacidification at the Library of Congress', in *Preservation of Library Materials* (1987), Vol. 1, pp. 137-140.
38   Karl Nyren, 'The DEZ Process and the Library of Congress', *Library Journal* (15 September 1986): 33-35; William J. Welsh, 'In Defense of DEZ: LC's Perspective', *Library Journal* (January 1987): 62-63; 'LC Agrees to Outside Review of the DEZ Process', *Library Journal* (1 February 1987): 20. See also the bibliography in *Library Resources and Technical Services* 31, 4 (1987): 381.
39   US Congress. Office of Technology Assessment, *Book Preservation Technologies* (Washington, D.C.: USGPO, 1988).
40   George Cunha, 'LC's Deacidification Process Leased to Chemical Giant', *American Libraries* (September 1989): 721; 'Deacidification', *Abbey Newsletter* 15, 3 (May 1991): 37; 'LC Regroups after Rejecting Deacidification Bids', *American Libraries* (October 1991); 831.
41   Cunha, 'Mass Deacification for Libraries' (1987) *op. cit.*, p. 436.
42   Harris, *op. cit.*, pp. 63-65; see also Richard D. Smith, 'Mass Deacidification: The Wei T'o Way', *College and Research Libraries* 45 (1984): 588-593. Illustrations of the process are given in Richard D. Smith, 'Mass Deacidification at the Public Archives of Canada', in *Conservation of Library and Archival Materials and the Graphic Arts*, ed. Guy Petherbridge (London: Butterworths, 1987), pp. 125-137. The

Canadian application is described in Marianne Scott, 'Mass Deacidification at the National Library of Canada', in *Preservation of Library Materials* (1987), Vol. 1, pp. 134-136.

43 Jean-Marie Arnoult, 'Mass Deacidification at the Bibliothèque Nationale', in *Preservation of Library Materials* (1987), Vol. 1, pp. 129-133; Cunha, 'Mass Deacidification for Libraries: 1989 Update', *op. cit.*, p. 60.

44 'Union Carbide Acquires Wei T'o Rights', *Abbey Newsletter* 13, 7 (1989): 129-130.

45 Susan Sayre Batton, 'Nonaqueous Deacidification at Princeton, 1982-1989: A Progress Report', *Abbey Newsletter* 14, 5 (August 1990): 80-83.

46 Sources used are Ed. King, 'New Hope for Decayed Paper', *Library Conservation News* 12 (1986): 1-2; David W.G. Clements, 'Paper Strengthening at the British Library', in *Preservation of Library Materials* (1987), Vol. 1, pp. 152-155; Wilson, *op. cit.*, p. 52; Cunha, 'Mass Deacidification for Libraries: 1989 Update', *op. cit.*, pp. 61, 69-70; C.E. Butler, D.W.G. Clements and C.A. Millington, 'Paper Strengthening at the British Library', in *Preservation and Technology* (London: National Preservation Office, 1989), pp. 65-74.

47 'Effects of Gamma Rays on Book Preservation', *Library Journal* (January 1990): 19; 'Successful Trials on Paper Restoration Techniques', *Library Association Record* 91, 11 (1989): 618.

48 'Mass Deacidification: Big Order for New Player Will Test Process', *American Libraries* (May 1989): 389; Cunha, 'Mass Deacidification for Libraries: 1989 Update', *op. cit.*, pp. 47-55.

49 GraceAnne A. DeCandido, 'New Book Deacidification Process Prototype Soon to Be Available', *Library Journal* (15 February 1988): 112-113; Cunha, 'Mass Deacidification for Libraries: 1989 Update', *op. cit.*, pp. 35-47.

50 Cunha, *ibid.*, pp. 56-59.

51 Toby Murray, 'FMC Dedicates Paper Preservation Demonstration Plant', *Conservation Administration News* 42 (July 1990): 1-2; Robert S. Wedinger, 'Lithco Develops Deacidification/Strengthening Process', *Alkaline Paper Advocate* 2, 4 (October 1989): 39-40.

52 Otto Wächter, 'Paper Strengthening at the National Library of Austria', in *Preservation of Library Materials* (1987), Vol. 1, pp. 141-145; Gerhard Banik, 'Problems of Mass Conservation of Newsprint in Libraries', in *Newspaper Preservation and Access* (München: K.G. Saur, 1988), Vol. 1, pp. 216-226.

53 Cunha, 'Mass Deacidification for Libraries: 1989 Update', *op. cit.*, p. 64 and Appendix B.

54 Diana Grimwood-Jones, 'Preservation', in *British Librarianship and Information Work 1981-1985: Volume 2*, ed. David W. Bromley and Angela M. Allott (London: Library Association, 1988), pp. 280-281.

55 Susan E. Bello, *Cooperative Preservation Efforts of Academic Libraries* (Urbana- Champaign, Ill.: Graduate School of Library and Information Science, University of Illinois, 1986); Carolyn Clark Morrow, 'National Preservation Planning and Regional Cooperative

Conservation Efforts', in *Conserving and Preserving Library Materials, op. cit.*, pp. 37-56.

56   Richard W. McCoy, 'Cooperative Preservation Activities of the Research Libraries Group (RLG)', in *Preservation of Library Materials* (1987), Vol. 1, pp. 83-88; *RLG Preservation Manual*. 2nd ed. (Stanford, Calif.: Research Libraries Group, 1986).

57   'Preservation Considerations of RLG Member Libraries', *RLG Preservation Manual, ibid.*, p. 92.

58   Pamela W. Darling and Duane E. Webster, *Preservation Planning Program: An Assisted Self-Study Manual for Libraries*. Expanded 1987 ed. (Washington, D.C.: Association of Research Libraries, Office of Management Studies, 1987).

59   'Guidelines for Minimum Preservation Efforts in ARL Libraries', *SPEC Kit* 138 (1987): 1-4.

60   Hans-Peter Geh, 'Conservation/Preservation: An International Approach', *Library Resources and Technical Services* 30, 1 (1986): 31-35; Merrily A. Smith, 'The IFLA Core Programme on Preservation and Conservation (PAC)', *IFLA Journal* 12, 4 (1986): 305-306; 'IFLA Core Programme on Preservation and Conservation', *International Preservation News* 1 (1987): 1-2.

61   'New PAC Regional Centers in Japan and Australia', *International Preservation News* 4 (August 1990): 1-3.

62   Merrily A. Smith, 'Annual Report 1990 of the IFLA PAC Programme', *IFLA Journal* 17, 2 (1991): 170.

63   *Ibid.*, pp. 170-175.

64   Carolyn Clark Morrow, 'National Preservation Planning and Regional Cooperative Conservation Efforts', in *Conserving and Preserving Library Materials, op. cit.*, pp. 43-49, describes centres in the United States.

65   Fay Zipkowitz, 'Saving Paper Treasures: The Northeast Document Conservation Center', *Library and Archival Security* 7, 2 (1985): 15-20; Ann Russell, Karen Motylewski and Gay Tracy, 'Northeast Document Conservation Centre: A Leader in Preservation', *Library Resources and Technical Services* 32, 1 (1988): 43-47.

66   Richard Frieder, 'Preservation Activity in the CIC', *Conservation Administration News* 39 (October 1989): 11, 31.

67   Gregor Trinkaus-Randall, 'Statewide Preservation Planning in Massachusetts', *Conservation Administration News* 44 (January 1991): 8-9.

68   'British Library to Set Up National Preservation Office', *Library Conservation News* 6 (1985): [3].

69   David W.G. Clements, 'The National Preservation Office in the British Library', *IFLA Journal* 12, 1 (1988): 25-32; Marie Jackson, 'The National Preservation Office', *Conservation Administration News* 38 (1989): 14.

70   *The Commission on Preservation and Access* [brochure] (Washington, D.C.: The Commission, 1989). The Commission's annual reports and *Newsletter* are an important source of information about preservation and should be sought out by readers.

71   Tom Clareson, 'OCLC's Preservation Program', *Conservation Administration News* 44 (January 1991): 6-7, 25.
72   Crispin Jewett, 'Conspectus: A Means to Library Co-operation', *Library Conservation News* 22 (1989): 4-6.
73   Crispin Jewett, 'Developing Conspectus', *Library Conservation News* 23 (1989): 2-3, 6.

Chapter 10

Developing a Library Preservation Program

Introduction

The introduction to this book notes four premises on which the book is based:

1   that preservation is a management responsibility, at the highest level;
2   that all collections need a preservation plan;
3   that the preservation plan must be adequately funded as part of the ongoing budget;
4   that preservation must be the concern of all library staff at every level and a part of all library routines: it is not just a technical specialist matter which takes place in a separate laboratory.

Preservation must not be limited to large research libraries or archives, but must be a high priority for every librarian. That this has not been the case in the past is firmly stated by one of the many librarians, Scottish in this instance, writing in recent years on preservation:

> many currently in senior management positions know little of even the bare essentials for an environment conducive to document preservation. Worse, many lower-grade staff actually inflict gratuitous damage on existing bookstocks by malhandling, clumsy or excessive photocopying, injudicious rebinding and improper storage conditions.[1]

The key question which this chapter addresses is how preservation can be integrated into all aspects of library management and into every library procedure. Other related questions are raised and the answers indicated in preceding chapters: those of why preservation should be integrated into library management, and of what techniques are at our command.

Preservation is a library management problem and must be considered in relation to other library management decisions. Consider a few examples. We know that books are best housed at temperatures lower than those at which humans thrive: if we choose to lower the temperatures of the stack areas, what is the effect on the humans who work in that area? What is the additional cost of maintaining the temperature at the lower level? Is there a cost saving? If the reading room temperature is lowered, will the library have to supply hot rum toddies to users who complain of the cold? If a flimsily bound thick monograph which is likely to be heavily used is received in the library, and is rebound as two thinner volumes to offer protection when being photocopied, what are the implications for other library procedures? Will it cause any problems in the cataloguing process? Will its separation into two volumes cause security problems? If one half of the work is lost or stolen, will the other half be completely useless?

The importance of having a policy statement for the library which clearly notes preservation as an essential part of that library's activities is noted in several places later in this chapter. Some examples here are not out of place. The National Library of New Zealand notes that its mission is 'to enrich the social, cultural and economic well-being of New Zealand by: ensuring equitable access to information and recorded knowledge [and] collecting, preserving and making available the documentary heritage of New Zealand.' The first of its functions is stated as: 'To collect, preserve and make available a comprehensive collection relating to New Zealand and its national heritage.'[2] A description of the contents of a preservation policy is given by Chapman, and a selection of preservation policy statements can be found in *Preservation Guidelines in ARL Libraries*.[3] That of the Columbia University Libraries begins with the unequivocal statement: 'The Columbia University Libraries is committed to the preservation of its collection.'[4]

Two further points, both already made in preceding chapters, are worth reiterating here. The first is that the aim of preservation is to make library materials usable; it is about helping items in library collections to last as long as they are wanted. In this definition preservation becomes the concern of all staff working in libraries and of all users of libraries, not only of the special materials librarian or conservator. The second point is that in the past library preservation has been reactive. It is essential that it become proactive, that is, that a large part of the resources available to preservation be applied to preventive preservation measures.

Integrating Preservation and Management: Some General Concerns

One of the basic texts about library technical services states unequivocally that 'there is no set pattern for the organization of a library preservation program.'[5] How the preservation program is organized and where it is placed in the overall library structure depend on a number of factors, organizational structure being only one. The establishment of preservation sections as separate units within the organization is of relatively recent origin, dating back to the 1970s, when preservation came to be considered as part of more general library concerns (most notably in North American libraries) and more specifically as part of the collection development function. More and more preservation departments are being established, as indicated by the example of member libraries of the Association of Research Libraries, where the number rose from twenty-seven in 1985 to seventy-three in 1989.[6]

Although there may be no set pattern for organizing the preservation program, some key ingredients necessary for the successful operation of such programs can be identified, and the steps essential in planning such a program can be isolated. Two essential ingredients are commitment on the part of the library's administration and staff, and the status of the preservation unit and its staff within the library. Although the initial impetus for the preservation program may not have come from the top, the continued support and commitment of the library's administration are necessary for the maintenance and well-being of preservation as a central activity. Commitment on the part of library staff at all levels is also essential. This is noted in Chapter 5.

The status of the preservation unit and its staff, and more particularly the status of the head of the preservation unit, within the library's hierarchy is another critical factor. The manager of the preservation program needs to be accorded a status high enough within the organization for that person to be privy to major administrative decisions, to be able to influence them, and to be in a position to implement those which are relevant. High status is also required to be effective in coordinating, liaising, advocating, planning and educating.

Carolyn Clark Morrow has examined seven case studies of successful preservation programs in libraries in the United States, and has established their common features which, it could reasonably be concluded, have contributed to their success. They are:

a redefining of the activities which constitute preservation (for example, including care and handling activities in addition to the more traditional repair activities);

hand in hand with the redefinition, a reorganisation of administration to better coordinate preservation activities;

employment of a professional (either a conservator or a librarian with preservation knowledge and experience) to develop and organise the program;

knowledgeable library staff, and the establishment of formal liaison between the preservation staff and the rest of the library staff;

an in-house treatment facility, for example, a workshop tailored to the need of the individual library.[7]

Funding of the preservation effort at adequate levels is required for success. It is instructive to note that Association of Research Libraries members are 'increasingly' spending '10 per cent of their materials budget on preservation', and some are spending higher amounts, ranging up to 50 per cent.[8] By comparison, university libraries in the US Midwest (in Indiana, Illinois and Ohio) spent on average 2.68 per cent of the total library expenditure on preservation.[9]

Steps in Implementing a Preservation Program

Writers on preservation planning are in general agreement about the steps which are needed to implement a successful library program. Robert Patterson notes that these are: first, to examine the environment in the library and the condition of the collection, and make recommendations; second, to prepare a disaster plan; third, to examine current practices (for example, binding, handling, processing, repair techniques) and recommend changes and ascertain additional requirements to meet current standards; fourth, to ascertain what professional conservation advice and expertise are available to the library; fifth, to develop a collection development approach for the library; sixth, to identify sources of funding; seventh, to establish an in-house clearinghouse for preservation information for staff; and, finally, to explore the feasibility of participating in regional or national cooperative conservation efforts.[10]

An experienced preservation administrator, Sally Buchanan, notes the general administrative concerns which are applicable to a preservation program; her list is similar to that of Patterson, above. She notes that the first step is to assess needs (through condition surveys – see Chapter 3). Next, priorities need to be established; here Buchanan suggests one useful way in which activities might be grouped for administrative purposes: maintenance of collections (both circulating and non-circulating collections), stabilization (of the environment, and through handling and housing), security (including disaster planning) and preservation of deteriorating volumes. The activities then need to be organized and funding sought (but note that some activities, for example disaster response planning, require relatively little financial support). The staffing requirements need to be addressed. Education of both staff and users is an essential step to ensure that both groups recognize the preservation program, which will make extra demands on them, as being worthwhile. Finally, evaluation of the program – of progress, and also regular monitoring – needs to be carried out.[11]

The need to establish priorities is an essential part of planning and implementing a preservation program. Here the concept of 'phased preservation' will assist. First developed at the Library of Congress in 1973 as 'phased conservation', this concept has proved to be of assistance in selecting materials for treatment, helping to avoid the selection of items which visibly need attention but which may not warrant a high priority if other factors such as use, value and rate of deterioration are also taken into account. (Chapter 8 notes in more detail issues relating to materials for treatment.) If the phased preservation concept is adopted, it needs to be integrated into the library's administrative structure.[12]

Responsibility for Developing and Implementing the Program

Once the steps to be carried out have been decided on, then the question arises of who does the planning and who implements the program. There are three possibilities. Specialists can be appointed, on a full-time or consultancy basis, to establish the program; a staff member can be charged with gaining experience in preservation and overseeing the preservation program (and hiring expertise on a consultancy basis where necessary); or a committee approach can be used. Specialist staff may be easier to locate on a consultancy basis than on a full-time permanent basis. The current shortage of trained conservation staff with sufficient library experience may mean that the best route to follow is to turn a professionally qualified librarian into a preservation librarian, that is, to assist that person to gain what preservation expertise he or she can. It can be said that ideally the preservation program should be under the control of a single administrator. This was certainly acknowledged to be an important factor in the success of the preservation program of the National Museums of Canada libraries. A full-time preservation officer 'focused' the efforts to achieve preservation objectives and also 'conferred a much higher profile on the preservation programme'.[13] However, the committee approach has met with considerable success in some libraries and is applicable to libraries of all sizes except the very smallest.

The preservation committee approach has been described in the library literature and is not therefore explained in any detail here.[14] It can be applied either in part or in full. That is, preservation programs can be planned, implemented and operated under the direction of a committee, or the committee approach can be applied only to some of the implementation stages. This latter approach is the basis in the United States of the 'assisted self-study' Preservation Planning Program of the Association of Research Libraries. It is intended for libraries with sufficient staff to assign about twenty-four people to the task, each spending on average five or six hours per week over four to six months. The self-study results in a detailed examination of the preservation needs of the library, essential for the further development of a preservation program. In outline, the Preservation Planning Program is made up of the following steps: preliminary matters (getting the plan organized); an assessment of environmental conditions; an assessment of the physical condition of the collections; an assessment of organizational issues; disaster control; identifying preservation resources in the library; and final reporting.[15]

The University of Texas at Austin General Libraries has used the committee approach to determine the initial needs of a preservation program.[16] The immediate result of this approach was that a report was produced which provided data about the nature and extent of preservation needs and made recommendations about implementing a preservation program. There were also less tangible results which may be of more lasting benefit to the institution. A number of staff members developed preservation expertise, and the general preservation awareness of the staff was heightened, as between 10 and 20 per cent of the total number of staff were involved in one way or another. The committee approach allows for a wide representation of interests, which can be increased if required by rotating the membership periodically. In the words of Mark E. Cain, author of the article describing the University of Texas at Austin experience, 'Libraries need not delay initiating a preservation program until they can afford fulltime staff for that purpose. Much groundwork can be laid by employees already onboard who have only a few hours each week to devote to the task in a committee framework.'[17] Another result of this approach is that it can indicate areas where improvements can be made in preservation without major expenditure and without new staff positions being established.

What Is in a Preservation Program?

The precise contents of an integrated preservation program will vary from library to library, but it is possible to indicate in general terms what its major components will be.[18] These are all described in detail in preceding chapters. There will be an understanding of the factors which affect the library's physical environment and an application of these factors to control that environment; a disaster prevention plan and recovery procedures; an emphasis on security; 'positive control' of binding; regular use of professional conservation expertise and facilities, perhaps in an in-house conservation laboratory in the largest libraries, but more likely using the services of conservators and facilities available on a contract basis; an in-house facility for preventive conservation and simple repair techniques to be carried out; an emphasis on treatment of the collections as a whole and not on single item treatment; a strong and ongoing staff training and education component; active participation in cooperative conservation efforts on a regional level and also on a national level if appropriate; and a concentration on finding alternative sources of funding for large-scale preservation activities such as major microfilming or reformatting projects.

Models for Integrating Preservation into Libraries

The rest of this chapter examines four models for integrating preservation into all aspects of library management. The first of these describes the preservation actions which can be introduced into small specialized libraries, such as special libraries with few staff members or some school libraries. The second model examined here is that of high-use collections, for example in public libraries, some school libraries and some academic libraries; again, the staffing levels are typically low. Next is noted lower-use retrospective collections where staffing is at a higher level, for example those in academic and state libraries. The fourth and final model is that of collections of national importance, for example those in national libraries and those in other libraries which have been identified (by a Conspectus approach, for instance) as of national importance.

It is important to note, before considering the first of the four models, that preservation attention is also necessary to personal collections. The extent to which this is the case will vary, from total lack of attention for a small working or recreational personal collection to full conservation treatment and air-conditioned storage facilities for a prestigious private collection, and perhaps especially for one which has been assembled with an eye to investment. For most of us, the reality is probably a few hundred books which we need to maintain as a collection of items for use, with some items of sentimental or personal value, rather than commercial value. The simple actions of preventive preservation are as relevant to these collections as they are to library collections: books should be kept away from sunlight and heat sources for precisely the same reasons as in library collections; they should be kept tidy on the shelves; they may need protective enclosures if fragile; and so on. Guidance for preservation of the personal collection is readily available. One of the more readable sources is Baynes-Cope's *Caring for Books and Documents*.[19] Price's *Stopping the Rot* contains much which can be applied to personal collections.[20]

Model 1: Small Specialized Libraries

Small libraries whose collections and clientele are of a specialized nature typically have a small number of staff (as low as one or two) and a limited user group. Such libraries are extremely unlikely to establish a position of preservation librarian, or to be able to devote anything more than a tiny part of the library's budget to preservation activities, but they share the same general preservation concerns as other libraries, that is, to keep the items in their collections usable for as long as is required. Their preservation requirements are of the same nature as for any other kind of library in the areas of: commercial binding; repair of damaged items; perhaps brittle book replacement; proper care, handling and housing; environmental monitoring and control; staff and user education; disaster planning; security; and possibly regional cooperation.[21]

What is most likely to be different about specialized libraries is the degree of attention to preservation which can be given, or indeed which is required by the nature of the collection and its use. As one example, law libraries typically have larger than usual numbers of leather bindings, frequently badly deteriorated, and 'a user population that requires having seven or eight items all open at once and piled on top of each other'.[22] Other special libraries may be less concerned about paper deterioration than about how to store magnetic tapes containing computer data for the next decade without that data becoming corrupt.

How, then, can special libraries with a small, hardworking staff and no additional finance for preservation activities integrate preservation into the administration of the library? Many simple actions which cost little or nothing will assist in the preservation of the items in the library's collection.[23] Perhaps the most important change is not financial, nor does it involve additional staff time, but is a matter of altering attitudes. The emphasis in special libraries is usually on the book or other item in the library's collection as a source of information, and little regard is given to the item as physical object. All staff members will need to participate in preservation activities.

In addition to this change in perception there are concrete actions which can be carried out. The first group of these relates to the environment in which the items are housed. In order to keep temperature and humidity levels stable, it is vital that air-conditioning equipment is well maintained on a regular basis. If the library has any control over the matter, the temperature level should be set as low as possible, consistent with the comfort of staff and clients. It is especially important that air-conditioning equipment is not turned off when the building is unoccupied, for example at evenings and weekends. It is useful to keep on the best possible terms with building maintenance staff. Light levels also need to be controlled. This can be achieved by methods as simple as drawing curtains to cut down on the level of direct sunlight, of turning off lights in rooms or stack areas when they are not required, and of replacing fluorescent tubes when they fail with tubes which emit low levels of ultraviolet light. A disaster plan, perhaps not highly detailed, should be drawn up. Special libraries are not immune from water and fire damage, as a quick look through the preservation literature will indicate.

A second group of actions relates to housekeeping and other ongoing procedures. Regular effective cleaning of the library is essential. If at all possible, eating and drinking in the library, including by staff at their desks, should be banned; smoking must also be forbidden. Attention should be paid to storage to ensure that shelving adequately supports the items shelved on it and does not damage them. Neatness in the library is important, not least for its effect in encouraging clients to take care of items in the library. Sending out binding to commercial binders is an ongoing procedure in many special libraries, albeit in small quantities. The librarian should become acquainted with the different kinds of bindings and know which are offered by his or her commercial binder. This knowledge becomes especially important for volumes which will be heavily photocopied. Some repairs will be carried out on occasion. It is important that materials used for repair are not the cause of further damage to the items. It may be possible to establish regular repair and maintenance routines in some libraries. Many special libraries rely heavily on interlibrary loan, or are heavy lenders of items in their collections, and should take special care of the way in which they pack items for posting or transporting by other means.

Many special libraries have some items in their collections which are of special significance as artefacts and which may need to be preserved in their original condition. Examples might be a special document, such as the minutes of the first meeting of the company's board of directors, or photographs relating to the early years. Many banks have archives of historical significance, and some employ preservation consultants or conservators. Special items in deteriorated condition may require protective enclosures or other conservation treatments, and the services of a consultant conservator could be required. There may be a case for applying for special financial assistance outside the library's normal budget. Microfilming or preservation photocopying may also be a solution. Microfilming in particular may have the further attraction of saving space, often at a premium in special libraries. Again it might be possible to seek additional funding outside the normal budget for a discrete special project.

Model 2: High-Use Collections

The second model is that of libraries where the collection is predominantly a high-use one, such as in public libraries, some school libraries and some academic libraries. Such collections often consist largely of recently published items, and the problems of aging stock that are found in research libraries are less noticeable. Most of such collections circulate, and items are typically used heavily and are discarded when too worn or when not deemed to be popular. However, there are often also some older materials for longer-term retention, for example local historical material. Such libraries usually have some kind of repairing program, and material is sent out to commercial binders.

Two examples which are described in the literature, one actual and one hypothetical, are noted here. The real example is a public library of 225,000 volumes in the United States, at Wellesley Free Library, Massachusetts. It is a collection of relatively new items, most being published after 1960, with the newest materials being in the children's books and adult fiction areas of the collection. Seventy-eight per cent of the total collection was assessed as being in excellent condition, and much of the remaining 22 per cent was in need of minor repairs.[24] The hypothetical example is the 'Level 1' library proposed by Carolyn Clark Morrow: a 'small college library or large public library with a heavily used core collection of standard works and current resources and a small retrospective collection. Includes a small collection of rare books, manuscripts and unique local materials.'[25] The staff levels in both models are typically low and the possibility of additional financial resources for preservation slender. In general what has been noted above for the first model, special libraries, also applies here: attention must be paid to environmental control, binding, a good minor repair program, storage and handling, packaging and transportation of items, care with photocopying, and training and education.

Morrow suggests a possible organization chart for her hypothetical example. The position of library director has reporting to it a technical services librarian, who has responsibility for a conservation technician (one full-time equivalent position) and part-time assistants (one and a half full-time equivalent positions).[26] Elsewhere Morrow and Dyall note that a library of this nature is likely to carry out these preservation procedures: commercial library binding for material of long-term interest, for example material in its historical collection; in-house repair for the material in the circulating collection, fiction for instance – tightening hinges, replacing torn end-sheets, some replacement of spines, some recasing using the original cases; for local history material, some protective enclosures, mending of tears and encapsulation is likely to be carried out.[27]

The Wellesley Free Library has used the results of its condition survey to promote the concept that its collection is a capital asset of the community, and that extra capital funds to increase collection maintenance procedures were needed. In addition, annual budget increases to continue preservation activities were sought. The main activities which have been carried out are: a reappraisal of outdated repair methods and repair materials; a new repair area was outfitted and staff were trained in better repair techniques; procedures for preparation of materials added to the collection were revised; and binding specifications were revised. Collection development procedures were revised to include 'preservation criteria'; the level of staffing for maintenance activities, including cleaning, was increased; and a public program on preservation education was to be established.[28]

Some other possible preservation activities which could be carried out are the purchase of multiple copies of heavily-used works, perhaps also restricting the use of one copy so that it is retained intact for future use; boxing and encapsulation of fragile material; and perhaps microfilming or preservation photocopying for some categories of material such as local newspapers.

Model 3: Lower-Use Retrospective Collections

This model is for collections where there is a large component of retrospective low-use items which it is considered necessary to retain. This is commonly found in academic libraries, such as the hypothetical example described by Morrow as her 'Level 3' library:

> University or large college library with a heavily used core collection of standard works and current resources and a moderately used retrospective collection. Includes several small branch or departmental libraries and a small separate collection of rare books and manuscripts.[29]

Typically such libraries have more staff and considerably higher budgets than do those in the second model above, and therefore they have potentially more flexibility to divert staff and funding to preservation activities without recourse to additional funding. Extra funding will still be required for major initiatives in the preservation field. There are many examples of libraries of this kind which have established preservation programs. This is especially the case in North American libraries, where the nature and extent of the library preservation problem were first noted and where the procedures to address it were first developed.

Model three libraries have, of course, the same need to attend to the preservation concerns already noted above – environmental control, binding, an effective minor repair program, storage and handling, packaging and transportation of items, care with photocopying, and training and education. Three aspects in particular are likely to require more attention, given the retrospective nature of collections in model three libraries: book repair, collection development, and reformatting.

Book repair is only one part of an integrated preservation program. It is an essential element for heavy use collections in order to maintain items in them in usable condition for as long as they are required. As many of these items will be 'retired' to a low-use retrospective collection when their immediate use lessens, the quality of the repairs and the nature of the materials used in them assume greater importance. There needs to be an emphasis on the archival life of the materials and on the longer-term effects of the repairs. Morrow and Dyall give one hypothetical example of a medium-sized academic library with a relatively new collection. The main preservation emphasis is on repair procedures for books damaged through ordinary use, heavily used reference books and reserve materials, and on other minor repairs. They suggest a staffing level of one full-time technician to oversee the repair program and also the binding preparation, plus part-time student assistants.[30] They propose another example, this time a large university library with departmental libraries. There is a newly established preservation committee, but no significant increase in funding or personnel, at least in the immediate future. The long-term requirement is to establish a full-scale preservation program, but the immediate needs are best served by halting the inappropriate repairs at present being carried out, and retraining the repair staff to perform repairs which are more appropriate to the longer-term preservation needs of the collections.[31]

Collection development aspects need to be considered as part of the preservation program where there is a requirement for items to be retained in retrospective collections. This is noted in the fourth model below.

Model three libraries may be in a position to implement an information reformatting program, using preservation photocopying or microfilming. They should also be able to commit staff time to searching actively for replacement copies, either paper or microform, for heavily deteriorated items. The cost of these activities is a significant factor, and a model for determining costs of preservation actions is given in a 1991 article by Harris, Mandel and Wolven.[32]

One possible organizational structure for preservation activities, limited to repair and binding, in a medium-sized academic library is noted above (Morrow and Dyall's Library A). Another possible structure is Morrow's

'Level 3' library, this time for a more comprehensive preservation program. In this the Preservation Librarian reports to the Head of Technical Services, who in turn reports to the library's Director. The Preservation Librarian has informal links with subject specialists and the Preservation Committee. Reporting to the Preservation Librarian are a technician responsible for materials preparation, including binding preparation (one full-time equivalent position), and a technician responsible for collection maintenance (one full-time equivalent). The materials preparation technician oversees two clerical full-time equivalent positions and part-time assistants (two full-time equivalent positions), and the collections maintenance technician oversees a conservation technician (one full-time equivalent positions) and part-time assistants (two full-time equivalent positions).[33]

Many examples are described in the literature and should be sought by anyone who is intending to establish a preservation program.[34] One especially comprehensive case is a program for the University of Connecticut Libraries.[35] Here the structure recommended is a Preservation Officer overseeing eight and a half positions: 1) bindery preparation, two positions; 2) shelving preparation, two positions; 3) repair, two positions; 4) brittle book replacements, two and a half positions.

Most of the preservation programs described in the literature are of libraries in the United States. It is useful to note two examples of Australian university libraries, for the situation is probably typical of institutions in countries which have developed an awareness of preservation problems more recently than their counterparts in the United States. Both collections contain deteriorating nineteenth-century and early twentieth-century material. Attention to the air-conditioning system was needed to provide better control of temperature and relative humidity levels, which fluctuated too much and were often too high. Cleaning was inadequate, and significant improvements in its level and frequency were recommended. Storage equipment was generally acceptable, but some improvements in shelving practices were suggested. More minor binding repair needed to be carried out and applied to items at an earlier stage in their deterioration process. Improvements in handling, especially during photocopying, were needed urgently. The disaster plans were in one case in an embryonic stage and in the other non-existent. For one of these libraries a consultant recommended that an efficient, cost-effective preservation program be established. Specific procedures which should be adopted were to implement a disaster response and recovery plan, to upgrade cleaning and fumigation, to improve the performance of the air-conditioning system, and to design and implement a user education program in order to improve handling and general behaviour in the library. An ongoing budget for treatment and remedial storage should be established, as should a preservation committee.

Model 4: Collections of National Importance

The fourth and final model is that of collections of national importance, such as those found in national libraries or those held in other libraries which have been identified (by a Conspectus approach, for instance) as of national importance. Such collections are to be retained for as long as possible and consequently require the highest level of preservation attention possible. They will probably contain some items of artefactual value, but also a considerable number of items whose value individually is not great but which are important to the collection as a whole. Typically, collections of national importance are located in large institutions which command large budgets and significant staff resources. Many, but not all, have a preservation unit already established, even though it may be largely concerned with binding or with artefact conservation.

In these collections the preservation concerns already noted in the above sections (environmental control, disaster response and recovery planning, staff and user education, and so on) will need to be addressed, and, because the collections themselves and the libraries in which they are housed are usually large, the scope and size of the procedures established to address these concerns will be greater. The disaster response planning process, for example, may involve in the order of one year of a staff member's time to develop, and its full implementation, including the training of staff, may require several more years. In addition to these procedures there are others which are more likely to be carried out in collections of national importance: considerable attention to preservation is likely to be paid in the context of collection development, reformatting may be carried out, and research and development work may take place.

Selection is the first preservation decision of the many which will be made in relation to an item in a collection. A collection development policy should have been established for the collection (but often is not).[36] Using this to provide a context, selection should then take into account the physical condition of the item and the permanence of the format. The physical condition is especially relevant for material received as a gift or on exchange and for out-of-print items, for which the preservation implications of selecting a deteriorated item may be the expenditure of a considerable amount of money (on repairs, binding or providing a protective enclosure) to bring that item up to a condition where it can be expected to last for as long as possible. In some cases there may be a choice of format, for example paperback or case binding, paper or microfilm, and here the collection development policy should give guidance on the preferred choice with respect to its permanence. Selectors and acquisitions staff have a further role to play, by alerting preservation staff to items received which have special preservation requirements. Examples of this could include a volume issued with several loose maps which will need special attention in binding, or an item whose binding is especially fragile and which will require a protective enclosure before it can be placed on the shelves.

Microfilming or other reformatting technologies are more likely to be used in collections where long-term preservation is an important objective. There will also be a higher level of artefact conservation carried out than in libraries in the model three category. Research into preservation and the development of new techniques may also be carried out. Examples of this are the application of optical technology for information preservation by the Library of Congress, the development of a new method of paper strengthening by the British Library, and the application of a mass deacidification process by the National Library of Canada, as noted in Chapter 9.

The kinds of collections we are concerned with can exist in many kinds of libraries, and the preservation units in these libraries may take one of a very large number of different organizational forms. It is impossible to describe them all here, but some possibilities are noted below.

One example is that of a small specialized research library. Because the emphasis is on not altering the physical state of items, that is, on retaining the value of the artefact, emphasis could be placed on a program of basic techniques such as protective enclosures and encapsulating fragile single sheet items. This could be carried out by lower level staff, after appropriate training, under the direction of a curator. The advice of a conservator to establish the program should be sought. A longer-term aim could be to establish a conservator's position in the library.[37] Morrow provides two hypothetical examples in this category. The first is her 'Level 4', a

> specialized research library or separate special collections library associated with a large research library. Includes collections of rare books, manuscripts, photographs, ephemera and other unique materials pertaining to one or several particular fields. Includes secondary research materials and reference works in support of the collections. Active exhibition program and popular collections that are heavily used.[38]

Here the possible structure could be an administrative conservator reporting to the Director, with links to the subject specialists and curators, and with responsibility for: 1) a paper conservator, overseeing a conservator dealing with photographs and two conservation technicians; 2) a book conservator, overseeing two conservation technicians; 3) a librarian responsible for information preservation, overseeing one technician, one clerical position and two microfilm technicians.

Morrow's second example, her 'Level 5', is a

> large research library with diversified collections organized into one central or main library receiving moderate use and numerous branch or departmental libraries receiving heavy use. Includes a large separate collection of rare books, manuscripts and photographs.

Her suggested organizational structure is a Preservation Librarian responsible through the Head of Technical Services to the Director, and with links to the Preservation Committee and to the Head of Collection Development. Three positions report to the Preservation Librarian: 1) a librarian responsible for information preservation, overseeing one technician, one clerical position and one assistant; 2) a librarian responsible for materials preparation, overseeing one technician, two clerical positions and four assistants; 3) a conservator, overseeing three conservation technicians and three assistants.

A 1990 summary of organizational structures of preservation sections in Association of Research Libraries member libraries showed that there was no one standard model. Trends noted were the centralizing of functions such as collection maintenance and bindery preparation into one preservation unit, and at the same time a greater permeation of preservation concepts into all aspects of all library practice. Two dominant organizational structures were reported: where there was a full-time preservation administrator, that person reported to the Associate Director for Collection Development; and where the preservation administrator was part-time, the reporting line tended to be to the Library Director. The report noted, however, that 'there remains a multiplicity of organizational patterns' in ARL libraries. The preservation administrator's time is increasingly being spent on strategic planning activities, in addition to day-to-day administration of the preservation unit.[39]

Many examples of preservation activities in collections of national importance are described in the literature.[40]

Conclusion

In what direction is the field of library preservation heading? Fascinating as it is to conjecture, prophecy is at best an imprecise art. Many have written on this topic, and some general directions can be perceived. It is of interest to note some of these as a conclusion to this book.[41]

The application of new technologies to preservation will become more widespread, but only after the problems associated with them – of archival standards of permanence, and compatibility between systems – have been more effectively addressed. There will be an increasing use of the older technology of microfilming, until – say by the year 2000 – digitizing equals it in popularity. However, despite the increasing use and availability of these technologies, the originals will still be retained wherever possible.

Mass deacidification processes will be more widely available and more widely used, but mass paper strengthening methods will not be wholly successful. More permanent paper will be manufactured and used in book production, to the benefit of libraries.

All major libraries will have a disaster preparedness plan. There will be increased emphasis on education for preservation in library schools. Preservation administrators will be more likely to be librarians with preservation training than conservators, as a detailed knowledge of libraries and their administration will be more important to effective preservation programs than will mastery of manual skills. Contracting out of preservation services will probably increase.

Let us end this book as we began it, by quoting John Feather.

International conferences, Unesco reports and European Commission plans can sometimes seem a little remote from the work of the ordinary librarian or archivist, struggling to keep a decaying collection in a condition in which it can be used, often in an inadequate building and almost always with insufficient funds. The perception is understandable, but it is false. A profession, which is, by definition, self-regulating, creates for itself the climate in which it conducts its activities. Within the broad scope of providing the service demanded by its clients, it largely determines its own agenda. In the last 20 years, and more markedly so during the 1980s, the library profession in many countries has apparently reached the conclusion, through its various representative bodies, that preservation is an area of significant and serious professional concern.... A consensus is emerging which will carry us through the new decade and into a new century. There is a broad general agreement that preservation is important, not least because our central professional activity – to transfer information from source to user – will be frustrated if we lose the media which contain the information. Therefore we need to be able to determine whether to preserve information in its original format, or whether to reformat it and preserve the surrogate. We need to have the technologies which will permit the reformatting to take place, and then to preserve the surrogates themselves. We need to be able to repair, restore and preserve those damaged originals which we prefer not to sacrifice. In short, ten years of revitalized concern for the physical media of information have forced us to rethink the way in which we manage our information resources.[42]

Notes

1   Antonia Bunch, 'Conservation and the Library Community', *Library Review* 35 (1986): 58.
2   National Library of New Zealand, *Report...for the Year Ended 31 March 1989* (Wellington: Government Printer, 1989), p. 14.
3   Patricia Chapman, *Guidelines on Preservation and Conservation Policies in the Archives and Libraries Heritage* (Paris: Unesco, 1990; *SPEC Kit* 137 (1987).
4   *Ibid.*, p. 17.
5   A. Dean Larsen, 'Preservation and Materials Processing', in *Library Technical Services: Operations and Management*, ed. Irene P. Godden (Orlando, Fla: Academic Press, 1984), p. 195.
6   Jutta Reed-Scott, 'Preservation Organization and Staffing', *SPEC Flyer* 160 (January 1990).

7   Carolyn Clark Morrow, *The Preservation Challenge: A Guide to Conserving Library Materials* (White Plains, N.Y.: Knowledge Industry Publications, 1983), pp. 115-117.

8   Reed-Scott, *op. cit.*

9   Robert S. Lamb, 'Library Preservation Survey', *Conservation Administration News* 45 (April 1991): 4-5.

10   Robert H. Patterson, 'Conservation: What We Should Do Until the Conservator and the Twenty-First Century Arrive', in *Conserving and Preserving Library Materials*, ed. Kathryn Luther Henderson, William T. Henderson (Urbana-Champaign, Ill.: Graduate School of Library and Information Science, University of Illinois, 1983), p. 14.

11   Sally A. Buchanan, 'Administering the Library Conservation Program', *Law Library Journal* 77, 3 (1984-1985): 569-574.

12   Peter Waters, 'Phased Preservation: A Philosophical Concept and Practical Approach to Preservation', *Special Libraries* 81, 1 (1990): 35-43.

13   Antony Pacey, 'Library Preservation: The Approach of the National Museums of Canada', *Canadian Library Journal* 47, 1 (1990): 27-33.

14   Some examples are Robert H. Patterson, 'Organizing For Conservation', *Library Journal* (15 May 1979): 1116-1119; Robert H. Patterson, 'Conservation: What We Should Do Until the Conservator and the Twenty-First Century Arrive', in *Conserving and Preserving Library Materials, op. cit.*, p. 14.

15   Pamela W. Darling and Duane E. Webster, *Preservation Planning Program: An Assisted Self-Study Manual for Libraries.* Expanded 1987 ed. (Washington, D.C.: Association of Research Libraries, Office of Management Studies, 1987).

16   Mark E. Cain, 'Analyzing Preservation Practices and Environmental Conditions: A Committee's Systems Approach', *Collection Management* 4, 3 (1982): 19-28.

17   *Ibid.*, p. 27.

18   George Martin Cunha and Dorothy Grant Cunha, *Library and Archives Conservation: 1980s and Beyond* (Metuchen, N.J.: Scarecrow Press, 1983), Vol. 1, p. 119; Chapman, *op. cit.*

19   A.D. Baynes-Cope, *Caring for Books and Documents.* 2nd ed. (London: British Museum, 1989).

20   Helen Price, *Stopping the Rot: A Handbook of Preventive Conservation for Local Studies Collections.* 2nd ed. (Sydney: Australian Library and Information Association, New South Wales Branch, 1989).

21   These are the points noted for law libraries in Buchanan, *op. cit.*

22   *Ibid.*, p. 570.

23   This section is based on the advice in Robert DeCandido and GraceAnne A. DeCandido, 'Micro-Preservation: Conserving the Small Library', *Library Resources and Technical Services* 29, 2 (1985): 151-160. Also essential reading is Wesley L. Boomgaarden, 'Preservation Planning for the Small Special Library', *Special Libraries* 76, 3 (1985): 204-211.

24   Anne L. Reynolds, Nancy C. Schrock and Joanna Walsh, 'Preservation: The Public Library Response', *Library Journal* (15 February 1989): 128-132.

25   Morrow, *op. cit.*, p. 87.

26   *Ibid.*

27   Carolyn Clark Morrow and Carole Dyall, *Conservation Treatment Procedures: A Manual of Step-by-Step Procedures for the Maintenance and Repair of Library Materials.* 2nd ed. (Littleton, Colo.: Libraries Unlimited, 1986), 'Library D' pp. 180-181. Similar advice can be found in Marcia Duncan Lowry, *Preservation and Conservation in the Small Library* (Chicago, Ill.: Library Administration and Management Association, ALA, 1989).

28   Reynolds, Schrock and Walsh, *op. cit.*

29   Morrow, *op. cit.*, p. 88.

30   Morrow and Dyall, *op. cit.*, Library A, p. 179.

31   *Ibid.*, Library C, p. 180.

32   Carolyn Harris, Carol Mandel and Robert Wolven, 'A Cost Model for Preservation: The Columbia University Libraries' Approach', *Library Resources and Technical Services* 35, 1 (1991): 33-54.

33   Morrow, *op. cit.*, p. 88.

34   Some are present in *SPEC Kit 66*, *SPEC Kit 160*, and in *Conservation Administration News.*

35   Jan Merrill-Oldham, *Conservation and Preservation of Library Materials: A Program for The University of Connecticut Libraries* (Storrs, Conn.: University of Connecticut Library, 1984).

36   G.E. Gorman and B.R. Howes, *Collection Development for Libraries* (London: Bowker-Saur, 1989), p. xiii.

37   Morrow and Dyall, *op. cit.*, Library B, pp. 179-180.

38   Morrow, *op. cit.*, 'Level 4' and 'Level 5', pp. 89-90.

39   Reed-Scott, *op. cit.*

40   Some of these are Brian Hutton, 'Preserving Scotland's Heritage', *Library Conservation News* 19 (1988): 1-3; Joseph Schir, 'Preservation at the National Library of Malta', *COMLA Newsletter* 61 (1988): 2-3; John P. Baker, 'Preservation Programs of the New York Public Library: Part One, The Early Years', *Microform Review* 10, 1 (1981): 25-28; 'Part Two, From the 1930s to the '60s', *Microform Review* 11, 4 (1982): 22-30.

41   Gleaned from Peter Waters, 'The Florence Flood of 1966 Revisited', in *Preserving the Word: The Library Association Conference Proceedings, Harrogate 1986*, ed. R. Palmer (London: Library Association, 1987), 127-128; Donald B. McKeon, 'Conservation for Libraries and Archives 1981-2001: Considerations of Future Developments and Personnel', *Restaurator* 6 (1984): 139-146; Reed-Scott, *op. cit.*; and Gay Walker, 'One Step Beyond: The Future of Preservation Microfilming', in *Preservation Microfilming: Planning and Production: Papers from the RTSD Preservation Microfilming Institute...1988* (Chicago, Ill.: Association for Library Collections and Technical Services, ALA, 1989), pp. 71- 72.

42   John Feather, *Preservation and the Management of Library Collections* (London: Library Association, 1991), pp. 105-106.

Select Bibliography

This bibliography lists a wide range of publications relating to preservation of library materials. It is not intended to be comprehensive. Additional references may be located by using the bibliographies listed in section 1 below, and through the standard library abstracting and indexing services. The references in this bibliography have been organized according to the chapters of this book. Each item appears only under one heading.

Writings about preservation continue to proliferate at a rapid rate. As the quantity of writings increases rapidly, their quality becomes more uneven. Those using this book and the references in this bibliography must judge for themselves how appropriate the information contained in them is. In particular, procedures and solutions described are constantly being re-evaluated and altered, often rapidly. The reader must therefore make every attempt to stay up-to-date with the literature of preservation. Regular critical reading of the preservation literature, and in particular of the periodicals in the field (*Abbey Newsletter* and *Conservation Administration News* are two good examples), is essential in order to be informed on current thinking about the value of existing procedures and the applications of new techniques. It is also vital to seek expert advice, from a conservator or experienced librarian with preservation expertise, before attempting to apply procedures and techniques described in some of the writings listed below.

1   Bibliographies and Literature Reviews

'A Basic Reading List on Permanence of Paper'. *Alkaline Paper Advocate* 2, 1 (1989): 14.

Bourke, Thomas A. 'The Reproduction of Library Materials in 1990'. *Library Resources and Technical Services* 35, 3 (1991): 307-318.

Bowling, Mary B. 'Literature on the Preservation of Nonpaper Material'. *American Archivist* 53, 2 (1990): 340-348.

Crawford-de Sa, Elizabeth and Cloonan, Michèle Valerie. 'The Preservation of Archival and Library Materials: A Bibliography of Government Publications, Part I'. *Conservation Administration News* 46 (1991): 16-17, 30-31.

Cunha, George Martin and Cunha, Dorothy Grant. *Library and Archives Conservation: 1980s and Beyond.* 2 vols. Metuchen, N.J.: Scarecrow Press, 1983. Vol. 2 is the bibliography.

Fox, Lisa B. *A Core Collection in Preservation.* Chicago, Ill.: American Library Association, 1988.

Fox, Lisa B. 'A Two-Year Perspective on Library Preservation: An Annotated Bibliography'. *Library Resources and Technical Services* 30, 3 (1986): 290-318.

Futscher, Joan M. *Preservation Microfilming: Bibliography.* Washington, D.C.: National Preservation Program Office, 1988.

Hendriks, Klaus B. and Whitehurst, Anne. *Conservation of Photographic Materials: A Basic Reading List.* Ottawa: National Archives of Canada, 1988.

Jones, Maralyn. 'More Than Ten Years After: Identity and Direction in Library Preservation'. *Library Resources and Technical Services* 35, 3 (1991): 294-306.

Kesse, Erich J. 'The Reproduction of Library Materials in 1989'. *Library Resources and Technical Services* 34, 4 (1990): 467-475.

Longstreth, Karl E. 'The Preservation of Library Materials in 1988: A Review of the Literature'. *Library Resources and Technical Services* 33, 3 (1989): 217-226.

Longstreth, Karl E. 'The Preservation of Library Materials in 1989: A Review of the Literature'. *Library Resources and Technical Services* 34, 4 (1990): 455-465.

Mihram, Danielle. 'Paper Deacidification: A Bibliographic Survey'. *Restaurator* 7, 2 (1986): 81-98; 7, 3 (1986): 99-118.

Montori, Carla J. 'Library Preservation in 1986: An Annotated Bibliography'. *Library Resources and Technical Services* 31, 4 (1987): 365-385.

Sinclair, James and Carpenter, John. *Disaster Planning for Libraries: A Bibliography.* Sydney: State Library of New South Wales, 1987.

Swartzburg, Susan G. 'Basic Preservation Bibliography'. *Conservation Administration News* 44 (1991): 10-12.

2   Periodicals

Abbey Newsletter. Provo, Utah, 1975- .

Alkaline Paper Advocate. Provo, Utah, 1988- .

Commission on Preservation and Access *Newsletter.* Washington, D.C., 1988- .

Conservation Administration News. Tulsa, Oklahoma, 1979- .

Library Conservation News. London, 1983- .

Microform Review. Westport, Conn., 1972- .

National Preservation News. Washington, D.C., 1985- .

Restaurator. Copenhagen, 1969- .

3   General Writings on Preservation

Banks, Paul N. 'Preservation of Library Materials'. In *Encyclopedia of Library and Information Science*, Vol. 23, 180-222. New York: Dekker, 1978.

Baynes-Cope, A.D. *Caring for Books and Documents*. 2nd ed. London: British Museum, 1989.

Brown, Norman B. 'Preservation in the Research Library: Its Past, Present Status, and Encouraging Future'. In Gorman, Michael, *et al. Technical Services Today and Tomorrow*, 105-129. Englewood, Colo.: Libraries Unlimited, 1990.

Bunch, Antonia. 'Conservation and the Library Community'. *Library Review* 35 (1986): 56-61.

Cluff, E. Dale. 'The Role and Responsibility of the Library in Preservation and Conservation.' In *Conserving and Preserving Library Materials*, ed. Kathryn Luther Henderson and William T. Henderson, 181-196. Urbana-Champaign, Ill.: Graduate School of Library and Information Science, University of Illinois, 1983.

Conservation and Collection Management: Proceedings of a Seminar at Loughborough University of Technology...1987. London: National Preservation Office, British Library, 1988.

Conservation in Crisis: Proceedings of a Seminar at Loughborough University of Technology, 16-17 July 1986. London: National Preservation Office, British Library, 1987.

Conservation in the Library: A Handbook of Use and Care of Traditional and Nontraditional Materials, ed. Susan Garretson Swartzburg. Westport, Conn: Greenwood Press, 1983.

Conservation of Library and Archival Materials and the Graphic Arts, ed. Guy Petherbridge. London: Butterworths, 1987.

Conserving and Preserving Library Materials, ed. Kathryn Luther Henderson and William T. Henderson. Urbana-Champaign, Ill.: Graduate School of Library and Information Science, University of Illinois, 1983.

Cunha, George Martin and Cunha, Dorothy Grant. *Library and Archives Conservation: 1980s and Beyond*. 2 vols. Metuchen, N.J.: Scarecrow Press, 1983.

Darling, Pamela W. and Webster, Duane E. *Preservation Planning Program: An Assisted Self-Study Manual for Libraries*. Expanded 1987 ed. Washington, D.C.: Association of Research Libraries, Office of Management Studies, 1987.

Dureau, J.M. and Clements, D.W.G. *Principles for the Preservation and Conservation of Library Materials*. The Hague: IFLA, 1986.

Feather, John. 'Preservation and Conservation: A Professional Issue for the 1990s'. *New Zealand Libraries* 46, 2/3 (1989): 17-25.

Feather, John. *Preservation and the Management of Library Collections*. London: Library Association, 1991.

Glossary of Basic Archival and Library Conservation Terms: English with Equivalents in Spanish, German, Italian, French and Russian, ed. Carmen Crespo Nogueira; comp. Committee on Conservation and Restoration, International Council on Archives. München: K.G. Saur, 1988.

Gracy, David B. 'Between Muffins and Mercury...: The Elusive Definition of "Preservation"'. *New Library Scene* 9, 6 (1990): 1, 5-7.

Grimwood-Jones, Diana. 'Preservation'. In *British Librarianship and Information Work 1981-1985: Volume Two*, ed. David W. Bromley and Angela M. Allott, 270-284. London: Library Association, 1988.

Hazen, Dan C. 'Preservation in Poverty and Plenty: Policy Issues for the 1990s'. *Journal of Academic Librarianship* 15, 6 (1990): 344-351.

Library Conservation: Preservation in Perspective, ed. John P. Baker and Marguerite C. Soroka. Stroudsburg: Dowden, Hutchinson and Ross, 1978.

Morrow, Carolyn Clark. *The Preservation Challenge: A Guide to Conserving Library Materials*. White Plains, N.Y.: Knowledge Industry Publications, 1983.

Newspaper Preservation and Access: Proceedings of the Symposium Held in London...1987, ed. Ian P. Gibb. 2 vols. München: K.G. Saur, 1988.

Preservation: A Survival Kit. London: National Preservation Office, 1986?

Preservation of Library Materials: Conference Held at the National Library of Austria, Vienna, April 7-10, 1986, ed. Merrily A. Smith. 2 vols. München: K.G. Saur, 1987.

Preservation Planning Program: Resource Notebook, comp. Pamela W. Darling; rev. ed. Wesley L. Boomgaarden. Washington, D.C.: Association of Research Libraries, 1987.

Preserving the Word: The Library Association Conference Proceedings, Harrogate 1986, ed. R. Palmer. London: Library Association, 1987.

Randall, Thea. 'Preservation and Conservation'. In *Local Studies Collections: A Manual*, Vol. 2, ed. Michael Dewe, 140-172. Aldershot: Gower, 1991.

Ritzenthaler, Mary Lynn. *Archives and Manuscripts: Conservation: A Manual on Physical Care and Management*. Chicago, Ill.: Society of American Archivists, 1983.

RLG Preservation Manual. 2nd ed. Stanford, Calif.: Research Libraries Group, 1986.

Roberts, Matt T. and Etherington, Don. *Bookbinding and the Conservation of Books: A Dictionary of Descriptive Terminology*. Washington, D.C.: Library of Congress, 1982.

Swartzburg, Susan G. *Preserving Library Materials: A Manual*. Metuchen, N.J.: Scarecrow Press, 1980.

Wilson, Alexander. *Library Policy for Preservation and Conservation in the European Community: Principles, Practices and the Contribution of New Information Technologies*. München: K.G. Saur, 1988.

4   Overview: The Problem, Causes and Solutions (Chapter 1)

Agresto, John. 'Preserving Our Heritage'. *National Preservation News* (July 1986): 10-13.

Barrow, William J. *Deterioration of Book Stock: Causes and Remedies: Two Studies on the Permanence of Book Paper*. Richmond, Va: Virginia State Library, 1959.

Barrow, William J. *Manuscripts and Documents: Their Deterioration and Restoration*. 2nd ed. Charlottesville, Va: University Press of Virginia, 1972.

Brown, Jay Ward. 'The Once and Future Book: The Preservation Crisis'. *Wilson Library Bulletin* (May 1985): 591-596.

Council on Library Resources. Committee on Preservation and Access. *Brittle Books: Report of the Committee on Preservation and Access*. Washington, D.C.: Council on Library Resources, 1986.

Darling, Pamela W. 'Will Anything Be Left?: New Responses to the Preservation Challenge'. *Wilson Library Bulletin* (November 1981): 177-181.

Darling, Pamela W. and Ogden, Sherelyn. 'From Problems Perceived to Programs in Practice: The Preservation of Library Resources in the U.S.A., 1956-1980'. *Library Resources and Technical Services* 25, 1 (1981): 9-29.

Higginbotham, Barbra Buckner. 'The "Brittle Books Problem": A Turn-of-the-Century Perspective'. *Libraries and Culture* 25, 4 (1990): 496-512.

Higginbotham, Barbra Buckner. *Our Past Preserved: A History of American Library Preservation, 1876-1910*. Boston, Mass.: G.K. Hall, 1990.

McDonald, Larry. 'Forgotten Forebears: Concern with Preservation, 1876 to World War I'. *Libraries and Culture* 25, 4 (1990): 483-495.

Merrill-Oldham, Jan. 'Preservation Comes of Age: An Action Agenda for the '80s and Beyond'. *American Libraries* 16 (December 1985): 770-772.

Ogden, Sherelyn. 'The Impact of the Florence Flood on Library Conservation in the United States of America: A Study of the Literature Published 1956-1976'. *Restaurator* 3, 1/2 (1979): 1-36.

Waters, Peter. 'The Florence Flood of 1966 Revisited'. In *Preserving the Word: The Library Association Conference Proceedings, Harrogate 1986*, ed. R. Palmer, 113-128. London: Library Association, 1987.

Waters, Peter. 'Phased Preservation: A Philosophical Concept and Practical Approach to Preservation'. *Special Libraries* 81, 1 (1990): 35-42.

Williams, Gordon. 'The Preservation of Deteriorating Books'. Part I *Library Journal* (1 January 1966): 51-56; Part II *Library Journal* (15 January 1966): 189-194.

Wilson, Alexander. 'For This and Future Generations: Managing the Conflict between Conservation and Use'. *Library Review* 31 (1982): 163-172.

5 Why Library Materials Deteriorate (Chapter 2)

Abt, Jeffrey. 'Objectifying the Book: The Impact of Science on Books and Manuscripts'. *Library Trends* 36, 1 (1987): 23-38.

Adams, Randolph G. 'Librarians as Enemies of Books'. *Library Quarterly* 7 (1937): 317-331.

Bansa, Helmut. 'The Conservation of Modern Books'. *IFLA Journal* 9, 2 (1983): 102-113.

Blades, William. *The Enemies of Books*. London: Trübner, 1880.

Brown, Lewis H. 'Preservation in Original Format: The Role of Paper Quality'. In *Preservation of Library Materials: Conference Held at the National Library of Austria, Vienna, April 7-10, 1986*, ed. Merrily A. Smith, Vol. 1, 49-57. München: K.G. Saur, 1987.

Browning, B.L. 'The Nature of Paper'. In *Deterioration and Preservation of Library Materials*, ed. Howard W. Winger and Richard D. Smith, 18-30. Chicago, Ill.: University of Chicago Press, 1970.

Butler, Randall R. '"Here Today...Gone Tomorrow": A pH Investigation of Brigham Young University's 1987 Library Acquisitions'. *College and Research Libraries* 51, 6 (1990): 539-547.

Curtin, Bonnie, Harger, Elaine and Yasue, Akio. 'The pH of New Library Books: Monitoring Acquisitions at Columbia University'. *Alkaline Paper Advocate* 1, 4 (1988): 30.

Grove, Lee E. 'Paper Deterioration: An Old Story'. *College and Research Libraries* 26 (1964): 365-374.

Hills, Richard L. *Papermaking in Britain 1488-1988: A Short History*. London: Athlone Press, 1988.

Hollinger, William K. 'The Chemical Structure and Acid Deterioration of Paper'. *Library Hi Tech* 1, 4 (1984): 51-57.

Hunter, Dard. *Papermaking: The History and Technique of an Ancient Craft*. New York: Dover, 1978 (first published 1947).

Lundeen, Gerald W. 'Preservation of Paper Based Materials: Present and Future Research and Developments in the Paper Industry'. In *Conserving and Preserving Library Materials*, ed. Kathryn Luther Henderson and William T. Henderson, 73-85. Urbana-Champaign, Ill.: Graduate School of Library and Information Science, University of Illinois, 1983.

McCrady, Ellen. 'Why Collections Deteriorate: Putting Acidic Paper in Perspective'. *Alkaline Paper Advocate* 1, 4 (1988): 31-32.

McCrady, Ellen. 'Wood Is Good'. *Library Conservation News* 20 (1988): 4-5.

Mosher, Paul H. 'Book Production Quality: A Librarian's View, or, the Self-Destructing Library'. *Library Resources and Technical Services* 28, 1 (1984): 15-19.

Pascoe, M.W. *Impact of Environmental Pollution on the Preservation of Archives and Records: A RAMP Study*. Paris: Unesco, 1988.

Poole, Frazer G. 'Foreword'. In Barrow, W.J. *Manuscripts and Documents: Their Deterioration and Restoration.* 2nd ed., xi-xxvii. Charlottesville, Va: University Press of Virginia, 1972.

Preservation of Historical Records [report of the] Committee on Preservation of Historical Records. Washington, D.C.: National Academy Press, 1986.

Priest, D.J. 'Paper and Its Problems'. *Library Review* 36 (1987): 164-173.

Rutledge, John and Owen, Willy. 'Changes in the Quality of Paper in French Books, 1860-1914: A Study of Selected Holdings of the Wilson Library, University of North Carolina'. *Library Resources and Technical Services* 27, 2 (1983): 177-187.

Society of Arts. Committee on Leather for Bookbinding. *Report of the Committee on Leather for Bookbinding.* London: George Bell for the Society of Arts, 1905.

Thompson, Lawrence S. 'Paper'. In *Encyclopedia of Library and Information Science*, Vol. 21, 333-364. New York: Dekker, 1977.

Trevitt, John. 'Permanence in Publishers' Edition Binding'. In *Preserving the Word: The Library Association Conference Proceedings, Harrogate 1986*, ed. R. Palmer, 90-94. London: Library Association, 1987.

Wessel, Carl J. 'Deterioration of Library Materials'. In *Encyclopedia of Library and Information Science*, 7, 69-120. New York: Dekker, 1972.

Wessel, Carl J. 'Environmental Factors Affecting the Permanence of Library Materials'. In *Deterioration and Preservation of Library Materials*, ed. Howard W. Winger and Richard D. Smith, 39-84. Chicago, Ill.: University of Chicago Press, 1970.

Westbrook, Lynn. *Paper Preservation: Nature, Extent, and Recommendations.* Urbana-Champaign, Ill.: Graduate School of Library and Information Science, University of Illinois, 1985.

Williams, John C. 'A Review of Paper Quality and Paper Chemistry'. *Library Trends* 30 (1981): 203-224.

6 Surveying the Library (Chapter 3)

Bond, Randall, *et al.* 'Preservation Study at the Syracuse University Libraries'. *College and Research Libraries* 48, 2 (1987): 132-147.

Buchanan, Sarah and Coleman, Sandra. *Deterioration Survey of the Stanford University Libraries Green Library Stack Collection* (1979). In *Preservation Planning Program Resource Notebook*, comp. Pamela W. Darling; rev. ed. Wesley L. Boomgaarden, 189-221. Washington, D.C.: Association of Research Libraries, Office of Management Studies, 1987.

Cain, Mark E. 'Analyzing Preservation Practices and Environmental Conditions: A Committee's Systems Approach'. *Collection Management* 4, 3 (1982): 19-28.

Chrzastowski, Tina, *et al.* 'Library Collection Deterioration: A Study at the University of Illinois at Urbana-Champaign'. *College and Research Libraries* 50, 5 (1989): 577-584.

Cunha, George M. *Methods of Evaluation to Determine the Preservation Needs in Libraries and Archives: A RAMP Study with Guidelines.* Paris: Unesco, 1988.

Cunha, George. 'What an Institution Can Do to Survey Its Conservation Needs'. In *Preservation Planning Program Resource Notebook,* comp. Pamela W. Darling; rev. ed. Wesley L. Boomgaarden, 17-20. Washington, D.C.: Association of Research Libraries, Office of Management Studies, 1987.

DeCandido, Robert. 'Condition Survey of the United States History, Local History and Genealogy Collection of the New York Public Library'. *Library Resources and Technical Services* 33, 3 (1989): 274-281.

King, Richard G., Jr. 'Deterioration of Book Paper: Results of Physical and Chemical Testing of the Paper in 2280 Monographs from the Collections of the University of California Libraries.' In *Advances in Library Administration and Organization,* Vol. 2, 119-149. Greenwich, Conn: JAI Press, 1983.

Nainis, Linda and Bedard, Laura A. 'Preservation Book Survey in an Academic Law Library'. *Law Library Journal* 78, 2 (1986): 243-259.

Pollock, Michael. 'Surveying the Collections'. *Library Conservation News* 21 (1988): 4-6.

Reynolds, Anne L., Schrock, Nancy C. and Walsh, Joanna. 'Preservation: the Public Library Response'. *Library Journal* (15 February 1989): 128-132.

Smith, Merrily A. and Garlick, Karen. 'Surveying Library Collections: A Suggested Approach with Case Study'. *Technical Services Quarterly* 5, 2 (1987): 3-18.

Walker, Gay. 'Notes on Research and Operations: Assessing Preservation Needs'. *Library Resources and Technical Services* 33, 4 (1989): 414-419.

Walker, Gay, *et al.* 'The Yale Survey: A Large-Scale Study of Book Deterioration in the Yale University'. *College and Research Libraries* 46, 2 (1985): 111-132.

7 Controlling the Environment (Chapter 4)

Air Quality Criteria for Storage of Paper-Based Archival Records. NBSIR-83-2795. Washington, D.C.: National Bureau of Standards, 1983.

Banks, Joyce M. *Guidelines for Preventive Conservation.* Ottawa: Committee on Conservation/Preservation of Library Materials, 1987.

Bansa, Helmut. 'The Conservation of Library Materials in Tropical and Sub-tropical Conditions'. *IFLA Journal* 7,3 (1981): 264-267.

Boss, Richard. 'Collection Security'. *Library Trends* 33 (1984): 39-48.

Bowser, Eileen. 'Motion Picture Film'. In *Conservation in the Library*, ed. Susan Garretson Swartzburg, 139-153. Westport, Conn.: Greenwood Press, 1983.

Brezner, Jerome and Luner, Philip. 'Nuke 'em!: Library Pest Control Using a Microwave'. *Library Journal* (15 September 1989): 60-63.

Harris, Carolyn L. and Banks, Paul N. 'The Library Environment and the Preservation of Library Materials'. *Facilities Manager* 6, 3 (1990): 21-24.

Hendriks, Klaus B. *The Preservation and Restoration of Photographic Materials in Archives and Libraries: A RAMP Study with Guidelines*. Paris: Unesco, 1984.

Hendriks, Klaus B. 'Storage and Handling of Photographic Materials'. In *Preservation of Library Materials: Conference Held at the National Library of Austria, Vienna, April 7-10, 1986*, ed. Merrily A. Smith, Vol. 2, 55-66. München: K.G. Saur, 1987.

Hickin, Norman. *Bookworms: The Insect Pests of Books*. London: Sheppard Press, 1985.

Larsgaard, Mary Lynette. 'Chapter 4: Storage, Care, and Repair'. In her *Map Librarianship: An Introduction*. 2nd ed., 163-197. Littleton, Colo.: Libraries Unlimited, 1987.

Lawson, Peter. 'Freezing as a Means of Pest Control'. *Library Conservation News* 20 (1988): 6.

Lincoln, Alan Jay and Lincoln, Carol Zall. *Library Crime and Security: An International Perspective*. New York: Haworth Press, 1987.

Lund, Thomas D. 'The Physical Aspects of Newspaper Collection Management: Some Problems and Their Solution'. In *Newspapers in the Library: New Approaches to Management and Reference Work*, ed. Lois N. Upham, 29-36. New York: Haworth Press, 1988.

McWilliams, Jerry. 'Sound Recordings'. In *Conservation in the Library*, ed. Susan Garretson Swartzburg, 163-184. Westport, Conn.: Greenwood Press, 1983.

Metcalf, Keyes D. 'The Design of Book Stacks and the Preservation of Books'. *Restaurator* 1 (1969): 115-125.

Morris, John. 'Protecting the Library from Fire'. *Library Trends* 33 (1984): 49-56.

Padfield, Timothy. 'Climate Control in Libraries and Archives'. In *Preservation of Library Materials: Conference Held at the National Library of Austria, Vienna, April 7-10, 1986*, ed. Merrily A. Smith, Vol. 2, 124-138. München: K.G. Saur, 1987.

Paris, Judith and Boss, Richard W. 'Videodiscs'. In *Conservation in the Library*, ed. Susan Garretson Swartzburg, 189-203. Westport, Conn.: Greenwood Press, 1983.

Parker, Thomas A. 'Integrated Pest Management for Libraries'. In *Preservation of Library Materials: Conference Held at the National Library of Austria, Vienna, April 7-10, 1986*, ed. Merrily A. Smith, Vol. 2, 103-123. München: K.G. Saur, 1987.

Pickett, A.G. and Lemcoe, M.M. *Preservation and Storage of Sound Recordings.* Washington, D.C.: Library of Congress, 1959.

Practice for Storage of Paper-Based Library and Archival Documents. Z39.XX-1984, section 3.4. ANSI Draft Standard.

Recommendations for Storage and Exhibition of Archival Documents. BS 5454: 1989. London: British Standards Institution, 1989.

Reilly, James M. *Care and Identification of 19th-Century Photographic Prints.* Rochester, N.Y.: Eastman Kodak, 1986.

Rempel, Siegfried. *The Care of Photographs.* New York: Nick Lyons Books, 1987.

Rempel, Siegfried. 'Cold and Cool Vault Environments for the Storage of Historic Photographic Materials'. *Conservation Administration News* 38 (1989): 6-7, 9.

Schrock, Nancy Carlson and Sundt, Christine L. 'Slides'. In *Conservation in the Library*, ed. Susan Garretson Swartzburg, 103-128. Westport, Conn.: Greenwood Press, 1983.

Stehkämper, Hugo. '"Natural" Air Conditioning of Stacks'. *Restaurator* 9, 4 (1988): 163-177.

Stewart, Eleanore. 'Freeze Disinfestation of the McWilliams Collection'. *Conservation Administration News* 32 (1988): 10-11, 25.

Swan, Alice. 'Conservation of Photographic Print Collections'. *Library Trends* 30 (1981): 267-296.

Swartzburg, Susan G. and Boyle, Deirdre. 'Videotape'. In *Conservation in the Library*, ed. Susan Garretson Swartzburg, 155-161. Westport, Conn.: Greenwood Press, 1983.

Thompson, Lawrence S. 'Library Pests'. *Library and Archival Security* 7, 1 (1985): 15-24.

Trinkhaus-Randall, Gregor. 'Preserving Special Collections through Internal Security'. *College and Research Libraries* 50, 4 (1989): 448-454.

Wall, Thomas B. 'Nonprint Materials: A Definition and Some Practical Considerations on Their Maintenance'. *Library Trends* 34 (1985): 129-140.

Walsh, Timothy. 'Air-Conditioning for Archives'. *Archives and Manuscripts* 8, 2 (1980): 70-78.

Ward, Alan. *A Manual of Sound Archive Administration.* Aldershot: Gower, 1990.

Wood Lee, Mary. *Prevention and Treatment of Mold in Library Collections with an Emphasis on Tropical Climates: A RAMP Study.* Paris: Unesco, 1988.

8   An Attitude of Respect: Careful Handling and Education (Chapter 5)

Banks, Paul N. 'Education in Library Conservation'. *Library Trends* 30, 2 (1981): 189-202.

Bansa, Helmut. 'The Awareness of Conservation: Reasons for Reorientation in Library Training'. *Restaurator* 7, 1 (1986): 36-47.

Barnes, Melvyn. 'In-House Conservation Education'. In *Conservation in Crisis: Proceedings of a Seminar at Loughborough University of Technology, 16-17 July 1986*, 35-43. London: National Preservation Office, British Library, 1987.

'Basic Preservation Procedures'. *SPEC Kit* 70 (1981).

Burdick, Amrita J. 'Library Photocopying: the Margin for Caring'. *New Library Scene* 5, 3 (1986): 17-18.

'Care and Handling of Library Materials: A User's Guide to Preserving the Yale University Library's Research Collections'. *SPEC Kit* 113 (1985): 77.

Chepesiuk, Ronald. 'Education of an Apprentice: Conservation at Johns Hopkins'. *Wilson Library Bulletin* (September 1985): 43-45.

Conway, Paul. 'Archival Preservation: Definitions for Improving Education and Training'. *Restaurator* 10 (1989): 47-60.

Dureau, Jeanne-Marie. 'Approaches to Training in Preservation and Conservation'. In *Preservation of Library Materials: Conference Held at the National Library of Austria, Vienna, April 7-10, 1986*, ed. Merrily A. Smith, Vol. 2, 10-19. München: K.G. Saur, 1987.

Education and Training for Preservation and Conservation: Papers of an International Seminar... 1986, ed. Josephine Riss Fang and Ann Russell. München: K.G. Saur, 1991.

Feather, John and Lusher, Anne. 'Education for Conservation in British Library Schools: Current Practices and Future Prospects'. *Journal of Librarianship* 21, 2 (1989): 129-138.

Feather, John and Lusher, Anne. *The Teaching of Conservation in LIS Schools in Great Britain*. London: British Library Research and Development Department, 1988.

Foster, Jocelyn. 'Are You a Book Batterer?' *College and Research Library News* 44, 4 (1983): 117.

Greenfield, Jane. *The Care of Fine Books*. New York: Nick Lyons Books, 1988.

Harris, Carolyn. 'Education for Preservation Administration: The Role of the Conservation Education Program of Columbia University's School of Library Science'. *Conservation Administration News* 42 (1990): 8-9, 24; 43 (1990): 4-5, 29.

Havard-Williams, Peter. 'Conservation in Library and Information Science Education'. *Library Conservation News* 10 (1986): 5, 9.

Kathpalia, Y.P. *A Model Curriculum for the Training of Specialists in Document Preservation and Restoration: A RAMP Study with Guidelines*. Paris: Unesco, 1984.

McCrady, Ellen. 'Notes on Operations: History of the Abbey Publications'. *Library Resources and Technical Services* 35, 1 (1991): 104-108.

McCrank, Lawrence J. 'Conservation and Collection Management: Educational Problems and Opportunities'. *Journal of Education for Librarianship* 22, 1/2 (1981): 20-43.

Marcum, Deanna B. *Preservation Education Institute Final Report August 2-4, 1990*. Washington, D.C.: Commission on Preservation and Access, 1990.

Preservation Education Directory. 6th ed., comp. Christopher D.G. Coleman. Chicago, Ill.: Association for Library Collections and Technical Services, ALA, 1990.

'Preservation Education in ARL Libraries'. *SPEC Kit* 113 (1985).

Smith, Merrily A. 'Care and Handling of Bound Materials'. In *Preservation of Library Materials: Conference Held at the National Library of Austria, Vienna, April 7-10, 1986*, ed. Merrily A. Smith, Vol. 2, 45-53. München: K.G. Saur, 1987.

Trinkhaus-Randall, Gregor and Jackson, Patience Kenney. 'Limiting the Use of Bookdrops: A Preservation Necessity'. *New Library Scene* 10, 1 (1991): 1, 5.

Turner, John R. 'Teaching Conservation'. *Education for Information* 6 (1988): 145-151.

Users' Guide to the Conservation of Library Materials (Stanford University Libraries, 1980). In *Preservation Planning Program: Resource Notebook*, comp. Pamela W. Darling; rev. ed. Wesley L. Boomgaarden, 175-184. Washington, D.C.: Association of Research Libraries, 1987.

White, Howard S. 'A Copier Easy on Books'. *American Libraries* 15 (November 1984): 726.

Wilman, H. 'Document Delivery without Damage'. *Interlending and Document Supply* 13, 4 (1985): 112-115.

9   Disaster Preparedness (Chapter 6)

Anderson, Hazel and McIntyre, John E. *Planning Manual for Disaster Control in Scottish Libraries and Record Offices*. Edinburgh: National Library of Scotland, 1985.

Barton, John P. and Wellheiser, Johanna G. *An Ounce of Prevention: A Handbook on Disaster Contingency Planning for Archives, Libraries and Record Centres*. Toronto: Toronto Area Archivists Group Education Foundation, 1985.

Belyaeva, Irina. 'Phased Conservation at the Library of the USSR Academy of Sciences'. *Conservation Administration News* 46 (1991): 1, 3, 7.

Bohem, Hilda. *Disaster Prevention and Disaster Preparedness*. Berkeley, Calif.: University of California, 1978.

Buchanan, Sally. *Disaster Planning: Preparedness and Recovery for Libraries and Archives: A RAMP Study with Guidelines*. Paris: Unesco, 1988.

Burgess, Dean. 'The Library Has Blown Up!' *Library Journal* (1 October 1989): 59-61.

Disaster in Libraries: Prevention and Control, ed. Max W. Borchardt. Camberwell, Vic.: CAVAL, 1988.

England, Claire and Evans, Karen. *Disaster Management for Libraries: Planning and Process*. Ottawa: Canadian Library Association, 1988.

Fortson-Jones, Judith. *Disaster Prevention and Recovery Plan Nebraska State Historical Society* (1980). In *Disaster Prevention and Preparedness, Problems in Archives Kit X* (1982).

Hill, Robert. 'Salvage on the Move'. *Library Conservation News* 16 (1987): 3, 8.

Jenkin, Ian Tregarthern. *Disaster Planning and Preparedness: An Outline Disaster Control Plan*. Boston Spa: British Library, 1987.

'Leningrad Library Fire'. *Abbey Newsletter* 12, 4 (1988): 59-61.

Lenzuni, Anna. 'Coping with Disaster'. In *Preservation of Library Materials: Conference Held at the National Library of Austria, Vienna, April 7-10, 1986*, ed. Merrily A. Smith, Vol. 2, 98-102. München: K.G. Saur, 1987.

McCleary, John M. *Vacuum Freeze-Drying, a Method Used to Salvage Water-Damaged Archival and Library Materials: A RAMP Study with Guidelines*. Paris: Unesco, 1987.

McIntyre, J.E. 'Disaster Control Planning at National Level'. In *Preservation of Library Materials: Conference Held at the National Library of Austria, Vienna, April 7-10, 1986*, ed. Merrily A. Smith, Vol. 1, 39-42. München: K.G. Saur, 1987.

Miller, R. Bruce. 'Libraries and Computers: Disaster Prevention and Recovery'. *Information Technology and Libraries* 7, 4 (1988): 349-358.

Morentz, James W. 'Computerizing Libraries for Emergency Planning'. *Special Libraries* 78, 2 (1987): 100-104.

Morris, John. *The Library Disaster Preparedness Handbook*. Chicago, Ill.: American Library Association, 1986.

Olson, Nancy B. 'Hanging Your Software Up to Dry'. *College and Research Libraries News* 47, 10 (1986): 634-636.

Parker, A.E. 'The Freeze-Drying Process: Some Conclusions'. *Library Conservation News* 23 (1989): 4-6, 8.

'Special Report: Fire at the USSR Academy of Sciences Library'. *Library Journal* (15 June 1988): 10, 12.

Strong, Gary E. 'Rats! Oh No, Not Rats!' *Special Libraries* 76, 2 (1987): 105-111.

Sung, Carolyn Hoover, Leonev, Valerii Pavlovich and Waters, Peter. 'Fire Recovery at the Library of the Academy of Sciences of the USSR'. *American Archivist* 53 (1990): 298-312.

Ungarelli, Donald L. 'Insurance and Prevention: Why and How?'. *Library Trends* 33 (Summer 1984): 57-67.

Waters, Peter. *Procedures for Salvage of Water-Damaged Library Materials.* 2nd ed. Washington, D.C.: Library of Congress, 1979.

Watson, Tom. 'Out of the Ashes: The Los Angeles Public Library'. *Wilson Library Bulletin* (December 1989): 34-38, 41.

10   Preserving the Artefact (Chapter 7)

Basic Conservation of Archival Materials: A Guide. Ottawa: Canadian Council of Archives, 1990.

Baynes-Cope, A.D. 'Ethics and the Conservation of Archival Documents'. *Journal of the Society of Archivists* 9, 4 (1988): 185-187.

Cains, Anthony and Swift, Katherine. *Preserving Our Printed Heritage: The Long Room Project at Trinity College Dublin.* Dublin: Trinity College Library, 1988.

Christensen, John O. 'Extended Life for Popular Paperbacks'. *Library Journal* (1 October 1989): 65-66.

Crespo, Carmen. *The Preservation and Restoration of Paper Records and Books: A RAMP Study with Guidelines.* Paris: Unesco, 1984.

Davis, Mary. 'Preservation Using Pesticides: Some Words of Caution'. *Wilson Library Bulletin* (February 1985): 386-388, 431.

Ellis, Roger. 'The Principles of Archives Repair'. In *Library Conservation: Preservation in Perspective*, ed. John P. Baker and Marguerite C. Soroka, 316-324. Stroudsburg: Dowden, Hutchinson and Ross, 1978.

Grauer, Sally. 'Recasing: A Discussion between Librarians and Binders'. *New Library Scene* 8, 4 (1989): 1, 5-8.

Greenfield, Jane. *Books: Their Care and Repair.* New York: Wilson, 1983.

Hadgraft, Nicholas. 'The Parker Library Conservation Project, 1983-1989'. *Library Conservation News* 24 (1989): 4-7.

Horton, Carolyn. *Cleaning and Preserving Bindings and Related Materials.* 2nd ed. Chicago, Ill.: American Library Association, 1969.

Hubbard, William J. *Stack Management: A Practical Guide to Shelving and Maintaining Library Collections.* Chicago, Ill.: American Library Association, 1981.

Library Binding Institute. *Library Binding Institute for Library Binding.* 8th ed. Rochester, N.Y.: Library Binding Institute, 1986.

Merrill-Oldham, Jan. 'Binding for Research Libraries'. *New Library Scene* 3, 4 (1984): 1, 4-6.

Merrill-Oldham, Jan and Parisi, Paul. *Guide to the Library Binding Institute Standard for Library Binding.* Chicago, Ill.: American Library Association, 1990.

Middleton, Bernard C. *The Restoration of Leather Binding.* Rev. ed. Chicago, Ill.: American Library Association, 1984.

Montori, Carla J. 'Managing the Library's Commercial Library Binding Program'. *Technical Services Quarterly* 5, 3 (1988): 21-25.

Morrow, Carolyn Clark and Dyall, Carole. *Conservation Treatment Procedures: A Manual of Step-by-Step Procedures for the Maintenance and Repair of Library Materials.* 2nd ed. Littleton, Colo: Libraries Unlimited, 1986.

Parisi, Paul A. 'Methods of Affixing Leaves: Options and Implications'. *New Library Scene* 3 (1984): 9-12.

Parisi, Paul A. and Merrill-Oldham, Jan. 'The LBI Standard for Library Binding: The Glossary'. *School Library Journal* 33, 2 (1986): 96-98.

Rebsamen, Walter. 'Binding'. *Library Trends* 30 (1981): 226-239.

Turner, John. 'Binding Arbitration: A Comparison of the Durability of Various Hardback and Paperback Bindings'. *Library Association Record* 88, 5 (1986): 233-235.

Walker, Gay. 'Library Binding as a Conservation Measure'. *Collection Management* 4, 1/2 (1982): 55-71.

Yezer, Frank. 'Housing, When and Why'. *Library Chronicle of the University of Texas at Austin* n.s. 44/45 (1989): 149-155.

11 Preserving the Intellectual Content (Chapter 8)

Atkinson, Ross. 'Preservation and Collection Development: Towards a Political Synthesis'. *Journal of Academic Librarianship* 16, 2 (1990): 98-103.

Atkinson, Ross W. 'Selection for Preservation: A Materialistic Approach'. *Library Resources and Technical Services* 30, 4 (1986): 341-353.

Avedon, Don M. 'International Standards for Microforms'. In *Preservation of Library Materials: Conference Held at the National Library of Austria, Vienna, April 7-10, 1986*, ed. Merrily A. Smith, Vol. 1, 68-77. München: K.G. Saur, 1987.

Borck, Helga. 'Microforms', In *Conservation in the Library*, ed. Susan Garretson Swartzburg, 129-138. Westport, Conn.: Greenwood Press, 1983.

Bossuat, Marie-Louise. 'International Bibliographic Control of Microforms'. In *Preservation of Library Materials: Conference Held at the National Library of Austria, Vienna, April 7-10, 1986*, ed. Merrily A. Smith, Vol. 1, 71-77. München: K.G. Saur, 1987.

Bourke, Thomas A. 'To Archive or Not to Archive'. *Library Journal* (15 October 1989): 52-54.

Byrne, Sherry. 'Guidelines for Contracting Microfilming Services'. *Microform Review* 15, 4 (1986): 253-264.

Byrnes, Margaret M. 'Preservation and Collection Management: Some Common Concerns'. *Collection Building* 9, 3/4 (1989): 39-45.

Cady, Susan A. 'The Electronic Revolution in Libraries: Microfilm Déjà Vu?'. *College and Research Libraries* 51, 4 (1990): 374-386.

Calmes, Alan. 'New Confidence in Microfilm'. *Library Journal* (15 September 1986): 38-42.

Chace, Myron B. 'Preservation Microfiche: A Matter of Standards'. *Library Resources and Technical Services* 35, 2 (1991): 186-190.

Child, Margaret S. 'Further Thoughts on "Selection for Preservation: A Materialistic Approach"'. *Library Resources and Technical Services* 30, 4 (1986): 354-362.

Chapman, Patricia and Kenna, Stephanie. 'Substitution Microforms: A Survey of the Policies and Practices in UK Libraries'. *Library Association Record* 90, 5 (1988): 282, 285.

Clarkson, Christopher. 'Conservation Priorities: A Library Conservator's View'. In *Conservation of Library and Archival Materials and the Graphic Arts*, ed. Guy Petherbridge, 235-238. London: Butterworths, 1987.

Cribbs, Margaret A. 'The Invisible Drip: How Data Seeps Away in Various Ways'. *Online* 11, 2 (1987): 15-26.

Darling, Pamela W. 'Developing a Preservation Microfilming Program'. In *Microforms in Libraries: A Reader*, ed. James A. Diaz, 323-333. Weston, Conn.: Microform Review, 1975.

Day, Michael William. *Preservation Problems of Electronic Text and Data*. Loughborough, Leics.: East Midlands Branch, Library Association, 1990.

Dean, John F. 'Conservation and Collection Management'. *Journal of Library Administration* 7, 2-3 (1986): 129-141.

Dupont, Jerry. 'De-Romancing the Book: The Pyrrhic Victory of Microforms'. *Microform Review* 19, 4 (1990): 192-197.

Ferris, Valerie. 'Don't Film It If You're Not Recording It!' *Library Conservation News* 22 (1989): 3, 8.

Foxon, David F. 'Priorities: A Bibliographer's View'. In *Conservation of Library and Archival Materials and the Graphic Arts*, ed. Guy Petherbridge, 221-225. London: Butterworths, 1987.

Green, Paul R. 'A Schedule for the Cost-Evaluation of the Brittle Book Programme at Cornell University'. *Aslib Proceedings* 42, 11/12 (1990): 277-286.

Hazen, Dan C. 'Collection Development, Collection Management, and Preservation'. *Library Resources and Technical Services* 26, 1 (1982): 3-11.

Ilbury, T. 'Microfilm: Hardware, Storage, Standards and Technical Aspects'. In *Newspaper Preservation and Access: Proceedings of the Symposium Held in London...1987*, ed. Ian P. Gibb, Vol. 1, 201-205. München: K.G. Saur, 1988.

'Intrinsic Value in Archival Records'. In *A Modern Archives Reader: Basic Readings in Archival Theory and Practice*, ed. Maygene Daniels and Timothy Walch, 91-99. Washington, D.C.: National Archives and Records Service, 1984.

Jacobs, Donna. 'Nineteenth-Century Periodicals: Preservation Decision Making at College Libraries'. *College and Research Libraries* 52, 3 (1991): 263-274.

Kruger, Betsy. 'Automating Preservation Information in RLIN'. *Library Resources and Technical Services* 32, 2 (1988): 116-126.

Landau, Herbert B. 'Microform vs. CD-ROM: Is There a Difference?' *Library Journal* (1 October 1990): 56, 58-59.

Lesk, Michael. *Image Formats for Preservation and Access*. Washington, D.C.: Commission on Preservation and Access, 1990.

Lynch, Clifford A. and Brownrigg, Edwin B. 'Conservation, Preservation and Digitization'. *College and Research Libraries* 47, 4 (1986): 379-382.

Lynn, M. Stuart. 'Preservation and Access Technology: The Relationship between Digital and Other Media Conversion Processes: A Structured Glossary of Technical Terms'. *Information Technology and Libraries* 9, 4 (1990): 309-336.

McClung, Patricia A. 'Costs Associated with Preservation Microfilming: Results of the Research Libraries Group Study'. *Library Resources and Technical Services* 30, 4 (1986): 363-374.

McCrady, Ellen. 'The History of Microfilm Blemishes'. *Restaurator* 6, 3/4 (1984): 191-204.

Mallinson, John C. 'On the Preservation of Human- and Machine-Readable Records'. *Information Technology and Libraries* 7, 1 (1988): 19-23.

Manual of Archival Reprography, ed. Lajos Körmendy. München: K.G. Saur, 1989.

Oakley, Robert L. *Copyright and Preservation: A Serious Problem in Need of a Thoughtful Solution*. Washington, D.C.: Commission on Preservation and Access, 1990.

Ogden, Barclay. *On the Preservation of Books and Documents in Original Form*. Washington, D.C.: Commission on Preservation and Access, 1989.

Ogden, Barclay. *Selection for Preservation of Research Library Materials*. Washington, D.C.: Commission on Preservation and Access, 1989.

Olsson, Henry. 'Copyright Aspects of Reproduction'. In *Preservation of Library Materials: Conference Held at the National Library of Austria, Vienna, April 7-10, 1986*, ed. Merrily A. Smith, Vol. 2, 32-44. München: K.G. Saur, 1987.

Orr, Gloria J. 'Preservation Photocopying of Bound Volumes: An Increasingly Viable Option'. *Library Resources and Technical Services* 34, 4 (1990): 445-454.

Perez, Madeleine, Raymond, Andrew and Swartzell, Ann. 'The Selection and Preparation of Archives and Manuscripts for Microreproduction'. *Library Resources and Technical Services* 27, 4 (1983): 357-365.

Poe, Mya Thanda. 'Organizing and Implementing a Preservation Microfilming Program'. In *Preservation of Library Materials: Conference Held at the National Library of Austria, Vienna, April 7-10, 1986*, ed. Merrily A. Smith, Vol. 2, 20-21. München: K.G. Saur, 1987.

Preservation Microfilming: A Guide for Librarians and Archivists, ed. Nancy E. Gwinn. Chicago, Ill.: American Library Association, 1987.

Preservation Microfilming: Papers from the RTSD Preservation Microfilming Institute, New Haven, Connecticut, April 21-23, 1988. Chicago, Ill.: Association for Library Collections and Technical Services, ALA, 1989.

Price, Joseph W. 'Optical Disk Pilot Program at the Library of Congress'. In *Preservation of Library Materials: Conference Held at the National Library of Austria, Vienna, April 7-10, 1986*, ed. Merrily A. Smith, Vol. 1, 156-159. München: K.G. Saur, 1987.

Robinson, Lawrence S. 'Establishing a Preservation Microfilming Program: The Library of Congress Experience'. *Microform Review* 13 (1984): 239-244.

Roper, Michael. 'Policy for Format Conversion: Choosing a Format'. In *Preservation of Library Materials: Conference Held at the National Library of Austria, Vienna, April 7-10, 1986*, ed. Merrily A. Smith, Vol. 1, 59-67. München: K.G. Saur, 1987.

Smethurst, J.M. 'The Relationship between Acquisition, Retention and Preservation Policies'. In *Conservation and Collection Management: Proceedings of a Seminar at Loughborough University of Technology...1987*, 11-18. London: National Preservation Office, British Library, 1988.

Smith, Eldred. 'Why Microfilm Research-Library Collections When Electronic Data Bases Could Be Used?'. *Microform Review* 20, 1 (1991): 27-29.

Stevens, Norman D. 'The Role of Networks in the Preservation of Library Materials'. *Journal of Academic Librarianship* 7, 3 (1981): 171-172.

Sturges, Paul. 'Policies and Criteria for the Archiving of Electronic Publishing'. *Journal of Librarianship* 19, 3 (1987): 152-172.

Swartzell, Ann. 'Preservation Microfilming: In-house Initiated Microfilms'. *Conservation Administration News* 34 (1988): 6-7.

Tanselle, G. Thomas. 'Reproductions and Scholarship'. *Studies in Bibliography* 42 (1989): 22-54.

'Testing the Disk: Predictions of Longevity'. *National Preservation News* 3 (1986): 11-13.

Tomer, Christinger. 'Identification, Evaluation, and Selection of Books for Preservation'. *Collection Management* 3, 1 (1979): 45-54.

Tomer, Christinger. 'Selecting Library Materials for Preservation'. *Library and Archival Security* 7, 1 (1985): 1-6.

US Congress. Office of Technology Assessment. *Book Preservation Technologies*. Washington, D.C.: USGPO, 1988.

Waters, Donald J. *From Microfilm to Digital Imagery: On the Feasibility of a Project to Study...Converting...Library Materials From Microfilm to Digital Images*. Washington, D.C.: Commission on Preservation and Access, 1991.

Williams, B.J.S. 'Implications for Preservation of the Newer Information Media'. In *Conservation in Crisis: Proceedings of a Seminar at Loughborough University of Technology, 16-17 July 1986*, 57-64. London: National Preservation Office, British Library, 1987.

Williams, Lisa B. 'Selecting Rare Books for Physical Conservation: Guidelines for Decision Making'. *College and Research Libraries* 46, 2 (1985): 153-159.

Winterbottom, D.R. and Fiddes, R.G. *Life Expectancy of Write Once Digital Optical Discs*. Boston Spa: British Library Research and Development Department, 1989.

Wolff, Robin. 'Preservation Information in the USMARC Format'. *National Preservation News* 8 (1987): 5-6.

Yerburgh, Mark R. 'Studying All Those "Tiny Little Tea Leaves": The Future of Microforms in a Complex Technological Environment'. *Microform Review* 16, 1 (1987): 14-20.

12 Technological and Cooperative Strategies (Chapter 9)

Banik, Gerhard. 'Problems of Mass Conservation of Newsprint in Libraries'. In *Newspaper Preservation and Access: Proceedings of the Symposium Held in London...1987*, ed. Ian P. Gibb, Vol. 1, 216-226. München: K.G. Saur, 1988.

Banks, Paul N. 'Books in Peril: Cooperative Approaches to Conservation'. *Library Journal* (15 November 1976): 2348-2351.

Barrow, William J. *The Manufacture and Testing of Durable Book Paper*. Richmond, Va: Virginia State Library, 1960.

Batton, Susan Sayre. 'Nonaqueous Deacidification at Princeton, 1982-1989: A Progress Report'. *Abbey Newsletter* 14, 5 (1990): 80-82.

Bello, Susan E. *Cooperative Preservation Efforts of Academic Libraries*. Urbana-Champaign, Ill.: Graduate School of Library and Information Science, University of Illinois, 1986.

Boyd, Jane and Etherington, Don. *Preparation of Archival Copies of Theses and Dissertations*. Chicago, Ill.: American Library Association, 1986.

Butler, C.E., Clements, D.W.G. and Millington, C.A. 'Paper Strengthening at the British Library: Recent Developments in the Graft Copolymerisation Technique'. In *Preservation and Technology: Proceedings of a Seminar at York University, 20-21 July 1988*. London: National Preservation Office, British Library, 1989.

Child, Margaret. 'Is the Infrastructure in Place?' *National Preservation News* 7 (1987): 19.

Clapp, Verner W. 'The Story of Permanent/Durable Book-Paper, 1115-1970'. *Restaurator* suppl. 3 (1972).

Clements, David W.G. 'The National Preservation Office in the British Library'. *IFLA Journal* 12, 1 (1988): 25-32.

Clements, David W.G. 'Paper Strengthening at the British Library'. In *Preservation of Library Materials: Conference Held at the National Library of Austria, Vienna, April 7-10, 1986*, ed. Merrily A. Smith, Vol. 1, 152-155. München: K.G. Saur, 1987.

Cloonan, Michèle Valerie. 'Mass Deacidification in the 1990s'. *Rare Books and Manuscripts Librarianship* 5, 2 (1990): 95-103.

Cunha, George Martin. 'Current Trends in Preservation Research and Developments'. *American Archivist* 33, 2 (1990): 192-202.

Cunha, George Martin. 'Mass Deacidification for Libraries'. *Library Technology Reports* 23, 3 (1987).

Cunha, George Martin. 'Mass Deacidification for Libraries: 1989 Update'. *Library Technology Reports* 25, 1 (1989).

Dahlø, Rolf. 'Preventing Future Needs for Conservation'. *Library Conservation News* 25 (1989): 1-2.

'Effects of Gamma Rays on Book Preservation'. *Library Journal* (January 1990): 19.

Field, Jeffrey. 'The Role of the National Endowment for the Humanities' Office of Preservation in the National Preservation Effort'. *Microform Review* 14, 2 (1985): 81-86.

Field, Jeffrey. 'The US Newspaper Program'. In *Newspaper Preservation and Access: Proceedings of the Symposium Held in London...1987*, ed. Ian P. Gibb, Vol. 2, 356-366. München: K.G. Saur, 1988.

Frieder, Richard. 'Mass Deacidification: Now That It Is a Reality, What Next?'. *IFLA Journal* 17, 2 (1991): 142-146.

Geh, Hans-Peter. 'Conservation/Preservation: An International Approach'. *Library Resources and Technical Services* 30, 1 (1986): 31-35.

'Good Resolutions'. *Abbey Newsletter* 12, 2 (1988): 29-31.

Govan, J.F. 'Preservation and Resource Sharing: Conflicting or Complementary?' *IFLA Journal* 12, 1 (1986): 20-24.

Grove, Pearce S. 'A Revolution in Newspaper Access'. *Resource Sharing and Information Networks* 3, 1 (1985/1986): 101-114.

Gwinn, Nancy E. 'The Rise and Fall of Cooperative Projects'. *Library Resources and Technical Services* 29, 1 (1985): 80-86.

Haas, Warren J. 'National Preservation Programs'. In *Preservation of Library Materials: Conference Held at the National Library of Austria, Vienna, April 7-10, 1986*, ed. Merrily A. Smith, Vol. 1, 112-118. München: K.G. Saur, 1987.

Hutton, Brian. 'Preserving Scotland's Heritage'. *Library Conservation News* 19 (1988): 1-3.

'IFLA Core Programme on Preservation and Conservation'. *International Preservation News* 1 (1987): 1-2.

'IFLA Permanent Paper Resolutions'. *Conservation Administration News* 40 (1990): 22.

Jewett, Crispin. 'Conspectus: A Means to Library Co-operation'. *Library Conservation News* 22 (1989): 4-6.

Jewett, Crispin. 'Developing Conspectus'. *Library Conservation News* 23 (1989): 2-3, 6.

Johansson, Eve. 'National Approaches to Newspaper Preservation: The United Kingdom'. In *Newspaper Preservation and Access: Proceedings of the Symposium Held in London...1987*, ed. Ian P. Gibb, Vol. 2, 342-351. München: K.G. Saur, 1988.

Kelly, George B., Jr. 'Non-Aqueous Deacidification of Books and Paper'. In *Conservation of Library and Archival Materials and the Graphic Arts*, ed. Guy Petherbridge, 117-123. London: Butterworths, 1987.

King, Ed. 'New Hope for Decayed Paper'. *Library Conservation News* 12 (1986): 1-2.

McCoy, Richard W. 'Cooperative Preservation Activities of the Research Libraries Group (RLG)'. In *Preservation of Library Materials: Conference Held at the National Library of Austria, Vienna, April 7-10, 1986*, ed. Merrily A. Smith, Vol. 1, 83-88. München: K.G. Saur, 1987.

McCrady, Ellen. 'Deacidification vs Microfilming'. *Abbey Newsletter* 14, 6 (1990): 112-113.

Morrow, Carolyn Clark. 'National Preservation Planning and Regional Cooperative Conservation Efforts'. In *Conserving and Preserving Library Materials*, ed. Kathryn Luther Henderson and William T. Henderson, 37-56. Urbana-Champaign, Ill.: Graduate School of Library and Information Science, University of Illinois, 1983.

A National Preservation Program: Proceedings of the Planning Conference. Washington, D.C.: Library of Congress, 1980.

Nyren, Karl. 'The DEZ Process and the Library of Congress'. *Library Journal* (15 September 1986): 33-35.

Preservation and Technology: Proceedings of a Seminar at York University, 20-21 July 1988. London: National Preservation Office, British Library, 1989.

Ratcliffe, F.W. 'Preservation: A Decade of Progress'. *Library Review* 36 (1987): 228-236.

Ratcliffe, F.W. *Preservation Policies and Conservation in British Libraries: Report of the Cambridge University Library Conservation Project*. Boston Spa: British Library, 1984.

Roosa, Mark. 'U.S. Promotes the Manufacture and Use of Permanent Paper'. *International Preservation News* 2 (1988): 1-3.

Russell, Ann. 'Northeast Document Conservation Center: A Case Study in Cooperative Conservation'. *American Archivist* 45, 1 (1982): 45-52.

Russell, Ann, Motylewski, Karen and Tracy, Gay. 'Northeast Document Conservation Centre: A Leader in Preservation'. *Library Resources and Technical Services* 32, 1 (1988): 43-47.

Scott, Marianne. 'Mass Deacidification at the National Library of Canada'. In *Preservation of Library Materials: Conference Held at the National Library of Austria, Vienna, April 7-10, 1986*, ed. Merrily A. Smith, Vol. 1, 134-136. München: K.G. Saur, 1987.

Smith, Merrily A. 'The IFLA Core Programme on Preservation and Conservation (PAC)'. *IFLA Journal* 12, 4 (1986): 305-306.

Smith, Richard D. 'Mass Deacidification at the Public Archives of Canada'. In *Conservation of Library and Archival Materials and the Graphic Arts*, ed. Guy Petherbridge, 125-137. London: Butterworths, 1987.

Smith, Richard D. 'Mass Deacidification Cost Comparisons'. *College and Research Libraries* 46 (1985): 122-123.

Smith, Richard D. 'Mass Deacidification: The Wei T'o Way'. *College and Research Libraries* 45 (1984): 588-593.

Sparks, Peter G. 'Mass Deacidification at the Library of Congress'. In *Preservation of Library Materials: Conference Held at the National Library of Austria, Vienna, April 7-10, 1986*, ed. Merrily A. Smith, Vol. 1, 137-140. München: K.G. Saur, 1987.

Sparks, Peter G. *Technical Considerations in Choosing Mass Deacidification Processes*. Washington, D.C.: Commission on Preservation and Access, 1990.

Sparks, Peter G. 'Technology in Support of Preservation'. In *Preservation of Library Materials: Conference Held at the National Library of Austria, Vienna, April 7-10, 1986*, ed. Merrily A. Smith, Vol. 1, 126-128. München: K.G. Saur, 1987.

Sparks, Peter G. and Smith, Richard D. 'Deacidification Dialogue'. *College and Research Libraries* 46 (1985): 9-11.

Strebel, Magda. 'The Need for Cooperation'. In *Preservation of Library Materials: Conference Held at the National Library of Austria, Vienna, April 7-10, 1986*, ed. Merrily A. Smith, Vol. 1, 79-82. München: K.G. Saur, 1987.

'Towards Permanent Paper: US Standard Reviewed'. *Library Conservation News* 9 (1985): 8-9.

'Union Carbide Acquires Wei T'o Rights'. *Abbey Newsletter* 13, 7 (1989): 129-130.

Wächter, Otto. 'Paper Strengthening at the National Library of Austria'. In *Preservation of Library Materials: Conference Held at the National Library of Austria, Vienna, April 7-10, 1986*, ed. Merrily A. Smith, Vol. 1, 141-145. München: K.G. Saur, 1987.

Welsh, William J. 'In Defense of DEZ: LC's Perspective'. *Library Journal* (January 1987): 62-63.

Wilson, Alexander. 'Collecting Policies and Preservation: United Kingdom'. In *Preservation of Library Materials: Conference Held at the National Library of Austria, Vienna, April 7-10, 1986*, ed. Merrily A. Smith, Vol. 1, 161-7. München: K.G. Saur, 1987.

Zipkowitz, Fay. 'Saving Paper Treasures: The Northeast Document Conservation Center'. *Library and Archival Security* 7, 2 (1985): 15-20.

13 Developing a Library Preservation Program (Chapter 10)

Baker, John P. 'Preservation Programs of the New York Public Library: Part One, The Early Years'. *Microform Review* 10, 1 (1981): 25-28.

Baker, John P. 'Preservation Programs of the New York Public Library: Part Two: From the 1930s to the '60s'. *Microform Review* 11, 4 (1982): 22-30.

Battin, Patricia. 'Preservation at the Columbia University Libraries'. In *The Library Preservation Program: Models, Priorities, Possibilities*, ed. Jan Merrill-Oldham and Merrily Smith. Chicago, Ill.: American Library Association, 1985.

Beard, John C. 'Preservation Problems in Public Libraries'. In *Preserving the Word: The Library Association Conference Proceedings, Harrogate 1986*, ed. R. Palmer, 46-50. London: Library Association, 1987.

Boomgaarden, Wesley L. 'Preservation Planning for the Small Special Library'. *Special Libraries* 76, 3 (1985): 204-211.

Buchanan, Sally A. 'Administering the Library Conservation Program.' *Law Library Journal* 77 (1984-85): 569-574.

Chapman, Patricia. *Guidelines on Preservation and Conservation Policies in the Archives and Libraries Heritage*. Paris: Unesco, 1990.

Cunningham-Kruppa, Ellen. 'The General Libraries Preservation Program: A Preliminary Report'. *Library Chronicle of the University of Texas at Austin*, n.s. 44/45 (1989): 157-163.

Darling, Pamela W. 'Creativity v. Despair: The Challenge of Preservation Administration'. *Library Trends* 30, 2 (1981): 179-188.

Darling, Pamela W. 'A Local Preservation Program: Where to Start'. *Library Journal* (15 November 1976): 2343-2347.

Darling, Pamela W. 'Planning for the Future'. In *The Library Preservation Program: Models, Priorities, Possibilities*, ed. Jan Merrill-Oldham and Merrily Smith, 103-110. Chicago, Ill.: American Library Association, 1985.

DeCandido, Robert and DeCandido, GraceAnne A. 'Micro-Preservation: Conserving the Small Library'. *Library Resources and Technical Services* 29, 2 (1985): 151-160.

Fox, Peter. 'Preservation Is for Everyone'. In *Preserving the Word: The Library Association Conference Proceedings, Harrogate 1986*, ed. R. Palmer, 33-36. London: Library Association, 1987.

'Guidelines for Minimum Preservation Efforts in ARL Libraries'. *SPEC Kit* 138 (1987): 1-4.

Harris, Carolyn, Mandel, Carol and Wolven, Robert. 'A Cost Model for Preservation: The Columbia University Libraries' Approach'. *Library Resources and Technical Services* 35, 1 (1991): 33-54.

Jones, Norvell M.M. and Ritzenthaler, Mary Lynn. 'Implementing an Archival Preservation Program'. In *Managing Archives and Archival Institutions*, ed. James Gregory Bradsher, 185-206. London: Mansell, 1988.

Larsen, A. Dean. 'Preservation and Materials Processing'. In *Library Technical Services: Operations and Management*, ed. Irene P. Godden, Chapter 6. Orlando, Fla: Academic Press, 1984.

Larsen, A. Dean. 'Preservation at the Brigham Young University Library'. In *The Library Preservation Program: Models, Priorities, Possibilities*, ed. Jan Merrill-Oldham and Merrily Smith. Chicago, Ill.: American Library Association, 1985.

The Library Preservation Program: Models, Priorities, Possibilities, ed. Jan Merrill-Oldham and Merrily Smith. Chicago, Ill.: American Library Association, 1985.

Liddle, David. 'Conservation: The Public Library View'. In *Conservation and Collection Management: Proceedings of a Seminar at Loughborough University of Technology...1987*, 29-38. London: National Preservation Office, British Library, 1988.

Lowry, Marcia Duncan. *Preservation and Conservation in the Small Library*. Chicago, Ill.: Library Administration and Management Association, ALA, 1989.

Merrill-Oldham, Jan. *Conservation and Preservation of Library Materials: A Program for The University of Connecticut Libraries*. Storrs, Conn.: University of Connecticut Libraries, 1984.

Milevski, Robert J. and Nainis, Linda. 'Implementing a Book Repair and Treatment Program'. *Library Resources and Technical Services* 31, 2 (1987): 159-176.

Mowat, Ian R.M. 'Preservation Problems in Academic Libraries'. In *Preserving the Word: The Library Association Conference Proceedings, Harrogate 1986*, ed. R. Palmer, 37-45. London: Library Association, 1987.

'Organizing for Preservation in ARL Libraries'. *SPEC Kit* 116 (1985).

Pacey, Antony. 'Library Preservation: The Approach of the National Museums of Canada'. *Canadian Library Journal* 47, 1 (1990): 27-33.

Patterson, Robert H. 'Conservation: What We Should Do Until the Conservator and the Twenty-First Century Arrive'. In *Conserving and Preserving Library Materials*, ed. Kathryn Luther Henderson and William T. Henderson, 9-18. Urbana-Champaign, Ill.: Graduate School of Library and Information Science, University of Illinois, 1983.

Patterson, Robert H. 'Organizing for Conservation'. *Library Journal* (15 May 1979): 1116-1119.

Peterson, Kenneth G. 'Preservation at the Morris Library, Southern Illinois University'. In *The Library Preservation Program: Models, Priorities, Possibilities*, ed. Jan Merrill-Oldham and Merrily Smith. Chicago, Ill.: American Library Association, 1985.

'Planning for Preservation'. *SPEC Kit* 66 (1980).

'Preservation Guidelines in ARL Libraries', *SPEC Kit* 137 (1987).

'Preservation Organization and Staffing'. *SPEC Kit* 160 (1990).

Rosenthal, Joseph A. 'Preservation at the University of California Libraries at Berkeley'. In *The Library Preservation Program: Models, Priorities,*

Possibilities, ed. Jan Merrill-Oldham and Merrily Smith. Chicago, Ill.: American Library Association, 1985.

Schmude, Karl G. 'The Politics and Management of Preservation Planning'. *IFLA Journal* 16, 3 (1990): 332-335.

Seaton, D.G. 'Conservation in High-Use Collections'. *Interlending and Document Supply* 11, 1 (1983): 7-11.

Stam, David H. 'Finding Funds to Support Preservation'. In *The Library Preservation Program: Models, Priorities, Possibilities*, ed. Jan Merrill-Oldham and Merrily Smith. Chicago, Ill.: American Library Association, 1985.

Walker, Gay. 'Advanced Preservation Planning at Yale'. *Microform Review* 18, 1 (1989): 20-28.

Watson, Duane A. 'The Divine Library Function: Preservation'. *School Library Journal* 33, 3 (1986): 41-45.

Winkle, Becky. 'Preservation on a Shoestring'. *American Libraries* 16 (December 1985): 778-779.

Wortman, William A. *Collection Management: Background and Principles*. Chicago, Ill.: American Library Association, 1989.

Index

About the Author

Ross Harvey BMus (Hons), PhD, DipNZLS, ANZLA, ALAA is a Senior Lecturer at the Graduate Department of Librarianship, Archives and Records at Monash University and Director of the Centre for Bibliographical and Textual Studies. He taught at the Library School of the National Library of New Zealand and has worked in various New Zealand libraries, most recently as the Newspaper Librarian at the National Library. He has published in the fields of musicology, newspaper history and preservation, and compiled the *Union List of Newspapers Preserved in Libraries...in New Zealand* (Wellington: National Library of New Zealand, 1987), *A Bibliography of Writings about New Zealand Music Published to the End of 1983* (Wellington: Victoria University Press, 1985) and *Music at National Archives* (Christchurch: University of Canterbury School of Music, 1991). He is an editor of the Bibliographical Society of Australia and New Zealand *Bulletin*.